T0178149

Lecture Notes of the Institute for Computer Sciences, Social Informatics and Telecommunications Engineering   540

The LNICST series publishes ICST's conferences, symposia and workshops.

LNICST reports state-of-the-art results in areas related to the scope of the Institute.

The type of material published includes

- Proceedings (published in time for the respective event)
- Other edited monographs (such as project reports or invited volumes)

LNICST topics span the following areas:

- General Computer Science
- E-Economy
- E-Medicine
- Knowledge Management
- Multimedia
- Operations, Management and Policy
- Social Informatics
- Systems

Ana Lucia Martins · Joao C. Ferreira ·
Alexander Kocian · Ulpan Tokkozhina ·
Berit Irene Helgheim · Svein Bråthen
Editors

Intelligent Transport Systems

7th EAI International Conference, INTSYS 2023
Molde, Norway, September 6–7, 2023
Proceedings

 Springer

Editors
Ana Lucia Martins ⓘ
ISCTE-University Institute of Lisbon
Lisbon, Portugal

Joao C. Ferreira ⓘ
ISCTE-University Institute of Lisbon
Lisbon, Portugal

Alexander Kocian ⓘ
University of Pisa
Pisa, Italy

Ulpan Tokkozhina ⓘ
University of Lisbon
Lisbon, Portugal

Berit Irene Helgheim ⓘ
Molde University College
Molde, Norway

Svein Bråthen ⓘ
Molde University College
Molde, Norway

ISSN 1867-8211   ISSN 1867-822X (electronic)
Lecture Notes of the Institute for Computer Sciences, Social Informatics
and Telecommunications Engineering
ISBN 978-3-031-49378-2   ISBN 978-3-031-49379-9 (eBook)
https://doi.org/10.1007/978-3-031-49379-9

This Springer imprint is published by the registered company Springer Nature Switzerland AG
The registered company address is: Gewerbestrasse 11, 6330 Cham, Switzerland

Paper in this product is recyclable.

Preface

We are delighted to introduce the proceedings of the seventh edition of the International Conference on Intelligent Transport Systems (INTSYS 2023) from the European Alliance for Innovation (EAI). We returned to presential mode and the conference took place in Molde from 6th – 7th September, hosted by Molde University College, Specialized University in Logistics (MUC). MUC offers several programs in IT, Logistics and Transport. It has a high research profile within these areas within both academic and applied research.

This conference brought together researchers, developers, and practitioners from around the world who are leveraging and developing Intelligent Transportation Systems (ITS) to increase efficiency, safety, and mobility, and to tackle Europe's growing emission and congestion problems.

The theme of INTSYS 2023 was "Intelligent Transportation Systems: Challenges for 2030". This edition received 39 submissions from which the technical program of INTSYS 2023 accepted 16 full papers. All 16 papers were presented in oral sessions at the main conference tracks. All of the accepted papers were subjected to a double-blind peer-review process with a minimum of four reviews for each paper. Concerning the committees, it was a great pleasure to work with the excellent organizing team of the EAI, which was essential for the success of the INTSYS 2023 conference. In particular, we would like to express our gratitude to Veronika Kissova and the EAI staff, for all the support she provided in all subjects. We thank Molde University College for their support of the conference. We would also like to express our gratitude to all the members of the Technical Program Committee, who helped in the peer-review process of the technical papers and ensured a high-quality technical program. We would like to thank the extensive list of external reviewers from several areas of expertise and numerous countries worldwide. A special acknowledgement must be addressed to all the authors for their effort in producing such good-quality papers and for the extremely rich and positive feedback shared at the conference. We strongly believe that the INTSYS conference provides a good forum for all researcher, developers, and practitioners to discuss all science and technology aspects that are relevant to ITS. We also expect the future INTSYS conferences to be as successful and stimulating as indicated by the contributions presented in this volume.

September 2023

Ana Lucia Martins
Joao C. Ferreira
Alexander Kocian
Ulpan Tokkozhina
Berit Irene Helgheim
Svein Bråthen

Organization

Steering Committee

Ana Lúcia Martins	Iscte – University Institute of Lisbon, Portugal
Joao C. Ferreira	Iscte – University Institute of Lisbon, Portugal
Alexander Kocian	University of Pisa, Italy

Organizing Committee

General Chair

Berit Irene Helgheim	Molde University College, Norway

General Co-chair

Svein Bråthen	Molde University College, Norway

TPC Chairs

Ana Lucia Martins	Iscte – University Institute of Lisbon, Portugal
Alexander Kocian	University of Pisa, Italy

TPC Co-chair

João C. Ferreira	Iscte – University Institute of Lisbon, Portugal

Web Chair

Sergei Teryokhin	Molde University College, Norway

Publicity and Social Media Chair

Carlos M. P. Sousa	Molde University College, Norway

Workshop Chair

Miguel Nunes   Iscte – University Institute of Lisbon, Portugal

Sponsorship and Exhibit Chair

Ana Madureira   ISEP – Porto, Portugal

Publication Chair

Ulpan Tokkozhina   Iscte – University Institute of Lisbon, Portugal

Panel Chair

Bjørn Jæger   Molde University College, Norway

Tutorial Chairs

Frederica Gonçalves   University of Madeira, ITI/LARSys, Portugal
Miguel Nunes   Iscte – University Institute of Lisbon, Portugal

Demo Chairs

Bruno Mataloto   Iscte – University Institute of Lisbon, Portugal
Mary Nsabagwa   Makerere University, Uganda

Posters and PhD Track Chairs

Luis Elvas   Iscte – University Institute of Lisbon, Portugal
Benjamin Sakita   Molde University College, Norway

Local Chair

Deodat Edward Mwesiumo   Molde University College, Norway

Technical Program Committee

Adreano Lino   Federal University of Western Pará, Brazil
Alexander Kocian   University of Pisa, Italy
Ana Lúcia Martins   Iscte – University Institute of Lisbon, Portugal

Ana Madureira	ISEP, Portugal
Aravazhi Agaraoli	Molde University College, Norway
Atilla Altintas	Chalmers University of Technology, Sweden
Benjamin Sakita	Molde University College, Norway
Berit Irene Helgheim	Molde University College, Norway
Bruno Mataloto	Iscte – University Institute of Lisbon, Portugal
Bjørn Jæger	Molde University College, Norway
Carlos M. P. Sousa	Molde University College, Norway
Dagmar Caganova	Slovak University of Technology in Bratislava, Slovakia
Deodat Edward Mwesiumo	Molde University College, Norway
Diana Mendes	Iscte – University Institute of Lisbon, Portugal
Frederica Gonçalves	University of Madeira, Portugal
Gabriel Pestana	INOV, Portugal
Ghadir Pourhashem	Slovak University of Technology in Bratislava, Slovakia
Giuseppe Lugano	University of Žilina, Slovakia
Joao C. Ferreira	Iscte – University Institute of Lisbon, Portugal
Lia Oliveira	ESCE-IPVC, Portugal
Lubos Buzna	University of Žilina, Slovakia
Luis Elvas	Iscte – University Institute of Lisbon, Portugal
Marek Kvet	University of Žilina, Slovakia
Michal Kohani	University of Žilina, Slovakia
Michal Kvet	University of Žilina, Slovakia
Miguel Nunes	Iscte – University Institute of Lisbon, Portugal
Miroslav Svitek	Czech Technical University in Prague, Czech Republic
Pavan Kumar Mishra	National Institute of Technology, Raipur, India
Peter Brida	University of Žilina, Slovakia
Peter Holečko	University of Žilina, Slovakia
Peter Jankovic	University of Zilina, Slovakia
Peter Pocta	University of Zilina, Slovakia
Porfirio Filipe	ISEL, Portugal
Rahul Sharma	TECMIC, Portugal
Rosaldo Rosseti	FEUP, Portugal
Sergei Teryokhin	Molde University College, Norway
Sofia Kalakou	Iscte – University Institute of Lisbon, Portugal
Svein Bråthen	Molde University College, Norway
Tatiana Kováčiková	University of Žilina, Slovakia
Teresa Grilo	Iscte – University Institute of Lisbon, Portugal
Tomas Brandão	Iscte – University Institute of Lisbon, Portugal
Ulpan Tokkozhina	Iscte – University Institute of Lisbon, Portugal

Veronika Sramova   University of Žilina, Slovakia
Vitor Monteiro   University of Minho, Portugal
Vitoria Albuquerque   Nova University, Portugal

Conference Manager

Veronika Kissova EAI - European Alliance for Innovation, Slovakia

Contents

Transportation

Drivers, Barriers, and Enablers of Digital Transformation in Maritime Ports Sector: A Review and Aggregate Conceptual Analysis

Benjamin Mosses Sakita[✉], Berit Irene Helgheim, and Svein Bråthen

Molde University College – A Specialized University in Logistics, 6410 Molde, Norway
benjamin.m.sakita@himolde.no, benjamin_mosses@yahoo.com

Abstract. This paper develops a conceptual framework for digital transformation in the maritime ports sector. The study combines a systematic literature review and aggregate conceptual analysis to explicate drivers, barriers, and enablers of digital transformation. Our literature review is grounded in maritime ports' existing albeit scant empirical evidence. Our attempt bridges the existing gap in ports literature review that has included articles from sources outside the maritime industry's domain. We deploy aggregate conceptual analysis on 35 maritime port related empirical literature and rank emerging concepts with respect to digital transformation phenomenon. We then synthesize 32 concepts deemed essential for the effective implementation of digital transformation in the ports sector. In doing so, four thematic categories emerge: i) drivers, ii) barriers, iii) enablers, and iv) digital transformation idiosyncrasies in ports. In terms of contribution, this study is one of the earliest efforts to aggregate factors related to digital transformation in the maritime ports sector. Our findings provide actionable insights that enable managers of maritime ports, stakeholders, and policymakers to successfully navigate the digital transformation process. For researchers, directions for future research are offered.

Keywords: Digital transformation · Digital transformation dimensions · Literature review · Maritime ports

1 Introduction

Maritime ports are indispensable enablers of international freight transport and pivotal nodes in global supply chains. Being inextricably intertwined in national socio-economic and geo-political systems (Haraldson *et al.*, 2021; Inkinen *et al.*, 2021), ports face increasing pressure to evolve and pace up with relentless global dynamics (Ippoliti *et al.*, 2018; Wang and Sarkis, 2021). For instance, drivers like the desire to streamline the efficiency of ports processes and operations, sustainability pressures from domestic and international regulatory bodies such as IMO (Inkinen *et al.*, 2021; Lee *et al.*, 2019; UNCTAD, 2019), competitions across ports, and pressures from trading partners, push ports to redefine their business and engagement models (Gausdal *et al.*, 2018).

© ICST Institute for Computer Sciences, Social Informatics and Telecommunications Engineering 2024
Published by Springer Nature Switzerland AG 2024. All Rights Reserved
A. L. Martins et al. (Eds.): INTSYS 2023, LNICST 540, pp. 3–33, 2024.
https://doi.org/10.1007/978-3-031-49379-9_1

Furthermore, the trends in shipping industry such as changes in the size and capacity of vessels warrant modern equipment at ports to streamline loading, offloading, and other related operations in the ports perimeter. Given the complexity of ports' operations and multiplicity of actors, the viable way for ports to adapt to global dynamics hinges on their ability and willingness to explore and exploit novel digital technological solutions. Indeed, the latter have increasingly become an imperative source of sustainability and competitive advantage (Heilig *et al.*, 2017; Seo *et al.*, 2023; Yusheng Zhou *et al.*, 2023). For instance, ports of Hamburg in Germany and Gothenburg in Sweden have made significant strides in their digital transformation (DT) initiatives. Through the introduction of digital twin and the use of sensor technologies, the Port of Hamburg has been able to monitor on-ground operations including current conditions of major port infrastructure utilization real-time, thereby reducing potential downtime, and optimizing waiting times for vessels and trucks (HPA, 2023; Min, 2022; Molavi *et al.*, 2020). Having learned the importance of attaining critical mass in achieving successful digital transforming, the port of Hamburg introduced homePORT digital initiative with the aim of involving port stakeholders in innovation co-creation (HPA, 2023). Likewise, the Port of Gothenburg through its Port Optimizer digital initiative has been able to integrate stakeholders' disparate data sources into a unique data source that helps the port, and its stakeholders address challenges such as data provenance and quality, and visibility of cargo in transit. This has enabled the Port to improve its productivity from ship to shore and terminal to hinterland customers (Dalaklis *et al.*, 2022). Consequently, ports are increasingly under pressure to undertake DT as part of strategic readjustment and adaptation.

In ports' context, DT refers to a process where port organizations and their related ecosystems deliberately explore and exploit affordances of novel technologies such as cloud computing, sensors, internet of things (IoT), big data, artificial intelligence, virtual and augmented reality, cybersecurity, blockchain, and analytics among others, to reinforce their communication, connectivity, information capturing and sharing, and analytical capabilities; thus, adapting to relentless competitive dynamics (Baum-Talmor and Kitada, 2022; Gómez Díaz *et al.*, 2023; Heikkilä *et al.*, 2022; Lin, 2023; Min, 2022; Parola *et al.*, 2020). The use of these novel technological solutions has enabled Ports of Rotterdam, Hamburg, and Quebec to transition into smart ports which are characterized by efficient use of port assets, intelligent port problem solving, and energy efficiency (Min, 2022; Molavi *et al.*, 2020).

Unlike traditional IT systems, novel digital technologies pervade beyond individual organizational boundaries which complicates their adoptions as it pertains to accountability and economic rent distribution. Thus, the process of DT is regarded as disruptive because adopting novel technological solutions are not merely the end in itself, it pervades and warrants rethinking of several organizational aspects like business process, business model, structure, people, products and services, and engagement model (Raza *et al.*, 2023; Tijan *et al.*, 2021). It is for this reason that many port organizations grapple with successful implementation of DT initiatives. In fact, the pace at which ports uptake digital technologies is generally slow and fragmented (Heilig and Voß, 2017; Jović *et al.*, 2022; Kapidani *et al.*, 2020; Sanchez-Gonzalez *et al.*, 2019; Tijan *et al.*, 2021; Y. Zhou *et al.*, 2020). Furthermore, the fragmentation of DT trajectories among ports is evidenced in contexts where only a fraction of ports such as Hamburg in Germany,

Singapore in Singapore, Antwerp in Belgium, Rotterdam in the Netherlands, Qingdao in China, Nagoya in Japan, Long beach in the United States, and Gothenburg in Sweden, to mention but a few, are actively involved in the adoption and exploitation of novel technological solutions. Examples of digitalization initiatives in these ports include: the application of mobile technology and wireless connectivity by the port of Singapore to streamline cargo flows efficiency, communication, and workforce satisfaction (Molavi *et al.*, 2020); the use of OnTrack application by the port of Rotterdam, which has enabled it to improve the efficiency of the planning process and train scheduling prediction benefiting both railway operators, traction suppliers and hinterland water terminals (Karaś, 2020); and the use of *iNose* technology at the port of Antwerp which has enabled it to monitor air quality in the port given its high throughput of chemical cargos (Karaś, 2020). These ports have one thing in common – a relentless exploitation of novel technological solutions. On the contrary, about 80% of active maritime ports are still bogged down with rudimentary digital solutions such as spreadsheets and whiteboards in performing their daily operations (Heikkilä *et al.*, 2022; Min, 2022), consequently defeating the efforts to address the mounting call for efficiency, safety and security.

In practice, many ports have been applying digital technologies for many years, i.e., terminal operating systems, port community systems, electronic data interchange (EDI), and RFID (Heilig and Voß, 2017) to develop for instance, traceability systems for maritime operations (Lin, 2023). However, latest technological breakthroughs, increase in global freight transport, and complexity in maritime supply chains, have rendered conventional ports digital systems inadequate (Seo *et al.*, 2023). Given the mounting environmental dynamics such as the COVID -19 pandemic (Y. Zhou *et al.*, 2020), there have been growing concerns on the slow acquisition of Industry 4.0 digital technologies which arguably exacerbates ports' inefficiencics and stifles their efficacy in facilitating efficient cargo flows and associated information through global supply chains (Dalaklis *et al.*, 2022; Hsu *et al.*, 2023). For instance, the ultra large container vessel is 24,000 TEUs strong and requires modern port equipment and streamlined operations across a range of port stakeholders. As central nodes with value added logistics, ports and their disparate stakeholders must synchronize their actions to effectuate meaningful value creation and capture (Heilig *et al.*, 2017; Jeevan *et al.*, 2020; Nikghadam *et al.*, 2021).

Typically, port organizations and their stakeholders (i.e., customs, customs agents, shipping lines, shipping agents, clearing and freight forwarders, terminal operators, etc.) (Denktas-Sakar and Karatas-Cetin, 2012) hardly share common interests, similar management principles, and sets of behavior – a tendency that chokes concerted efforts to undertake DT unanimously (Carlan *et al.*, 2017). For instance, Heilig *et al.* (2017) showcased how an innovative *SmartPORT* initiative at the port of Hamburg fell through due to lack of collaboration from the stakeholders. The authors insinuated that, for digital technologies to take root, important costs and benefits considerations must be made upfront and impact assessment be conducted to determine an appropriate way to reward different stakeholder groups based on their interests.

Similarly, the need to preserve information confidentiality as a means to expropriate value is not uncommon as evidenced by Zeng *et al.* (2020)'s empirical work that found out that freight forwarders refrained from using an open digital platform for container bookings in that regard. While DT introduces transparency and visibility for orchestrators, it also jeopardizes the source of power inherent in asymmetrical information which other value chain actors leverage. Nevertheless, human and technical challenges to implementing DT initiatives go beyond a mere intent of acquiring novel technologies. Port organizations must holistically consider how such endeavors impact such aspects as strategy, scope, and (digital) leadership (Raza *et al.*, 2023).

While extant literature abounds with studies on barriers, drivers, and success factors of DT (Brunila *et al.*, 2021; Carlan *et al.*, 2017; Tijan *et al.*, 2021; Vairetti *et al.*, 2019; Y. Zhou *et al.*, 2020), there is a lack of exhaustive review and compilation of antecedents to DT in maritime ports sector. Although Tijan *et al.* (2021) attempted to conduct a literature review on barriers, drivers and success factors of DT in maritime transport sector, their analysis included studies that came from outside the field of maritime domain (i.e., manufacturing, automobile, and insurance sectors). Such analysis confounds the understanding of contextual factors only pertinent to maritime domain, and systemically precludes other scholars from building on it. A recent study by (Jović *et al.*, 2022) also notes and underscores the drawback implicated in Tijan *et al.* (2021)'s work. As such, an extensive review that is exclusively based on the maritime sector is warranted. We therefore seek to bridge this gap by conducting a systematic literature review combining it with aggregate conceptual analysis (MacInnis, 2011). We then showcase peculiarities of undertaking DT in the face of multitude stakeholders and contextual dimensions and suggest a framework that provides a theoretical foundation and actionable managerial recommendations.

The remainder of this paper is articulated as follows: Sect. 2 describes a systematic literature review methodology. Section 3 presents the findings and synthesis. Section 4 places the results in perspective and provides actionable managerial and policy implications. Section 5 concludes the paper and outlines directions for further research.

2 Literature Review Methodology

This literature review aims to unearth the current state and trends of DT in maritime ports sector using context-specific empirical literature. To ensure the reliability and validity of our results, we adopted a rigorous and structured approach in accordance with (Tranfield *et al.*, 2003). Thus, this study deploys a three-phase approach to perform a content analysis of literature on DT in maritime ports. Phases 1 and 2 are described in Sect. 2, whereas Phase 3 is presented in Sect. 3. In the first phase, we identified a corpus of articles using specific keywords search strategy (see Fig. 1). In the second phase, we coded the content of the articles to extract important emerging concepts deemed pertinent to DT in maritime ports. Subsequently, we constructed a network analysis to determine the relationships between the concepts and their relative importance. In the third phase, following aggregation approach (MacInnis, 2011), we synthesized the concepts and developed a conceptual framework. These steps are detailed in the subsections that follow.

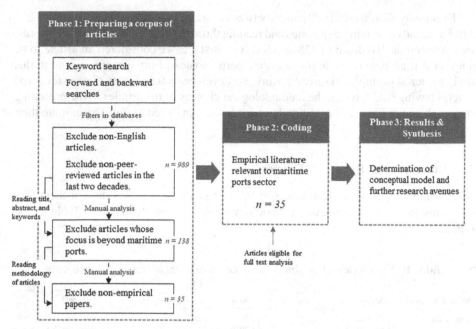

Fig. 1. Review methodology of this study. Source: Authors' own elaboration as adapted from (Tranfield *et al.*, 2003).

2.1 Phase 1: Preparing a Corpus of Articles

The articles search exercise commenced with inclusion and exclusion criteria focusing on specific keywords. We limited our search criteria to open access, peer-reviewed empirical academic articles on DT in the maritime ports from 2000 to February 2023. The inclusion criteria were formulated following the recommendations by (McWilliams *et al.*, 2005). Indeed, we resorted to including only peer-reviewed journal articles as these demonstrate rigor in quality assurance mechanisms and therefore, have a significant impact on new knowledge (Arduini and Zanfei, 2014; McWilliams *et al.*, 2005). Since non-english academic articles tend to have limited contribution to the international academic discourse, we excluded them in accordance with (Boselie *et al.*, 2005).

In line with Tranfield *et al.* (2003), we used "digital transformation" AND "maritime ports" as key search terms within title, abstract, keywords or full text from Science direct, Sage, ProQuest, Elsevier, Google Scholar, Web of Science, Semantic Scholar, and Research Gate databases using the filters we have described above. To broaden our search strategy, we extended the keyword combinations to phrases; "digitalization of maritime ports", "digitalization" OR "maritime business". Other synonyms of maritime ports such as "shipping ports", "maritime logistics", "maritime business", "maritime supply chains", "shipping industry", "smart ports", and "maritime sector" were alternatively used in the initial searching exercise. Additionally, variants "digitalization", "digitization", and "digitisation" were used. Furthermore, we performed backward and forward searches to expand the scope of relevant literature.

Eventually, we retrieved 989 papers between March 11, 2021, and February 20, 2023. After manually removing duplicates and reading through titles, abstracts, and keywords, we narrowed the list down to 138 articles. At this stage, we considered an article to be relevant if it addressed DT in the maritime ports' context. Furthermore, central to this study's interest in empirical research work, we developed a final list of 35 peer-reviewed articles having read through the methodological choices of the articles in the preceding step as shown in Fig. 1. The 35 articles were further analyzed by fully examining their text.

2.2 Description of Reviewed Articles

After reading all 35 empirical papers in full, we generated an overview of their contributions in terms of context, methodology, and trend as depicted in Table 1 and Fig. 2.

Table 1. An overview of empirical contributions in terms of context, methodology

Methods/Context	Africa	America	Asia	Australia	Europe
Case study	(Gekara and Nguyen, 2020)		(Lambrou et al., 2019; Zeng et al., 2020)		(Bisogno, 2015; Fedi et al., 2019; Gausdal et al., 2018; Inkinen et al., 2019, 2021; Philipp et al., 2019; Raza et al., 2023)
Mathematical modelling approach		(Molavi et al., 2020)	(Chowdhury et al., 2023; Hsu et al., 2023; Kashav et al., 2022; Seo et al., 2023; Zhou et al., 2020)		(Carlan et al., 2017; Zhang and Lam, 2019)
Mixed methods		(Vairetti et al., 2019)	(Iman et al., 2022)		(Kapidani et al., 2020; Philipp, 2020)
Others					(Bauk et al., 2017; Bavassano et al., 2020; Camarero Orive et al., 2020; Gómez Díaz et al., 2023; González-Cancelas, Molina, et al., 2020; González-Cancelas, Molina Serrano, et al., 2020)
Survey			(He et al., 2023; Kuo et al., 2021; Lin, 2023; Yang, 2019)	(Djoumessi et al., 2019; Gekara and Nguyen, 2018)	(Peynirci, 2021)
	(1) 3%	(2) 6%	(12) 34%	(2) 6%	(18) 51%

We can depict a lopsided distribution of empirical literature with European and Asiatic authors in the lead. These two regions accounted for 85% of all reviewed empirical papers. Africa had only one empirical work at the time of our review, below America and Australia which had two publications each. The three regions together scraped only 15% of the empirical work. In terms of methodological choices, we depict a diverse set of approaches the authors adopted across the regions. Case study has been the most utilized method and accounted for (11) 31.4% of the reviewed empirical research. This is perhaps justified by the novelty of DT phenomenon where researchers try to unravel its tenets. On the other hand, mathematical approaches such as analytical hierarchy process (AHP), fuzzy set qualitative comparative analysis (FsQCA), accounted for (8) 22.9% which also gives an indication of deliberate efforts to use expert opinions to understand the DT phenomenon better. About (4) 11% of the papers utilized mixed methods approach while (6) 17% deployed survey. Meanwhile, a myriad of other methods such as business observation tool (BOT), strengths, weaknesses, opportunities and threats (SWOT) accounted for (6) 17% of the reviewed papers.

With regard to the trend of publications over the past two decades, Fig. 2. Depicts that, the researchers in maritime domain only started to empirically measure the concept of DT in the European context in 2015. From then on, the trend of publications of empirical research on maritime industry's DT increased steadily and peaked in the year 2020 before the pandemic. According to our analysis, 23 empirical works had been conducted until then. The trend declined sharply with only 2 papers in 2021, presumably due to the pandemic and associated restrictions which might have precluded the traditional methods of collecting data. However, from 2022 to date, the trend has been rising again with about 10 papers published during this period possibly due to the normalization of human activities post-pandemic. Nevertheless, the trend depicts the scarcity of empirical literature on DT phenomenon and the pace at which academia is at odds with technological breakthroughs.

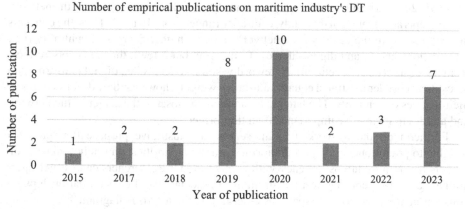

Fig. 2. Distribution of empirical papers on DT over the past two decades. Source: Authors' own elaboration from empirical literature review.

2.3 Phase 2: Coding Process

We read through the final list of 35 empirical peer-reviewed articles, in the process, jotting down all concepts that we deemed relevant to DT in maritime ports. We recorded these concepts with their respective authors in an excel spreadsheet. This exercise resulted in an initial list of 104 concepts. As each researcher coded the concepts independently, a consensus had to be reached and any disagreements resolved. Furthermore, in order to reduce the dimensions and duplications of concepts emerging in different articles, we aggregated all closely related concepts in accordance with (MacInnis, 2011) which resulted into 32 concepts that this study synthesized.

We then developed a network diagram to ascertain how these concepts related to each other. Firstly, we enumerated the concepts and respective authors in a fresh excel sheet, and then deployed a pivot table functionality to visualize and aggregate concepts co-occurrence with respect to each paper. The results of the pivot table enabled us to develop a weighted matrix of *nxm* dimensions, where n represented rows of 32 concepts, and m represented 35 papers. This matrix considered each concept against all others that have been mentioned by one paper for all papers.

Secondly, as we determined to use the *igraph* function in R software version 4.2.1, to generate network diagram of the concepts, we necessarily reduced the weighted concept matrix into a two-column matrix. For instance, agility co-occurred with other concepts in 33 articles 50 times, so we enumerated it fifty times against all co-occurring concepts. We repeated this exercise for all concepts in the weighted concept matrix and finally generated a 270x2 matrix that we fed into *igraph*. The outcome of this exercise is the network diagram which is illustrated in Fig. 3.

As shown in Fig. 3, the nodes of the network (in orange circles) represent 32 concepts while the arcs (connecting lines) represent interconnectedness amongst concepts. The numeric figures on the nodes were computed by an algorithm in *igraph* function in R-software and quantify the degree of centrality of each concept relative to others in the network. The degree of centrality indicates how important a concept is in a network (Q. Liu *et al.*, 2022). The higher the degree of centrality the closer to the center of the network the concepts are located. In this study, centrality ranged from 16 to 31. Thus, the concepts that are closest to the center of the network indicate higher degrees of centrality (i.e., information sharing and digital literacy, to mention but a few), than concepts furthest from the center (i.e., coopetition). Noteworthy, some concepts i.e., digital platforms and investment cost demonstrated equal quantitative weights, however, they differ in terms of their degrees of centrality. The latter is located much closer to the center of the network and alludes to its relative importance than the former.

Furthermore, the network diagram serves an illustrative purpose that provides insights to practitioners i.e., port authorities, public authorities, and policy makers on aspects that require utmost urgency with respect to DT. Researchers can further operationalize the concepts and test the strength of associations of causal relationships by considering the most critical aspects as emerging in the network diagram. This can further enlighten our understanding of nuances these factors present thereby informing a better management of DT endeavors.

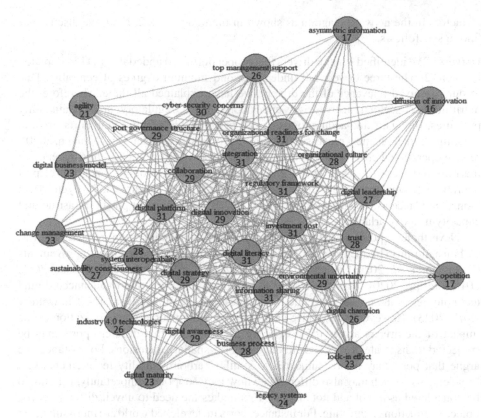

Fig. 3. Network diagram showing concepts' interrelationships and their centrality. Source: Authors' own elaboration from empirical literature review. (Color figure online)

3   Phase 3: Results and Synthesis

3.1   Drivers, Barriers, and Enablers of DT in Maritime Ports Sector

Based on our review of empirical peer-reviewed articles, we found that ports' DT is a function of many factors (i.e., the concepts in the network diagram) some of which exert opposing effects on implementation initiatives. We thematically aggregate these factors into drivers, barriers, and enablers, and provide anecdotal nuances of their interplays on maritime ports' DT. We started by computing the quartiles of the degrees of centrality and used them to categorize the concepts into high, medium, and low importance. The first group (high importance) consists of concepts whose degrees of centrality are equal to or above the third quartile. The second group (medium importance) consists of concepts whose degrees of centrality are above the first quartile and below the third quartile, while the last group consists of concepts whose degrees of centrality are equal to or less than the first quartile. The computation of quartiles of degree of centrality of each concepts permitted a more objective justification for our choice of explicating only selected factors in the proposed framework in Fig. 4. It also corroborates the visualized interrelationships of factors in the network diagram as shown in thematic Table 2. Next, we discuss our findings as follows.

Drivers. We identified 3 major drivers that propel ports into undertaking DT as depicted in Table 2. The three drivers fall under high and medium degrees of centrality. Due to our perceived relevance of the drivers, we have explained all three. Therefore, the maritime port sector is increasingly under competitive, regulatory, and sustainability pressures. Being a value-adding logistic node in the global supply chain, ports strive to reconfigure their business processes to improve productivity (Gekara and Nguyen, 2020), reduce operational costs (Gausdal et al., 2018), improve efficiency and transparency of maritime business (Y. Zhou et al., 2020), better measure, monitor, and control port operations (Camarero Orive et al., 2020; Carlan et al., 2017; Gekara and Nguyen, 2018; González-Cancelas, Molina Serrano, et al., 2020), and optimize ports' infrastructural capacity usage (Carlan et al., 2017).

Nevertheless, ports must fulfil regulatory and sustainability requirements such as carbon neutrality (Inkinen et al., 2021), and continuous safety and security improvements (Bavassano et al., 2020; Camarero Orive et al., 2020; Carlan et al., 2017; Gausdal et al., 2018; Philipp, 2020). These forces are so imminent that ports turn to advanced digital technologies as the potential avenue for addressing such global dynamics (Chowdhury et al., 2023). However, we exercise caution in providing cursory generalization of the impact of the drivers across the board. We acknowledge that different ports may be subjected to disparate drivers at different temporal-spatial dimensions. For instance, we argue that ports may not be subjected to similar carbon neutrality requirements in a broader sense which may also differentiate how they adopt DT. Importantly, DT should be considered as a tool and not an end. This makes the need to unveil different ports' objective functions interesting. For instance, ports in developed world are more subjected to strict environmental preservation including containing negative social externalities, as such, modern technologies may be sought to address the need to comply to environmental sustainability requirements. Nevertheless, implementation of DT initiatives in ports is a function of a complex interplay of barriers and enablers as described underneath.

Barriers. We identified 14 barriers to successful implementation of DT in the ports sector (see Table 2). Based on their degree of centrality, only a few barriers have been discussed underneath.

Information Sharing. This has emerged as one of the serious most barrier to DT. Arguably, open information sharing accelerates perceived infiltration of trade secrets and loss of power among stakeholders due to information dis-intermediation (Raza et al., 2023; Zeng et al., 2020). Indeed, ports ecosystems are complicated by a myriad of actors who have disparate competitive goals and therefore succumb to potential opportunistic appropriation which may preclude stakeholders' trust in each other regarding information sharing (Bavassano et al., 2020). Some actors may express a low inclination to share correct information relating to their business model, business process, products and services, and customers engagement model fearing that, these can be used against them and thus reduce their competitive efficacy (Zhang and Lam, 2019). For example, Y. Zhou et al. (2020) alluded that lack of mutual trust between shippers and shipping

Table 2. Synthesis of drivers, barriers, and enablers of DT in maritime ports sector

	Degree rank	Drivers	Barriers	Enablers
High degree centrality	31	Regulatory compliance		
	31		Information sharing	
	31		Digital literacy	
	31		Investment cost	
	31			Stakeholders integration
	31			Ports readiness for change
	30			Digital platform
	29		Cybersecurity concerns	
	29		Digital awareness	
	29		Port governance structure	
	29		Environmental uncertainty	
	29			Collaboration
	29			Digital innovation
	29			Digital strategy
Medium degree centrality	28	Port process optimization		
	28		System interoperability	
	28		Ports culture	
	28			Trust
	27	Sustainability consciousness		
	27			Digital leadership
	26			Industry 4.0 technologies
	26			Top management support
	26			Digital champion

(*continued*)

Table 2. (*continued*)

	Degree rank	Drivers	Barriers	Enablers
Low degree centrality	24		Legacy systems	
	23		Lock-in effect	
	23			Change management
	23			Digital business model
	23			Digital maturity
	21		Agility	
	17		Asymmetric information	
	17			Co-opetition
	16		Diffusion of innovation	

Source: Authors' own elaboration from empirical literature review.

companies has precluded open information sharing on container capacity which perceivably eliminates bargaining power of the latter and therefore their competitiveness. Undoubtedly, poor information management in the port ecosystem is costly as it may lead up to 20% increase in ports operational budget (Gausdal *et al.*, 2018). However, nascent technologies like blockchain may secure information sharing among stakeholders (Bavassano *et al.*, 2020; Lin, 2023). Certainly, information sharing is one of the cornerstones to successful implementation of DT as it influences other aspects such as collaboration among stakeholders.

Digital Literacy. The knowledge repository of maritime ports' stakeholders has a bearing on the perceived usefulness of advanced digital technologies, which also influence their pace of acquisition and deployment. Digital literacy is the extent to which port stakeholders use their cognitive abilities to exploit the affordances of digital technologies as they create and capture value along maritime supply chains. Operational and technical skills are increasingly becoming essential assets amid the ubiquity of novel digital technologies (Chowdhury *et al.*, 2023). However, people may have strong cognitive abilities, but may lack the necessary knowledge about digital tools and their potential contribution in the actual context where they are supposed to be used. Consequently, maritime ports experience low digital literacy amongst stakeholders and internal human capital (González-Cancelas, Molina Serrano, *et al.*, 2020; Inkinen *et al.*, 2021). Some researchers have attributed this deficiency of skills to the lack of training to both employees and stakeholders, which consequently impair an understanding of digital affordances in business improvement (Baum-Talmor and Kitada, 2022; Raza *et al.*, 2023; Zhang and Lam, 2019). For instance, Gekara and Nguyen (2020) revealed that digital initiatives to install container terminal operating system (CTOS) at the Port of Mombasa failed partly due to workforce's sabotage and limited technical knowhow on the users of the installed CTOS. The authors further argued that the workforce's limited knowledge and skills to operate the new system effectively instigated overdependence on the external system developer to resolve even the minor technical and operational glitches. They also reported that ports' workers often ignored using system devices such as hand-held terminals and vehicle mounted terminals because they found them difficult or unfamiliar (ibid). In contrast, ports stakeholders' digital literacy may stimulate adequate actions and investments during strategic decision-making process (Philipp, 2020) and harness appropriate cultural climate for digital innovation (Hsu *et al.*, 2023; Lambrou *et al.*, 2019).

Investment Cost. High investment and implementation costs have been cited as one of the most prominent roadblocks to implementing DT initiatives in maritime ports (Bavassano *et al.*, 2020; Carlan *et al.*, 2017; Gausdal *et al.*, 2018; Inkinen *et al.*, 2021; Nicoleta *et al.*, 2020). While some authors contend that industry 4.0 digital technologies are inexpensive, this contention may contradict important aspects relating to the organizational transformation such as training requirements for system users, systems (re)configurations and architecture that enhance the efficacy of existing IT systems uninterruptedly (Zhang and Lam, 2019), port size (Poulis *et al.*, 2020), and the extent of digital maturity of ports' IT repertoires (Heilig and Voß, 2017). Thus, hardware, software, and training costs may present significant barriers for ports with especially limited budget. For instance, Inkinen *et al.* (2019) revealed that all medium-sized ports in Finland lagged in digitalization endeavors. The authors attributed the slowness to the size of the ports and their close association with limited financial resources and constrained strategic choices. Likewise, unclear cost and benefit distribution among port stakeholders may considerably attenuate their cooperation in implementing DT initiatives (Carlan *et al.*, 2017; Lin, 2023; Seo *et al.*, 2023). For instance, Y. Zhou *et al.* (2020) investigated the barriers to blockchain implementation among Singaporean maritime organizations and revealed that capital expenditure on the blockchain project and requisite training and upskilling of employees constituted perceived high investment cost amongst the interviewed maritime professionals. The authors argued that investment in blockchain technology requires financial stability that the maritime industry may lack (ibid).

Cybersecurity Concerns. Latest digital solutions are arguably more secure (Hsu *et al.*, 2023; Inkinen *et al.*, 2021). However, interconnected devices on shared digital platforms increase the risk of costly malicious attacks and data breaches especially, when we consider the novelty and infancy of technologies such as blockchain (Lin, 2023; Yang, 2019). Increasingly, data and information have become sensitive strategic resources and aspects of operations warranting aggressive safeguarding (Gekara and Nguyen, 2018; Kuo *et al.*, 2021; Nicoleta *et al.*, 2020). Following this, stakeholders such as freight forwarders have expressed concerns about the confidentiality of their business data on a shared open platform for container booking processes (Zeng *et al.*, 2020) in case it becomes preyed upon (Raza *et al.*, 2023). Examples of malicious attacks are not uncommon in the maritime domain. For instance, the port of Antwerp in Belgium came under cyberattack when the perpetrators smuggled cocaine and heroin through legitimate cargos by hacking the port's IT systems (Chang *et al.*, 2020). Meanwhile, the shipping giants Maersk, MSC, Hapag Lloyd, ONE, and CMA CGM came under cyberattacks in 2017 (Afenyo and

Caesar, 2023). While these companies had been thought to have airtight cybersecurity systems, such attacks set a bad precedence for sectors such as ports which may aspire to venture into new technologies for which they have limited knowledge about. Thus, the perception of vulnerabilities inherent in new digital solutions daunts ports' stakeholders from implementing them (Gómez Díaz *et al.*, 2023; González-Cancelas, Molina, *et al.*, 2020; González-Cancelas, Molina Serrano, *et al.*, 2020). This fact exacerbates stakeholders' mistrust in advanced digital technologies' data management capabilities (Inkinen *et al.*, 2021). Thus, perceived digital security risks increases reluctance of maritime ports to experiment with and exploit digital technological solutions, consequently making ports and maritime supply chains uncompetitive (Kashav *et al.*, 2022).

Digital Awareness. Digital awareness represents ports' knowledge repository and inquisitiveness about the functioning and affordances of Industry 4.0 digital solutions. It is the extent to which maritime ports consciously recognize the potential of novel technological solutions and proactively engage in pursuit of their affordances. It may be rooted in the ports' experimental culture and quest to invoke new business models to stay competitive (Chowdhury *et al.*, 2023; Gómez Díaz *et al.*, 2023). In fact, ports' lack of digital awareness has been attributed to their staggering DT initiatives (Philipp, 2020). Yet, lack of knowledge and awareness of how digital technologies may affect maritime ports' businesses has been linked with their slow rate of acquisition (Lin, 2023). A few exceptions include container terminals such as Victoria International Container Terminal (VICT) in Melbourne Australia, Container Terminal Altenwerder (CTA) in Hamburg, Germany, Euromax Container Terminal in Rotterdam, Netherlands, and Norfolk International terminals in Virginia (Gekara and Nguyen, 2018) which are fully automated with modern digital technologies and are commonly regarded as the industry's best practice role models. Indeed, top executives' digital awareness is an essential internal dynamic capability that underscores the capacity to sense and shape opportunities and threats by reconfiguring intangible and tangible ports assets (Raza *et al.*, 2023).

Port Governance Structure. The influence of port governance models on DT trajectories are discernible through their influence on organizational structure (Lambrou *et al.*, 2019; Zhang and Lam, 2019), technological integration (Inkinen *et al.*, 2021), and decision-making processes (Zeng *et al.*, 2020). This barrier varies greatly on a continuum between publicly owned and hybrid port models with private and public entities collaborating in the ownership and management of port operations (Philipp, 2020). Public port authorities encounter challenges due to bureaucratic decision-making processes and limited agility (Zeng *et al.*, 2020), hindering the rapid adoption of digital innovations (He *et al.*, 2023). However, their stability and long-term vision enable strategic planning for sustainable technology integration. On the other hand, private port operators driven by profitability and operational efficiency exhibit greater responsiveness to DT, investing readily in digital solutions to optimize processes and improve customer experience. The landlord port model, by segregating infrastructure ownership from operations, fosters DT through competition among terminal operators and the pursuit of cutting-edge technologies. Nevertheless, hybrid port governance models – combining elements of public and private sector involvement (He *et al.*, 2023; Inkinen *et al.*, 2021), offer both strategic planning and entrepreneurial spirit but may face complexities in decision-making. For instance, (Zeng *et al.*, 2020) found out that government power and organization ownership structure impacted the adoption of inter-organizational information systems in the maritime supply chain and that, actors must recognize disparities among various ownership structures.

Environmental Uncertainty. In this context, environmental uncertainty refers to an external outcome that may jeopardize the efficacy of ports' or its stakeholders' DT endeavors. Generally, environmental uncertainty should be a driving force that propels ports to acquire new digital solutions to mitigate risks (Kuo *et al.*, 2021). Oxymoronically, it acts as a barrier to effective implementation of DT in ports. Firstly, as myriads of policies, regulations, and trade agreements change constantly, they make it difficult for ports to know what digital tools and solutions will work in the future (Inkinen *et al.*, 2021; Raza et al., 2023; Y. Zhou et al., 2020). As ports are entwined in global economy and geopolitical events, their services increasingly fluctuate with these dynamics making it hard for them to determine return on investments of novel digital solutions (Gómez Díaz et al., 2023; Lin, 2023). For instance, the ongoing trade tensions between China and the US, and the Russian invasion of Ukraine impact both ports' businesses as well as those of stakeholders such as shipping lines and freight forwarders in terms of higher freight fees, longer transit times, and port congestion. Secondly, an unprecedented exponential growth in Industry 4.0 technologies presents uncertainty to ports regarding which digital solutions to adapt and how to implement them effectively as well as unified standards for data transmission, sharing, an interoperability (Lin, 2023). Meanwhile, embarking on novel technologies adds another layer of uncertainty regarding displacement of jobs and emergence of new skills requirements which can instigate resistance to change as digital talents are reportedly scarce and do not match the pace of DT (Gekara and Nguyen, 2018, 2020; Raza et al., 2023). Irrespective of the digital solutions that ports adopt, the existence of stable national broadband connectivity has been brought into the spotlight. For instance, the flickering internet connectivity (provided by another governmental agency) was reported to force the Port *of* Mombasa's workforce and its wider array of stakeholders to switch between digital and manual systems thereby suppressing the port's effort to automate its container terminal (Gekara and Nguyen, 2020). Furthermore, while blockchain for instance, can provide an opportunity for ports to streamline efficiency and enhance stakeholders experience, it also introduces a layer of uncertainty regarding interoperability, scalability, and potential disruptions to existing ports operations.

Enablers. These are factors that facilitate the attainment of successful DT in ports sectors. We identified 15 enablers of which we resorted to discussing only 6 of them based on their degrees of centrality.

Stakeholders' Integration. This refers to synchronization of port stakeholders' information and workflows and the way their disparate systems communicate with each other. The ports sector has a plethora of technologies relating to ports' operations, i.e., port community systems (PCS), single window systems (SWS), electronic data interchange (EDI), radio frequency identification, among others (Bauk *et al.*, 2017; Peynirci, 2021). These conventional technologies have been used by port authorities for years to integrate ports' actors. While they may lack scalability, retrofitability, and interoperability, they foster the adoption of advanced technologies such as digital twins, artificial intelligence, block chain, and internet of things (Hsu *et al.*, 2023; Lin, 2023; Raza *et al.*, 2023) as supporting baseline technologies. Considering the value creation logic that lies in stakeholders such as customs authorities, shipping lines, freight forwarders and the ports themselves, initiatives to integrate their interfaces may further strengthen value creation and capture of the ecosystem, engendering ports' competitiveness, and consequently bolstering inclination to embark on novel digital technologies (Carlan *et al.*, 2017; Hsu *et al.*, 2023; Seo *et al.*, 2023). Arguably, the more integrated the stakeholders are, the more likely they are to implement DT initiatives that further benefit them.

Ports and Stakeholders Readiness for Change. We define this as the extent to which maritime ports embrace changes and readily undergo digital metamorphism. The exploitation of novel and cutting-edge digital technologies lies in the complex interplay of management measures and employees' knowledge and skills, as well as functional information technology processes (Philipp, 2020). These elements increasingly require concerted efforts of maritime ports to embrace digital transformative changes. In fact, Philipp (2020) and González-Cancelas, Molina Serrano, *et al.* (2020) suggest that neither innovative digital technologies alone nor human aspects are a panacea to successful DT of maritime ports. They argue that successful implementation of DT in ports relies on such aspects as alignment of existing culture, structure, personnel, and tasks (Gómez Díaz *et al.*, 2023; González-Cancelas, Molina Serrano, *et al.*, 2020; Iman *et al.*, 2022) for all stakeholders involved. Yet, an empirical study by Bavassano *et al.* (2020) revealed a heterogeneity in implementing digital initiatives such as blockchain, among maritime stakeholders (i.e., shipping companies, port authorities, regulators) and attributed it to organizational and perceived market readiness aspects. The findings in this study underscore ports' attitudinal role towards change and the timeline upon which the change will materialize. For instance, some of the interviewed actors expressed concerns that it would take about 10 years for a blockchain initiative to materialize. Such a view exacerbates disinclination to invest in novel technologies (Bavassano *et al.*, 2020).

Digital Platform. This concept entails a collaborative electronic platform that pulls ports ecosystems' stakeholders together, thereby enabling a smooth information sharing as it pertains to freight movements, vessel arrival times, port call processes, as well as interactions with hinterland actors (Carlan *et al.*, 2017; Lambrou *et al.*, 2019). The implementations of digital platforms such as PortNet (Fedi *et al.*, 2019; Inkinen *et al.*, 2019), and blockchain technology (Bavassano *et al.*, 2020; Lin, 2023; Philipp *et al.*, 2019) have permitted the rationalization of port processes and bolstered coordination between ports and their stakeholders. In fact, digital platforms such as port community (PCS) systems and national single window systems (NSWS) are a precursor for more digitalized ports as they create paperless ports and streamline administrative procedures (Bisogno, 2015; Carlan *et al.*, 2017; Hsu *et al.*, 2023; Seo *et al.*, 2023). However, the development of common digital platforms among a diverse set of stakeholders is arguably a daunting task (Gekara and Nguyen, 2020; Inkinen *et al.*, 2019) because benefits and cost of such initiatives may not equally accrue and resonate with all stakeholders involved, unless powerful digital orchestrators emerge to spearhead the process. For instance, the Port of Rotterdam's vision 2030, has had long term strategic vision that incorporates stakeholders' opinions thereby obtaining their buy-in in initiatives that impact the port's ecosystem.

Collaboration. This is an extent to which maritime ports stakeholders synchronously pool resources (tangible and intangible) in implementing DT initiatives. Unequivocally, successful implementation of DT initiatives depends on well-coordinated efforts of most ports' stakeholders (Camarero Orive *et al.*, 2020; Raza *et al.*, 2023). Stakeholders' collaboration stems from shared innovation vision, commitment to open communication, mutual respect, and willingness to work together, lack of which exacerbates fragmented transformational initiatives (Carlan *et al.*, 2017; Kuo *et al.*, 2021; Lin, 2023). In this vein, Gekara and Nguyen (2020) found that container terminal automation initiative failed due to lack of collaboration from internal workforce and freight forwarders who were external users when they bypassed the installed system and maintained manual transaction of freight clearing documentations. Additionally, the self-organizing interplay of disparate actors, requires formal agreements for developing and implementing collaborative solutions (Inkinen *et al.*, 2021; Vairetti *et al.*, 2019), as well as commitment and willingness of experienced stakeholder partners with whom to spearhead the implementation of DT (Y. Zhou *et al.*, 2020). For instance, to achieve mutual trust and communication ports' stakeholders must collaborate in effectuating the enablements in blockchain technology (Gómez Díaz *et al.*, 2023; Lin, 2023; Raza *et al.*, 2023). To elaborate this, the Port of Antwerp collaborated with T-Mining, a blockchain solution provider on a digital project to secure the flow of documents through smart contracts which has enabled it to share real-time secured documents and related information with all interested parties (Chang *et al.*, 2020; Zhao *et al.*, 2023). Examples of the efficacy of collaboration can also be drawn from shipping sector where IBM created a blockchain digital solution, Trade-Lens in collaboration with Maersk a global shipping leader (Bavassano *et al.*, 2020). This solution has enabled real-time tracking and planning of shipping containers and the automation of shipping documents flows including letters of credit, commercial invoices, certifications, and bill of lading which are typically prone to fraud (Chang *et al.*, 2020). The TradeLens platform serves stakeholders such as port authorities, public authorities and freight forwarders and other shipping companies such as MSC, and CMA CGMA (González-Cancelas, Molina, *et al.*, 2020). However, due to disparities in resources and perceived benefits of adopting inter-organizational digital systems, port stakeholders will likely experience protracted and complicated negotiation process (Vairetti *et al.*, 2019).

Digital Innovation. A digital innovation captures the extent to which ports explore new ways of delivering superior products or services and differentiated stakeholders value by exploiting novel digital technologies. In fact, the outcome of a digital innovation is noted in its impact on processes (i.e., streamlining the efficacy of port processes) (Carlan *et al.*, 2017; Gausdal *et al.*, 2018), value creation and capture model (i.e., new digital business model) (Gausdal *et al.*, 2018), and engagement model (i.e., stakeholders experience) (Bavassano *et al.*, 2020; Philipp, 2020). Nevertheless, ports exploit digital innovation in aspects they deem the former fits best with strategic business needs (Gausdal *et al.*, 2018). For instance, the port of Antwerp, through its ambition to become a European leader in IoT has embarked on digital initiatives such as blockchain solution which has enabled it to automate end-to-end physical flow of containers, automate document flows, and integrate data silos (Chang *et al.*, 2020). Digital innovations such as track and trace, automatic identification systems (AIS), blockchain, electronic data interchange

(EDI), among others, have the potential of facilitating imperative ports' continuous DT (Bavassano *et al.*, 2020; Carlan *et al.*, 2017; Inkinen *et al.*, 2019; Lin, 2023).

Digital Strategy. ICT deployment strategies have a direct bearing on the extent to which maritime ports acquire and experiment with digital technological solutions. A digital strategy is the one that uses ICT infrastructure (both soft and hard) as a core of ports' business strategy reconfiguration. It deploys digital innovation and integrates it with core port processes thereby enabling them to create and capture superior value among its participating stakeholders (Lambrou *et al.*, 2019; Raza *et al.*, 2023). A particular digital strategy has a bearing on the outcome of DT initiatives. For instance, pathfinder ports (i.e., Rotterdam, Antwerp, Singapore, and Hamburg, among others) experiment with latest technological breakthroughs and take risks, thereby, influencing positively DT outcomes such as full port integration with all stakeholders of the industry (Bauk *et al.*, 2017; Hsu *et al.*, 2023; Kapidani *et al.*, 2020; Philipp, 2020; Raza *et al.*, 2023). On the contrary, late adopters or laggards, where majority of ports falls, have missing digital strategy and only adopt new technology necessary to safeguard their business operations (Bauk *et al.*, 2017; Inkinen *et al.*, 2019; Y. Zhou *et al.*, 2020). Between the two extremes are monitor ports, early majority (or adopter ports), and developer ports (Bauk *et al.*, 2017; Philipp, 2020). Effective digital strategy may enable ports to persevere transformational endeavors in the face of unprecedented failures. For example, Inkinen *et al.* (2019), in their empirical research on DT trajectories in Finish ports revealed that majority of the respondents affirmed to have adopted an observer's role as opposed to taking the leading role which has resulted to low digitalization outcomes among Finish ports. Besides, the authors revealed that Finish ports' DT evolves as a part of strategic choice which they openly argued was missing. The authors identified that, of the interviewed Finish ports, none had a designated person for digital service development (ibid).

To sum up, Fig. 4 presents an aggregated framework that conceptualizes the drivers, barriers, and enablers of DT in the maritime ports sector. As the framework shows, despite the pressure from competition, regulatory authorities, and sustainability consciousness, achieving DT is not straight forward. There are several barriers that can hinder that journey. However, several factors serve as enablers of DT implementation.

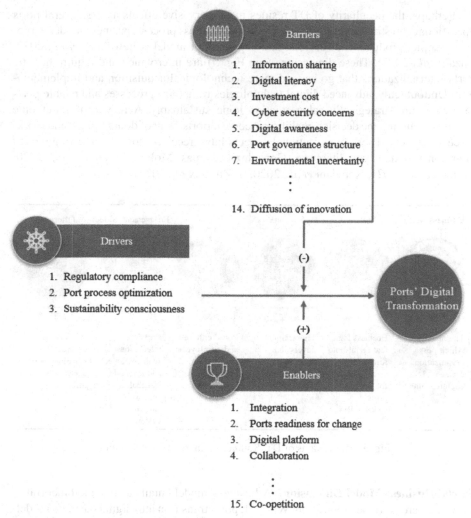

Fig. 4. Framework of drivers, barriers, and enablers of DT in the maritime ports. Source: Authors' own elaboration based on empirical literature.

3.2 DT Idiosyncrasies and Dimensions

DT in maritime ports refers to the process that results in a fundamental transition in the way ports operate, create, and expropriate value. Undeniably, DT of maritime ports is oxymoronic as it presents both opportunities and significant disruptions. Ports may leverage the affordances of advanced digital technologies to improve efficiency, safety, and sustainability. Contrarily, to leverage such affordances ports must conscientiously integrate novel technologies into their existing processes, infrastructure, and legacy systems while balancing the complexity of operations which involve numerous stakeholders (Chowdhury *et al.*, 2023). Moreover, coordinating and integrating disparate stakeholders' systems and processes may be a potentially daunting task.

Perhaps, the peculiarity of DT resides in its pervasive effects across several ports operational and structural aspects such as ports business process, business model, structure, people, products and services, and engagement model (Chowdhury *et al.*, 2023; Raza *et al.*, 2023). These dimensions (see Fig. 5) are intertwined and require holistic ports internalizations that go beyond mere technological acquisition and implementation. Undoubtedly, advanced digital technologies transform processes and enable ports to reconfigure strategically value creation logic sustainably. Achieving this outcome requires changing the decision-making processes, ports' way of doing things, and workforce's skillsets. These organizational aspects have received considerable fragmented attention in extant port literature (González-Cancelas, Molina Serrano, *et al.*, 2020; Inkinen *et al.*, 2021; Kapidani *et al.*, 2020; Y. Zhou *et al.*, 2020).

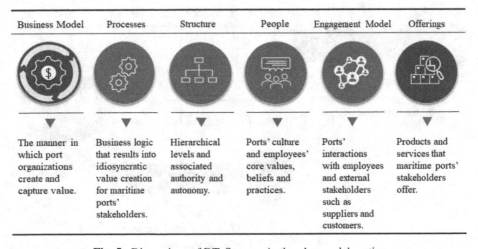

Business Model	Processes	Structure	People	Engagement Model	Offerings
The manner in which port organizations create and capture value.	Business logic that results into idiosyncratic value creation for maritime ports' stakeholders.	Hierarchical levels and associated authority and autonomy.	Ports' culture and employees' core values, beliefs and practices.	Ports' interactions with employees and external stakeholders such as suppliers and customers.	Products and services that maritime ports' stakeholders offer.

Fig. 5. Dimensions of DT. Source: Authors' own elaboration.

Ports' Business Model Dimension. A business model entails a strategic blueprint of how ports create value proposition. With DT, ports transition into digital business models from traditional business models (i.e., using digital platforms that optimize port's interactions with its external stakeholders). This adoption of business model enables ports to generate new value proposition and revenue streams (Kuo *et al.*, 2021; Sanchez-Gonzalez *et al.*, 2019; Seo *et al.*, 2023). Given the complexity of port processes and multiplicity of actors, ports need to develop a digital supply chain as a new business model in collaboration with shipping lines, governmental agencies, freight forwarders, customs authorities, among others. For instance, Chowdhury *et al.* (2023) and Seo *et al.* (2023) report that the port of Singapore introduced a digital platform, digitalport@SGTM which optimizes vessel, health, and immigration clearances. Meanwhile, the ports of Hamburg, Antwerp, and Rotterdam have implemented smartPORT, NxtPort, and PortXchange business models respectively, which streamline port operations such as real-time cargo tracking, customs clearance, berth availability, and vessel schedules (Gausdal *et al.*, 2018; Hsu *et al.*, 2023; Inkinen *et al.*, 2021). With digital technologies such as internet of things (IoT), sensors, and big data analytics, these ports can take strategic decisions that are grounded in real-time data thereby significantly minimizing port congestion and waiting times. Furthermore, the platforms streamline connectivity and transparent interactivity of all actors in a systematized way hence, engendering ecosystems competitiveness at large (Hsu et al., 2023). We contend that the DT needs of ports vary depending on their business models, which can be influenced by factors such as the complexity and volume of cargo they handle and their heterogeneity. For example, a large container port like Rotterdam in the Netherlands, may require advanced technologies such as automation and artificial intelligence to optimize cargo handling and reduce turnaround times. In contrast, a smaller port like Bremanger in Norway that handles bulk cargo may require simpler DT solutions such as digital documentation and real-time tracking of cargo.

Ports' Process(es) Dimension. It is a logical order of interrelated activities that ports, and its stakeholders perform to receive and discharge cargo to consignees. It relates to how ports bring value proposition to life and harness economic rent. DT has certainly had a significant bearing on the port processes. For instance, the introduction of digital technologies has facilitated greater automation of port processes, such as cargo handling, terminal management, and vessel scheduling. Automation such as digital twin has allowed the port of Hamburg to increase transparency of process management and reduce the degree of human interventions in the operations of port processes (Camarero Orive et al., 2020; Chowdhury et al., 2023). As port processes are inextricably intertwined in the actions of many stakeholders, DT has enabled ports to better integrate their operations with those of their stakeholders, such as customs authorities, shipping lines, freight forwarders, and railway and trucking companies. Such integration has engendered substantial coordination and collaboration amongst these value chain actors which have further enhanced efficiency and reduced delays in some pioneering ports such as Antwerp, Gothenburg, Qingdao, Rotterdam, etc. (Lin, 2023; Raza et al., 2023). Furthermore, the use of big data analytics enables ports to rationalize data captured by IoT and sensor devices to predict vessel arrival times, optimize assets utilization in cargo handling operations and improve productivity. However, stakeholders express mixed feelings about the pros and cons of digital technologies. For instance, Gausdal et al. (2018) in their empirical work on Norwegian maritime industry found that blockchain technology did not provide the right fit for the whole shipping industry. The authors contended that nuanced attention must be paid to specific actors' requirements in terms of size, goals, vision, financial capacity, and interest in a particular innovation (ibid). Therefore, the journey to digital maturity is long and winding as ports are said to be at different stages of implementation of DT initiatives (Inkinen et al., 2021; Philipp, 2020). At one extreme, there are ports that are digitizing documentation flow internally and across relevant stakeholders (i.e., the port of Dar es Salaam in Tanzania), at the other extreme, there are ports that have automated all their processes including integration with relevant stakeholders (i.e., Gothenburg port in Sweden).

Ports' Organizational Structure Dimension. DT allows ports to redefine hierarchical and functional structures due to increasing need for faster decision-making, process transparency, and open communication lines (Seo et al., 2023). The increasing use of digital platforms such as port community systems and electronic single windows (Peynirci, 2021) shifts structural power across stakeholders, however, affords ports greater vertical and horizontal collaborations and flexibility in value creation and capture (Philipp,

2020). For instance, the use of blockchain's smart contracts secures ports stakeholders' transactions when only relevant actors can verifiably effectuate their value creation equation. The level of transparency goes a long way to enforcing greater accountability meanwhile streamlining ports' operations. Moreover, open platforms such as those for container bookings have impacted the decision-making tactics of actors such as freight forwarders, shippers, and shipping lines, where they previously had to work with limited asymmetrical information (Zeng *et al.*, 2020) which arguably had been used as a source of bargaining power and competitiveness. The authors further revealed that freight forwarders expressed concerns that valuable customer information such as prices could be accessed and taken advantage of by the Onetouch (open platform) system's provider, hence their reluctance to use such system (Zeng *et al.*, 2020). Thus, storing data on the cloud and introducing other organizations in the value creation of freight forwarders seemed to infiltrate their sphere of influence. It follows that hierarchical organizational structure instigates bureaucracy that contradicts the need for agility and greater decentralized autonomy in decision-making. More horizontal structure will allow ports to establish cross-functional team structure that fosters collaboration by integrating both business and digital teams into a high-performing team. Furthermore, ports may have to restructure to accommodate the emergence of new roles which specialize in data analytics, automation, and artificial intelligence (Raza *et al.*, 2023; Zhang and Lam, 2019). As Kuo *et al.* (2021) stresses, organizational structure is pertinent building block of DT and therefore it is affected by it.

Ports' People Dimension. The ports' workforce are the ultimate users of any digital system as such, they directly impact their success of failure. DT, due to its evolutionary and combinatorial natures, may pejoratively instill fear of change and intensify negative attitudinal prejudices towards acceptance and use of digital solutions. In fact, this tendency may be more pronounced among maritime ports with low technological diffusion (Djoumessi *et al.*, 2019; Zeng *et al.*, 2020). Consequently, stalling efforts to implement digital initiatives at port level and across ports' stakeholders. Nonetheless, implementation of DT necessitates ports' workforce reskilling and upskilling because of changes in work cultures and practices (Gekara and Nguyen, 2018; Inkinen *et al.*, 2021; Y. Zhou *et al.*, 2020). For instance, of the very few remaining workforces in Australian ports require more analytical skills than physical skills as they need to adeptly interact with digital systems' diagnostics and intervention (Gekara and Nguyen, 2018). Furthermore, Gekara and Nguyen (2020) revealed that the failure of a digital initiative to automate Mombasa container terminal was partly due to limited steady training and skilling effort to the existing and new recruits after the digital project had been rolled out. Therefore, digital skills management and literacy are requisite conditions that may support ports' continuous adaptation through DT (Gekara and Nguyen, 2018).

Ports' Engagement Model Dimension. Engagement model entails a point of contact between the ports and its broad array of users. DT impacts how ports interact internally and externally with customers and other stakeholders (Kuo *et al.*, 2021). With DT, technologies such as big data, analytics, and IoT may allow ports to transition into digital channels or combine both physical and digital channels using social media and other e-commerce platforms. For instance, the use of big data may allow ports to garner and analyze large amounts of data about their operations such as ship arrivals and departures, cargo volumes, and whether conditions. This data can be used to optimize port operations such as scheduling cargo arrivals and departures and predicting and mitigating potential delays or disruptions. Likewise, analytics can afford ports a capability to synthesize vast amounts of data they generate thus gaining insights that permit data-driven decisions whereas, IoT can allow remote control of connected ports' devices such as cranes, trucks, and containers (Gekara and Nguyen, 2018). While social media platforms will enable ports to inform customers about cargo arrivals and departures, e-commerce can facilitate online transactions where port users can book cargo shipments, track their shipments, and make payments. This will enable ports to harness intelligent information real-time and thus take effective decisions to effect positive outcomes such as vessel arrival scheduling, and trucking appointments. Likewise, port users may garner information relating to the status of their shipments, pay port dues online, and communicate with port authorities in real-time. This dimension is closely interlinked with the automation of ports' business processes. The key is to collect intelligent information and disseminate it to appropriate stakeholders. For instance, the use of a single point of entrance of cargo manifest may save ports, clearing and forwarding companies, customs, and other public authorities, time and duplication of efforts.

Ports' Offerings Dimension. DT affects value added logistics that ports and its stakeholders provide to final consignees. Thus, ports can leverage digital technologies and harness more value in their service offerings. For instance, ports can use straddle carriers with integrated electronic data interchange (EDI) or IoT sensors to streamline identification, tracking and tracing of cargo movements both ship-to-shore and in the yards (Camarero Orive et al., 2020; Carlan et al., 2017). Moreover, the use of temperature-controlled warehouses may attract more cold-chain (i.e., perishable food and drink market). Meanwhile, artificial intelligence (AI) and sensor technologies may reduce energy consumption, thereby, enabling ports to sustainably cut cost and lessen environmental footprint (Raza et al., 2023). Robotic technology may reinforce value added activities such as weighing, repalletizing and wrapping, packaging and consolidation for onwards distribution. Technologies that allow ships to recharge electricity while on port call enable ports to reduce greenhouse gas footprint. Tracking and tracing technologies will allow ports to accurately share port traffic information with stakeholders such as trains, truckers, shipping lines, among others.

We posit that the preceding six dimensions underlie differing transformational trajectories within ports and across stakeholders. While there as some ports that have traversed and transformed in all dimensions (i.e., smart ports as Hamburg, Rotterdam, and Victoria International Container Terminal) (Kuo et al., 2021; Philipp, 2020), majority seem to chart sketchy paths which presumably underscore the many interacting factors as illustrated in Fig. 4.

4   Managerial and Policy Implications

4.1   One Size Does Not Fit All

We concur that DT as a tool does not fit all ports equally. It requires a nuanced analysis of its affordances and a more pragmatic understanding of its applicability in different contexts and conditions. While there has been an increasing need to improve efficiency and productivity in the maritime industry as a whole and ports in particular using novel digital technologies, we argue that not all ports may be suitable candidates for DT. One plausible explanation is that the capital expenditure involved in procuring new equipment and digital infrastructure (i.e., hardware and software) may extend to millions or even billions of dollars, far out of reach of many ports. Yet, ports that handle specialized cargo such as containerized, hazardous, perishable, or liquid bulk may require more significant investments in DT due to the need for specialized equipment, storage, and technology. For instance, implementing DT solutions in ports that handle high-value cargo such as chemicals as is the case with the Port of Antwerp in Belgium, may require significant investments in security, tracking, and monitoring, systems than ports that transit low-value cargo such as timber in the port of Riga in Latvia. Moreover, ports that handle less specialized cargo such as grain bulk may require less investment in DT and therefore investment cost in that respect may not be of concern. Again, the investment costs emanating from DT may not be a huge barrier for ports that handle large volumes of cargo than for ports which handle limited volumes of cargo because large economic rents that accrue from massive volumes may justify investments in DT that optimize operations. Thus, cosmetic improvements on manually operated systems – through digitization might be a more pragmatic approach for ports with limited cargo traffic to warrant significant investments in digital innovations. In fact, some ports may make-do with digitization of paper documentations, data, record keeping and other administrative and documentation formalities. Therefore, as the needs of different ports evolve, a transition towards more advanced DT may make more sense. With the findings in this study, we are convinced to have unfolded peculiarities of DT and provided anecdotal evidence and insights from meaningful cases in the port industry. Furthermore, we provide a caveat that the thematic drivers, enablers, and barriers of DT in maritime ports may play out differently across a range of ports around the world. For instance, the issue of internet connectivity is a much relevant environmental uncertainty aspect in contexts where ports experience weak and unstable connectivity because of over-reliance on governmental internet service providers who often may lack ambition to develop stronger networks and bandwidths (Gekara and Nguyen, 2020). In this vein, most emerging economies are currently transitioning into 3G and 4G internet technologies while their developed counterparts are charting 5G which provides low latency and much faster data transmissions. The latter supports interconnected devices such as automated guided vehicles, automated rubber-tired gantry cranes, remotely controlled ship-to-shore cranes, and analytics of large amounts of data generated by these devices (González-Cancelas, Molina, et al., 2020; Inkinen et al., 2021). Nevertheless, the need for internet connectivity is a must for all ports, large or small, as there are standard shipping documentations that must be shared with relevant stakeholders to rapidly clear cargos through ports. Several other caveats are discussed here under:

Regulatory compliance is a universal driver of DT, however, may be greeted with different action points. For instance, ports that exist in geographical locations such as Europe and America where there is a greater requirement for energy transition from fossil fuels to renewable energy may fast track DT initiatives as the means to comply to strict regulations and accommodate modern ships design and size. In this regard, ports in these locations may implement DT initiatives such as digital twin, IoT, A/VR, and AI to streamline port operations by reducing movements and congestions of ships and trucks which are prime candidates for CO2 emissions. On the other hand, ports in Africa may be subjected to slightly lax regulations where emphasis may be placed on digitizing documentation flows and automating selected aspects such as containers offloading, stacking, and delivery.

4.2 Stakeholders' Alignment Challenges in Ports DT

Throughout this paper, we have alluded to the importance of stakeholders' involvement in DT's success or failure. Examples such as those offered by Gekara and Nguyen (2020) on the failure of TOS initiative due to misalignment of goals across both internal port's personnel and external port users – the freight forwarders; and Heilig *et al.* (2017) on the failure of the port of Hamburg to get stakeholders to use smartPORT digital platform back in 2017, stress the importance of stakeholders' considerations. Moreover, ports such as Long beach and Los Angeles have continued to enter renegotiations with International longshore and warehouse union (ILWU) due to possible ramifications of introducing novel technological solutions on the existing workforce. These anecdotes illustrate the fact that digital technologies as tools are as good as the strength of the alignment of all port actors who may directly be impacted by such digital initiatives. In contrast, ports like Rotterdam, Antwerp, and Gothenburg have managed to develop programs that are inclusive in terms of integrating views of different stakeholders including developing collaborative solutions together. This consequently impacts the sense of ownership among stakeholders and entice their buy-in. Therefore, port authorities must look up to initiatives that involve major stakeholders such as workers associations, government agencies, shipping lines, and freight forwarders as an immediate solution to minimize the risk of system failure due to less optimal critical mass. They may also involve these stakeholders in identifying opportunities for collaboration and innovation.

4.3 Embracing Ports' Digital Ecosystem as a New Imperative Normal

Although DT endeavors are pervasive, they are idiosyncratic to different ports' stakeholders. For instance, ports can serve as central hubs for the development of digital technologies and infrastructure, establishing partnerships with other stakeholders to share data and knowledge to foster innovation and improve efficiency. Meanwhile, support from the shipping community may leapfrog digitalization projects in maritime ports because the former has made significant strides in implementing DT initiatives (Poulis *et al.*, 2020). Moreover, the involvement of professional consulting firms in the project management and training of workforce may lessen the pain points in implementing DT initiatives. It is arguably beneficial to adopt digital technologies with ecosystem's enablement, however, ports and its stakeholders (i.e., government agencies, shipping lines, logistics providers, etc.) must be ready and willing to share information which can be made possible through application programming interface (APIs). This will enable ports to enhance their operational efficiency and minimize delays in cargo handling. Moreover, attribution of value to such investment among disparate port stakeholders remains an unsolved puzzle (Bavassano *et al.*, 2020). Information asymmetry that some actors such as freight forwarders live off may stimulate increasing resistance to adopting an open platform by these critical stakeholders (Iman *et al.*, 2022; J. Liu *et al.*, 2021; Seo *et al.*, 2023; Zeng *et al.*, 2020). Importantly, government and regulators can significantly influence digitalization process by enacting friendly regulations and providing concessions and subsidies. For instance, governments can provide exemptions or tax incentives for ports and companies that invest in digital technology. A typical example is the port of Rotterdam in the Netherlands whose government had been instrumental in providing subsidies and incentives for the adoption of digital technologies. As a result, the Port of Rotterdam has become one of the most advanced and efficient ports in the world, with real-time tracking of vessels and cargo, automated cargo handling, and optimized cargo logistics. Meanwhile, workers associations can provide valuable insights into the needs and concerns of workers who are critical to port operations. They can participate in the development of training programs that help workers adapt to new digital technologies and ensure their rights and interests are protected.

4.4   Port-Wide Digital Leadership and Digital Talent Management

DT dictates unique skillsets that top executives need to steer transformational initiatives in the right direction. Likewise, digital knowledge is essential in talent acquisition, grooming, retention, and management of digital resources. Roles such as chief information/digital officers (CIO & CDO) are exceedingly trending as top requirements for a successful DT and go hand in hand with supportive lower-level structures of port organizations. Moreover, an employee-centric approach may stimulate employees' innovation and participation in the implementation of DT initiatives. Thus, primary users of digital technologies become the center stage of grooming and digital knowledge acquisition. Considering their position, ports' digital leaders should reasonably treat digital assets as core strategic resources and instill a digital mindset across the board. For instance, they may encourage collaboration among stakeholders such as shipping lines and customs authorities to share best practice and insights. They may also facilitate the adoption of digital solutions and platforms that enable secure and efficient information sharing among disparate stakeholders. Similarly, ports may establish innovation labs or incubators that can help them test and experiment with new technologies before deploying them on a large scale. Talent management may ensure that digitally adept workforce will be available to manage cybersecurity risks and respond with efficacy to any unprecedented malicious attacks such as hacking and cybervandalism. These steps will reduce the intensity of cybersecurity concerns as one of the major barriers that empirical literature asserts to cripple down DT initiatives among ports.

Furthermore, to overcome digital awareness challenge among port stakeholders, ports' digital leaders may strategize and acquire digital solutions that align with both internal and external stakeholders' requirements, meanwhile devising specific trainings to upskill and reskill personnel to ensure they can adeptly use adopted digital tools. Yet, to overcome environmental uncertainty barrier towards the adoption of DT, ports digital leaders can spearhead the culture of innovation and experimentation. This will afford ports agility in adapting to changing circumstances (i.e., continual emergencies of new technologies). Meanwhile, digital talent management will ensure that employees are equipped with the necessary skills and expertise to navigate uncertainty and respond effectively to new changes.

4.5 How Ports Can Sustain DT Endeavors

We argue that DT of ports is not an end in itself, that after having transformed all aspects of the port business ports can complacently relax. Instead, ports must espouse DT as a necessary facilitating mechanism to strategic reconfiguration and rejuvenation of their efficacy in ever-changing environmental dynamics such as the mounting need for data and physical infrastructure security, operational safety, process and procedural transparency, and sustainability. In fact, economics of transformation endeavors may be such that, ports may experience high investment and implementation costs in initial implementation initiatives. However, such costs may decline in subsequent transformations due to infused readiness for change and cumulative effect of previously acquired digital infrastructure (Carlan *et al.*, 2017). Furthermore, the role of ports' digital leaders should stretch across IT departments and complement the overall strategic vision of ports. The latter calls for a unified view of both port business and IT strategies and the convergence of C-suite managers' interests towards advancing ports objectives holistically and collaboratively. Arguably, no matter how good novel digital solutions are, if ports' workforce cannot support and use them effectively, the true benefits of DT can hardly ever be achieved.

As DT pervades all spheres of ports aspects such as structure, workforce culture, processes, and port services, ports top executives' and executors' change management skills become an ever-requisite talent. Nevertheless, to overcome eminent resistance to change by the workforce, transformation initiatives may be introduced phase-wise. In the meantime, giving the workforce an opportunity to rethink their roles, grow into them, and take necessary steps to equip themselves in case of subsequent transformational endeavors.

5 Conclusions and Directions for Further Research

In this paper, we have developed a framework based on empirical evidence from the maritime ports sector. We have delineated drivers, barriers, and enablers antecedents to successful implementation of DT in ports and demonstrated how each antecedent impacts materialization of digitalization initiatives. We have also cautioned that our framework of drivers, enablers, and barriers of DT in ports is contingent upon such factors as port size, complexity, nature of cargo handled, geographical location of ports, and heterogeneity. We have argued that the barriers may be accentuated or minimized on a continuum of these elements. Similarly, drivers can have different stresses across different ports. Therefore, our analysis adds a layer of granularity that helps practitioners and academic community understand the peculiarities of DT endeavors. While this study has only developed a framework of drivers, enablers, and barriers of DT, its strength lies in the exclusive analysis of peer-reviewed, empirical literature. Its benefits are twofold: firstly, it addresses the shortfall of (Tijan *et al.*, 2021) whose literature review included articled beyond the scope of maritime ports as explained elsewhere in this paper. Secondly, derivation of empirically generated factors forms a firm basis for the development of rigorous conceptual frameworks and hypothesis testing. Therefore, the foundation provided in this paper will incite the scientific community's quest to advance knowledge by testing associations and causal relationships among the factors this paper has deemed critical. A generalization of the results will help augment our understanding of the realities of DT in the maritime ports and complement existing fragmented anecdotal accounts.

Further studies may examine how value co-creation influences maritime ports' synchronized implementation of DT initiatives. Furthermore, future research on cybersecurity related to DT initiatives may demystify possible maritime ports' tenacity to go digital. Future research may investigate the role of prominent stakeholders—with mature DT initiatives in stimulating the implementation of DT in laggards. Other specific areas of interest include: (1) determining aspects of DT dimensions that require urgent implementation attention where a deeper analysis of singular dimensions and their nuances will be promising; (2) a deeper analysis of how individual port stakeholders' DT trajectories affect port ecosystem's holistic transformation endeavors and how these relationships can be empirically verified; 3) how collaborative agility can engender ports' ecosystems successful DT.

As DT is an evolving concept, to holistically understand its underlying tenets, further studies may examine the interplay of the factors in this study through quantitative and qualitative enquiries. Moreover, longitudinal research may robustly capture and clarify the interplay, e.g., moderating, mediating, or direct roles of the identified factors in the framework and address the gap between digital technological breakthroughs and organizational dynamics in implementing DT.

References

Afenyo, M., Caesar, L.D.: Maritime cybersecurity threats: gaps and directions for future research. Ocean Coast. Manag. **236**, 106493 (2023)
Arduini, D., Zanfei, A.: An overview of scholarly research on public e-services? A meta-analysis of the literature. Telecommun. Policy **38**(5–6), 476–495 (2014)
Bauk, S., Kapidani, N., Schmeink, A., Holtham, C.: Concerning intelligent ICT exploitation in some maritime business organizations: a pilot study. Naše More **64**(2), 63–68 (2017)
Baum-Talmor, P., Kitada, M.: Industry 4.0 in shipping: Implications to seafarers' skills and training. Transp. Res. Interdisc. Perspect. **13**, 100542 (2022)
Bavassano, G., Ferrari, C., Tei, A.: Blockchain: how shipping industry is dealing with the ultimate technological leap. Res. Transp. Bus. Manag. **34**, 1–8 (2020)
Bisogno, M.: Improving the efficiency of port community Systems through integrated information flows of logistic processes. Int. J. Digit. Account. Res. **15** (2015)
Boselie, P., Dietz, G., Boon, C.: Commonalities and contradictions in HRM and performance research. Hum. Resour. Manag. J. **15**(3), 67–94 (2005)
Brunila, O.-P., Kunnaala-Hyrkki, V., Inkinen, T.: Hindrances in port digitalization? Identifying problems in adoption and implementation. Eur. Transp. Res. Rev. **13**(1) (2021)
Camarero Orive, A., Santiago, J.I.P., Corral, M.M.E.-I., González-Cancelas, N.: Strategic analysis of the automation of container port terminals through BOT (business observation tool). Logistics **4**(1), 1–14 (2020)
Carlan, V., Sys, C., Vanelslander, T., Roumboutsos, A.: Digital innovation in the port sector: barriers and facilitators. Compet. Regulat. Netw. Ind. **18**(1–2), 71–93 (2017)
Chang, Y., Iakovou, E., Shi, W.: Blockchain in global supply chains and cross border trade: a critical synthesis of the state-of-the-art, challenges and opportunities. Int. J. Prod. Res. **58**(7), 2082–2099 (2020)

Chowdhury, M.M.H., Alshareef, M., Shaheen, M.M.A., Majumdar, S.: Smart port management practices and implementation: an interpretive structural modelling approach. Bangladesh Maritime J. **7**(1) (2023)

Dalaklis, D., Christodoulou, A., Ölcer, A.I., Ballini, F., Dalaklis, A., Lagdami, K.: The port of gothenburg under the influence of the fourth stage of the industrial revolution: implementing a wide portfolio of digital tools to optimize the conduct of operations. Maritime Technol. Res. **4**(3), 253844 (2022)

Denktas-Sakar, G., Karatas-Cetin, C.: Port sustainability and stakeholder management in supply chains: a framework on resource dependence theory. Asian J. Shipp. Logist. **28**(3), 301–319 (2012)

Djoumessi, A., Chen, S.-L., Cahoon, S.: Factors influencing innovation in maritime clusters: an empirical study from Australia. Mar. Policy **108**, 1–16 (2019)

Fedi, L., Lavissiere, A., Russell, D., Swanson, D.: The facilitating role of IT systems for legal compliance: the case of port community systems and container Verified Gross Mass (VGM). Supply Chain Forum: Int. J. (2019)

Gausdal, A., Czachorowski, K., Solesvik, M.: Applying blockchain technology: evidence from Norwegian companies. Sustainability **10**(6), 1–16 (2018)

Gekara, V., Nguyen, X.: New technologies and the transformation of work and skills: a study of computerisation and automation of Australian container terminals. N. Technol. Work. Employ. **33**(3), 219–233 (2018)

Gekara, V., Nguyen, X.: Challenges of implementing container terminal operating system: the case of the port of Mombasa from the belt and road initiative (BRI) perspective. J. Int. Logist. Trade **18**, 49–60 (2020)

Gómez Díaz, C., González-Cancelas, N., Camarero Orive, A., Soler Flores, F.: Digital governance approach to the Spanish port system: proposal for a port. J. Marine Sci. Eng. **11**(2), 311 (2023)

González-Cancelas, N., Molina, B., Soler-Flores, F.: Study to improve the digitalization of the Spanish port system through an affinity diagram. Deniz Taşımacılığı Lojistiği Dergisi **1**(2), 51–68 (2020)

González-Cancelas, N., Molina Serrano, B., Soler-Flores, F., Camarero-Orive, A.: Using the SWOT Methodology to Know the Scope of the digitalization of the Spanish Ports. Logistics **4**(3), 1–20 (2020)

Haraldson, S., Lind, M., Breitenbach, S., Croston, J.C., Karlsson, M., Hirt, G.: The port as a set of socio-technical systems: a multi-organisational view. In: Lind, M., Michaelides, M., Ward, R., Watson, R.T. (eds.) Maritime informatics. PI, pp. 47–63. Springer, Cham (2021). https://doi.org/10.1007/978-3-030-50892-0_4

He, X., Hu, W., Li, W., Hu, R.: Digital transformation, technological innovation, and operational resilience of port firms in case of supply chain disruption. Mar. Pollut. Bull. **190**, 114811 (2023)

Heikkilä, M., Saarni, J., Saurama, A.: Innovation in smart ports: future directions of digitalization in container ports. J. Marine Sci. Eng. **10**(12), 1925 (2022)

Heilig, L., Lalla-Ruiz, E., Voß, S.: Digital transformation in maritime ports: analysis and a game theoretic framework. NETNOMICS Econ. Res. Electron. Netw. **18**(2), 227–254 (2017)

Heilig, L., Voß, S.: Information systems in seaports: a categorization and overview. Inf. Technol. Manage. **18**(3), 179–201 (2017)

HPA. Port of Hamburg Magazine: The digital Transformation (2023). https://www.hafen-hamburg.de/en/port-of-hamburg-magazine/the-digital-transformation/

Hsu, C.-T., Chou, M.-T., Ding, J.-F.: Key factors for the success of smart ports during the post-pandemic era. Ocean Coast. Manag. **233**, 1–14 (2023)

Iman, N., Amanda, M.T., Angela, J.: Digital transformation for maritime logistics capabilities improvement: cases in Indonesia. Marine Econ. Manage. **5**(2), 188–212 (2022)

Inkinen, T., Helminen, R., Saarikoski, J.: Port digitalization with open data: challenges, opportunities, and integrations. J. Open Innov.: Technol. Mark. Complexity **5**(2), 30 (2019)

Inkinen, T., Helminen, R., Saarikoski, J.: Technological trajectories and scenarios in seaport digitalization. Res. Transp. Bus. Manage. (2021)

Ippoliti, C., et al.: SeaGIS abruzzo: a publicly available atlas of marine uses and natural resources in the adriatic sea region. Geospat. Health **13**(2) (2018)

Jeevan, J., Mohd Salleh, N.H., Mohd Zaideen, I.M., Othman, M.R., Menhat, M.N.S., Divine Caesar, L.: Application of geoeconomics in seaport operations: a theoretical proposal for post Covid-19 recovery strategy. Aust. J. Maritime Ocean Affairs **12**(4), 217–242 (2020)

Jović, M., Tijan, E., Brčić, D., Pucihar, A.: Digitalization in maritime transport and seaports: bibliometric, content and thematic analysis. J. Marine Sci. Eng. **10**(4), 486 (2022)

Kapidani, N., Bauk, S., Davidson, I.E.: Digitalization in developing maritime business environments towards ensuring sustainability. Sustainability **12**(21), 1–17 (2020)

Karaś, A.: Smart port as a key to the future development of modern ports. TransNav: Int. J. Marine Navig. Saf. Sea Transp. **14**(1) (2020)

Kashav, V., Garg, C.P., Kumar, R., Sharma, A.: Management and analysis of barriers in the maritime supply chains (MSCs) of containerized freight under fuzzy environment. Res. Transp. Bus. Manag. **43**, 100793 (2022)

Kuo, H.-M., Chen, T.-L., Yang, C.-S.: The effects of institutional pressures on shipping digital transformation in Taiwan. Maritime Bus. Rev. (2021)

Lambrou, M., Watanabe, D., Iida, J.: Shipping digitalization management: conceptualization, typology and antecedents. J. Shipp. Trade **4**(1), 1–17 (2019)

Lee, P., Kwon, O., Ruan, X.: Sustainability challenges in maritime transport and logistics industry and its way ahead. Sustainability **11**(5) (2019)

Lin, H.-F.: Blockchain adoption in the maritime industry: empirical evidence from the technological-organizational-environmental framework. Maritime Policy Manage. 1–23 (2023)

Liu, J., Zhang, H., Zhen, L.: Blockchain technology in maritime supply chains: applications, architecture and challenges. Int. J. Prod. Res. **58**, 1–17 (2021)

Liu, Q., Yang, Y., Ke, L., Ng, A.K.Y.: Structures of port connectivity, competition, and shipping networks in Europe. J. Transp. Geogr. **102**, 103360 (2022)

MacInnis, D.J.: A framework for conceptual contributions in marketing. J. Mark. **75**(4), 136–154 (2011)

McWilliams, A., Siegel, D., Van Fleet, D.D.: Scholarly journals as producers of knowledge: theory and empirical evidence based on data envelopment analysis. Organ. Res. Methods **8**(2), 185–201 (2005)

Min, H.: Developing a smart port architecture and essential elements in the era of Industry 4.0. Maritime Econ. Logist. 1–19 (2022)

Molavi, A., Lim, G.J., Race, B.: A framework for building a smart port and smart port index. Int. J. Sustain. Transp. **14**(9), 686–700 (2020)

Nicoleta, G.-C., Beatriz, M., Francisco, S.-F.: Study to improve the digitalization of the Spanish port system through an affinity diagram. J. Maritime Transp. Logist. **1**(2), 51–68 (2020)

Nikghadam, S., Molkenboer, K.F., Tavasszy, L., Rezaei, J.: Information sharing to mitigate delays in port: the case of the Port of Rotterdam. Maritime Econ. Logist. 1–26 (2021)

Parola, F., Satta, G., Buratti, N., Vitellaro, F.: Digital technologies and business opportunities for logistics centres in maritime supply chains. Marit. Policy Manag. **48**(4), 461–477 (2020)

Peynirci, E.: The rise of emerging technologies: a quantitative-based research on "maritime single window" in Turkey. Res. Transp. Bus. Manage. 100770 (2021)

Philipp, R.: Digital readiness index assessment towards smart port development. Sustain. Manage. Forum | NachhaltigkeitsManagementForum **28**(1–2), 49–60 (2020)

Philipp, R., Prause, G., Gerlitz, L.: Blockchain and smart contracts for entrepreneurial collaboration in maritime supply chains. Transp. Telecommun. J. **20**(4), 365–378 (2019)

Poulis, K., Galanakis, G.C., Triantafillou, G.T., Poulis, E.: Value migration: digitalization of shipping as a mechanism of industry dethronement. J. Shipp. Trade **5**(1), 1–18 (2020). https://doi.org/10.1186/s41072-020-00064-0

Raza, Z., Woxenius, J., Vural, C.A., Lind, M.: Digital transformation of maritime logistics: exploring trends in the liner shipping segment. Comput. Ind. **145**, 103811 (2023)

Sanchez-Gonzalez, P., Díaz-Gutiérrez, D., Leo, T., Núñez-Rivas, L.R.: Toward digitalization of maritime transport? Sens. (Basel Switz.) **19** (2019)

Seo, J., Lee, B.K., Jeon, Y.: Digitalization strategies and evaluation of maritime container supply chains. Bus. Process. Manag. J. **29**(1), 1–21 (2023)

Tijan, E., Jović, M., Aksentijević, S., Pucihar, A.: Digital transformation in the maritime transport sector. Technol. Forecast. Soc. Chang. **170**, 1–15 (2021)

Tranfield, D., Denyer, D., Smart, P.: Towards a methodology for developing evidence-informed management knowledge by means of systematic review. Br. J. Manag. **14**(3), 207–222 (2003)

UNCTAD. Digitalization in Maritime Transport: Ensuring Opportunities for Development (2019). https://unctad.org/system/files/official-document/presspb2019d4_en.pdf

Vairetti, C., González-Ramírez, R.G., Maldonado, S., Álvarez, C., Voβ, S.: Facilitating conditions for successful adoption of inter-organizational information systems in seaports. Transp. Res. Part A: Policy Pract. **130**, 333–350 (2019)

Wang, Y., Sarkis, J.: Emerging digitalisation technologies in freight transport and logistics: current trends and future directions. Transp. Res. E-Log **148**, 1–8 (2021)

Yang, C.-S.: Maritime shipping digitalization: blockchain-based technology applications, future improvements, and intention to use. Transp. Res. Part E: Logist. Transp. Rev. **131**, 108–117 (2019)

Zeng, F., Chan, H.K., Pawar, K.: The adoption of open platform for container bookings in the maritime supply chain. Transp. Res. Part E: Logist. Transp. Rev. **141**, 1–16 (2020)

Zhang, X., Lam, J.S.L.: A fuzzy Delphi-AHP-TOPSIS framework to identify barriers in big data analytics adoption: case of maritime organizations. Marit. Policy Manag. **46**(7), 781–801 (2019)

Zhao, N., Wang, Z., Ji, X., Fu, H., Wang, Q.: Analysis of a maritime transport chain with information asymmetry and disruption risk. Ocean Coast. Manag. **231**, 106405 (2023)

Zhou, Y., Li, X., Yuen, K.F.: Sustainable shipping: a critical review for a unified framework and future research agenda. Mar. Policy **148**, 1–15 (2023)

Zhou, Y., Soh, Y.S., Loh, H.S., Yuen, K.F.: The key challenges and critical success factors of blockchain implementation: Policy implications for Singapore's maritime industry. Mar. Policy **122**, 1–10 (2020)

Aircraft Cruise Alternative Trajectories Generation: A Mixed RRG-Clustering Approach

Jean-Claude Lebegue[1,2] (ID), Andréas Guitart[1(✉)] (ID), Céline Demouge[1] (ID),
Daniel Delahaye[1], Jacco Hoekstra[3], and Eric Feron[4]

[1] Ecole Nationale de L'Aviation Civile, Toulouse, France
{jean-claude.lebegue-ext,andreas.guitart,celine.demouge}@enac.fr,
daniel@recherche.enac.fr
[2] Sopra Steria, Toulouse, France
jean-claude.lebegue@soprasteria.com
[3] TU Delft, Delft, Netherlands
J.M.Hoekstra@tudelft.nl
[4] King Abdullah University of Science and Technology, Thuwal, Saudi Arabia
eric.feron@kaust.edu.sa

Abstract. Weather obstacles in the airspace can interfere with an aircraft's flight plan. Pilots, assisted by air traffic controllers (ATCs), perform avoidance maneuvers that can be optimized. This paper addresses the generation of alternative aircraft trajectories to resolve unexpected events. The authors propose a solution based on the RRG algorithm, K-means clustering, and Dynamic Time Warping (DTW) similarity metric to address the problem. The mixed algorithm succeeds in generating a set of paths with diversity in an obstacle constrained airspace between Paris-Toulouse and London-Toulouse airports. This tool could help to reduce the workload of pilots and ATCs when such a situation arises.

Keywords: metrics · RRG · alternative trajectory · clustering · similarity

1 Introduction

Aircraft trajectory optimization is one of the most important topics within the frame of air transport. To minimize fuel consumption, each airline computes an optimized flight plan. This optimization takes into account the aircraft's performance and the expected weather. This flight plan is followed as much as possible by the pilots. However, during a flight, an aircraft can be confronted with unexpected events that can disrupt the flight plan: weather obstacles, conflicts between aircraft, or "mechanical" failures. In the last case, pilots often have to land as soon as possible. This problem has been addressed in the European project SafeNcy [6,25,26,29]. In the two other cases, pilots led by air traffic controllers have to find solutions to avoid hazardous areas or to solve conflicts.

© ICST Institute for Computer Sciences, Social Informatics and Telecommunications Engineering 2024
Published by Springer Nature Switzerland AG 2024. All Rights Reserved
A. L. Martins et al. (Eds.): INTSYS 2023, LNICST 540, pp. 34–50, 2024.
https://doi.org/10.1007/978-3-031-49379-9_2

The resolution should be done fast, that is why these solutions are solely optimal. Moreover, in some very critical situations, it could be difficult to rapidly react and automation could help. We propose to address this problem by automatically generating, before the flight, alternative cruise trajectories to rapidly have a satisfactory solution.

Moreover, air transport is facing a new major challenge: reducing its environmental impact. Indeed, aviation is responsible for about 3–5% of total global warming [20]. Its impact is composed of CO_2 but also from non-CO_2 effects. Among these non-CO_2 effects, condensation trails (contrails) have the higher warming power [20]. Indeed, if they persist and form cirrus clouds, contrails can have a warming effect. Their impact is still not well known and contrail areas are still difficult to predict perfectly [10] even if ice-supersaturated areas are the most likely to be favorable to persistent contrails [14]. These areas can therefore be considered as hard obstacles such as thunderstorm areas, or be considered as soft obstacles areas where the crossing time must be limited. Contrails seem to have similarities with thunderstorm areas, that is why, the generation of alternative trajectories could be a solution to their avoidance.

Most of the works in the literature focus on the generation of one avoidance trajectory for a given situation. In these works, authors propose to cure the situation by computing one avoidance trajectory at the occurrence of the obstacles. In contrast, in this paper, we propose to generate several trajectories to prevent an unexpected event.

The objective of this research is to create a solution framework to design, for a given flight, efficient alternative cruise trajectories to ensure obstacle avoidance. Using the alternative trajectories, the aircraft will be able to deviate from its initial trajectory and join another trajectory. It can then resume the initial flight plan or continue to follow the new route. In this paper, the following requirements are considered:

- Alternative trajectories should not be too far (fuel is limited) to the optimal flight plan or too similar to each other. To avoid this, a similarity metric is defined.
- An alternative trajectory has at least one significant maneuver compared to the initial flight plan.
- At least one of the alternative paths has to avoid the obstacles.

The paper is organized as follows: Sect. 2 presents a state of the art about alternative trajectories generation and similarity metrics. Then, Sect. 3 details the proposed algorithm. Finally, in Sect. 4, the test results on contrails avoidance are presented.

2   Prior Works

This section presents prior works related to alternative path algorithms and some similarity metrics.

2.1   Path Generation Algorithms

Many approaches have been developed to find a solution to the path planning problem. Among them, optimal control [4,16,24], graph [2,21], or front propagation [22,27,28] approaches can be mentioned. This state-of-the-art focuses on sampling-based path planning methods. This type of methods has been first introduced by LaValle [19]. In his paper, he presents a new algorithm called Rapidly-exploring Random Tree (RRT). This algorithm generates a tree in order to find a path. The tree grows at each iteration by adding a new point. An extension of this method for graph generation called RRG has been developed by Karaman and Frazzoli [17]. It will be detailed in Sect. 3. More recently, Janson, Schmerling, Clark, and Pavone [15] proposed a new sampling-based path planning algorithm called Fast Marching Tree Star (FMT*). This method performs a forward propagation over several sampled points and creates a tree of paths. FMT* is asymptotically optimal and faster than the RRT algorithm. Initially used in robotics, these methods have recently also been used in aviation [3,9,11,12,26].

2.2   Alternative Path Algorithms

The alternative path problem is a well known graph problem in the literature, often referred to as the k-shortest path problem. Two main approaches have been used to tackle this problem: graph structure change [32] and ripple spreading [13]. The former approach starts by computing the shortest path between an Origin-Destination (OD) pair thanks to a shortest path algorithm (Dijkstra algorithm [7]). Then, each link of this shortest path is disconnected from the graph one at a time. At each disconnection, the shortest path is recomputed. This path is a potential k-shortest path. When all links have been disconnected and the potential shortest paths computed, the k-shortest paths are determined by sorting and selecting the k least cost paths from this set. Elsewhere, the latter approach generates k ripples from the origin node. When a ripple meets a node, it triggers a new ripple at this node. The process keeps going on until k ripples have reached the destination.

2.3   Similarity Metrics

The k-shortest paths achieved by one of the previous methods are often very similar. The number of overlapped links is important. A disruption on a shared link may impact several paths. This is the reason why attention was paid on the k dissimilar shortest path problem [1]. Several different similarity indices were developed to compare paths. Chondrogiannis, Bouros, Gamper, and Leser [5] use the overlap ratio as a measure of similarity. Considering two paths, it is the sum of the weights of the shared links over the length of one path. In [23], the authors define a lower bound length for two paths and a set of heuristics to avoid exploring some unnecessary paths to compute the k shortest paths with diversity. They use a wide variety of path similarity metrics from the literature (see Table 1 where $\ell(p_i)$ is the length of the path p_i and $p_i \cap p_j$ represents the overlap of the paths p_i and p_j). Finally, Talarico, Sörensen, and Springael [31] define a similarity metric to compare two solutions of the Vehicle Routing Problem (VRP). Their metric is similar to $sim_2(p_i, p_j)$ on the second row of Table 1, the difference is that the similarity of two VRP solutions is the maximum similarity between their routes.

Table 1. Path similarity metrics from the literature

Notation	Definition
$sim_1(p_i, p_j)$	$\frac{\ell(p_i \cap p_j)}{\ell(p_i \cup p_j)}$
$sim_2(p_i, p_j)$	$\frac{\ell(p_i \cap p_j)}{2\ell(p_i)} + \frac{\ell(p_i \cap p_j)}{2\ell(p_j)}$
$sim_3(p_i, p_j)$	$\sqrt{\frac{\ell(p_i \cap p_j)^2}{\ell(p_i)\ell(p_j)}}$
$sim_4(p_i, p_j)$	$\frac{\ell(p_i \cap p_j)}{\max(\ell(p_i), \ell(p_j))}$
$sim_5(p_i, p_j)$	$\frac{\ell(p_i \cap p_j)}{\min(\ell(p_i), \ell(p_j))}$

3 Alternative Path Generation

As presented in the introduction, the objective of this research is to design alternative trajectories that are the following characteristics:

- in all types of situations, at least one trajectory avoids the obstacles;
- two trajectories have at least one different significant maneuver;
- alternative trajectories have all a significant difference with the flight plan but are not too far from it.

To answer the two first issues, it is proposed to use the Rapidly-Exploring Random Graph (RRG) algorithm that can generate several paths between two points. Moreover, it is easily adaptable to consider the constraints of the problem. The third issue is solved by using clusterization and removing similar routes according to a metric.

3.1 Graph Generation

In the following paragraphs, a graph G will be represented by a set of nodes V and a set of edges E. Before presenting the details of the RRG algorithm, it is necessary to introduce its main functions. This algorithm uses 4 functions:

- The *sampling* function randomly or uniformly generates sample points in the space.
- The *steer* function brings a random point closer to the graph.
- The *nearest* function returns, for a given point x, the closest point in the graph.
- The *near* function returns, for a given point x, a set of nodes at distance lower than a radius r.

RRG algorithm was first introduced by Karaman and Frazzoli [17,18] and works in the same way as RRT. Figure 1 shows an iteration of the RRG algorithm. x_{new} is added to the vertex set V and a link is created between the new point x_{new} and its nearest neighbor $x_{nearest}$ as for the RRT algorithm. Then, new connections are added to the edges set E between x_{new} and all vertices x_{near} in V at a distance lower than a radius r depending on the cardinal of V. This radius is defined as follows:

$$r = \min\{\eta, \gamma_{RRG}(\log(|V|)/|V|)^{1/d}\}, \tag{1}$$

where:

$$\gamma_{RRG} > 2(1 + 1/d)^{1/d}(\mu(\chi_{free})/\zeta_d)^{1/d}, \tag{2}$$

with d the dimension of the space ($d = 2$ in this study), $\mu(\chi_{free})$ is the Lebesgue measure[1] of the obstacle-free space and ζ_d is the volume of the unit ball in the d-dimensional euclidean[2].

As for the RRT* algorithm, it is proven to be asymptotically optimal.

Improvements. In this study, it is proposed to adapt the RRG algorithm to the alternative trajectories generation.

To avoid too short maneuvers, it is proposed to modify the *near* function. As a reminder, this function returns the closest neighbors. If a neighbor is very close to the new point, it creates a very short connection. To avoid this phenomenon, the points at a distance lower than a radius r_{min} are not considered as neighbors. This radius is defined as follows:

$$r_{min} = r\alpha \left(1 - \frac{1}{i}\right), \tag{3}$$

where i is the iteration number and α is a coefficient in $[0, 1]$. The higher α is, the higher the radius r_{min} is, and therefore, the higher the connection lengths are. The connection linked x_{new} and $x_{nearest}$ is nevertheless kept to preserve the optimal connection. Figure 2 shows this change, only the points in the "donut" zone (in green) are considered neighbors. In this example, the second closest neighbor is therefore not connected.

The second modification of the RRG algorithm is on the sampling method. Most of the time, the samples are randomly generated in the whole space. To avoid obtaining too long trajectories, it is proposed to sample around the straight line linking the start and final positions. Figure 3 shows the proposed sampling area. This area is defined by the distance d_s to the straight line computed as follows:

$$d_s = \frac{d}{\beta}\left(1 - \sqrt{\frac{|d_o - d/2|}{d/2}}\right), \tag{4}$$

---

[1] $\mu([a1, b1] \times [a2, b2]) = (b1 - a1) * (b2 - a2)$ where $b1 > a1$ and $b2 > a2$.
  $\mu([a1, b1] \times [a2, b2] \times [a3, b3]) = (b1 - a1) * (b2 - a2) * (b3 - a3)$ where $b1 > a1$, $b2 > a2$ and $b3 > a3$.
[2] In 2D space, ζ_2 is the surface of a disk of radius 1 ($\zeta_2 = \pi$).

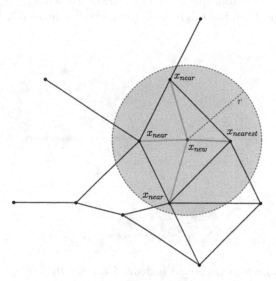

Fig. 1. RRG local optimization iteration: First, a connection linked x_{new} and its nearest neighbor $x_{nearest}$ is created (in red) and then, x_{new} is connected to the points x_{near} at a distance lower than r (in green). (Color figure online)

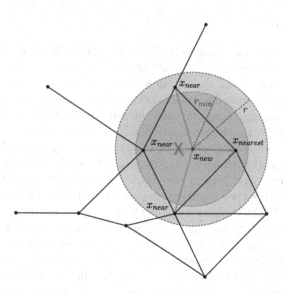

Fig. 2. RRG local optimization iteration with "donut": Connection linked x_{new} and $x_{nearest}$ is created as usual but the edge with the second closest point is not added to the graph.

where d is the distance from the origin O to the destination D, d_o is the distance on the straight line from the origin and β is a coefficient in $\mathbb{N}^*$.

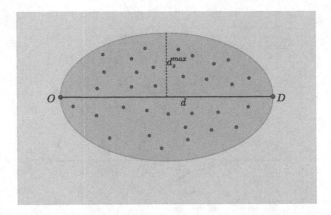

Fig. 3. The sampling area (in green) is defined around the straight line linking the origin O and the destination D by the distance d_s. (Color figure online)

This sampling reduces the graph propagation area. The number of samples can thus be lower and thus reduce the computation time of the graph.

3.2   Clustering

After generating all the alternative paths by the RRG algorithm, we remark that a lot of nodes were really close to each other (Fig. 4a). Having small groups of nodes gathered in small size space zone is not that relevant. For instance, if one node is in a weather zone, its closest nodes will also be in this area. Therefore, closest nodes are merged into only one centroid node (Fig. 4b). Performing this step is also beneficial for the post treatment on the similarity.

We choose a k-means algorithm for the clustering processing because it is an unsupervised method with only one parameter which is the number of clusters. Besides, there are no outliers in the data. Indeed, all the points belong to at least one path because they have been generated by the RRG algorithm. Figure 5 shows a run on a Paris-Toulouse trip for three sizes of clusters (20, 70, and 130). When the number of clusters is low (Fig. 5a), distant points can be grouped together as it is in the top right corner and in the bottom left corner. For 70 clusters (Fig. 5b), the paths are smoother than the previous clustering and there are less overlapping after replacing the points by their centroids. On Fig. 5c, the paths are more precise but also more similar because the clusters are smaller. A trade-off has to be done here between similarity and precision. Because this step is followed by a similarity post treatment, we can focus on precision.

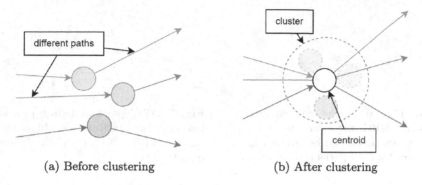

(a) Before clustering   (b) After clustering

Fig. 4. Three spatially close nodes from three different paths merged into one centroid before/after clustering

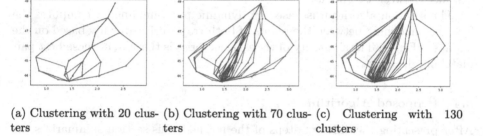

(a) Clustering with 20 clus- (b) Clustering with 70 clus- (c) Clustering with 130
ters   ters   clusters

Fig. 5. K-means clustering of the points generated by RRG algorithm for three different number of clusters (20, 70 and 130) for the Paris-Toulouse trip

3.3 Similarity Post Processing

The RRG algorithm generates lots of paths between origin and destination nodes. The clustering step merged very close points into centroids. However, some of the paths generated shared too many common links. Too similar paths (red paths on Fig. 6), will not allow a correct avoidance maneuvering of a weather obstacle by an aircraft because both paths will go through such a zone. These potential alternatives are finally not really alternatives. The idea behind this process is therefore to detect similar alternative paths among those generated and merge them.

The similarity metric used in this paper is Dynamic Time Warping (DTW). This method can compare two temporal sequences with potentially different speeds, and sizes. The algorithm computes the optimal matches between these two sequences. Let us consider two paths $\mathbf{x} = (x_i)_{0 \le i \le n}$ and $\mathbf{y} = (y_j)_{0 \le j \le m}$ connecting a departure airport to an arrival airport i.e. $x_0 = y_0$ and $x_n = y_m$. The DTW of $\mathbf{x}$ and $\mathbf{y}$ is defined by:

$$DTW(\mathbf{x}, \mathbf{y}) = min_{\mu \in \mathcal{M}_{\mathbf{x}, \mathbf{y}}} \sum_{(i,j) \in \mu} d(x_i, y_j), \tag{5}$$

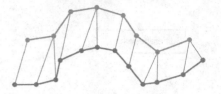

Fig. 6. Post treatment on generated paths by RRG algorithm to detect and remove similar paths (red paths) and keep diversity paths (green paths) (Color figure online)

Fig. 7. DTW point matching process between two trajectories (blue and orange) with different lengths (Color figure online)

with $\mathcal{M}_{\mathbf{x},\mathbf{y}}$ being the set of possible matching between paths $\mathbf{x}$ and $\mathbf{y}$. d is a distance between two points.

The solution algorithm is based on dynamic programming. It computes the best pair matching between the points of both trajectories greedily based on the distance (Fig. 7). The similarity of these trajectories is the sum of these best pair matching distances.

3.4   Proposed Algorithm

After presenting the different steps of the method, this section summarizes the complete alternative trajectories generation process (See Fig. 8 and Algorithm 1). The procedure is the following:

1. n_g graphs are generated with different values of maximum neighborhood radius η (Lines 2 to 5). This process computes short and long avoidance maneuvers to avoid small or big obstacles. An example with 2 graphs is given in Fig. 8a.
2. The n_g generated graphs are then clusterized to obtain a graph with more edges (Line 6). As explained in Sect. 3.2, a lot of nodes are very close. Close nodes are therefore merged to obtain only one graph (See Fig. 8b).
3. A post-process based on DTW is done to remove similar paths (See Fig. 8c and Line 7).
4. If an obstacle appears, the paths passing through the obstacle are removed from the graph to keep only those avoiding it (See Figs. 8d and e and Lines 8 to 10).

The first three steps are performed before the flight while computing the optimal flight plan. The last step can be used in different ways. It can be done when an unexpected event occurs (weather obstacle for instance). It can also be used to change the optimal flight plan by taking into account the contrail areas. This option is discussed in the next section.

Algorithm 1. Alternative paths generation algorithm

Require: $n \in \mathbb{N}^*$, $n_g \in \mathbb{N}^*$, H = $\{\eta_i : \eta_i > 0, i \in [\![1, n_g]\!]\}$

1: $\mathcal{G} \leftarrow \emptyset$
2: **for** $\eta \in$ H **do**
3:    $G = RRG(\eta, n)$
4:    $\mathcal{G} \leftarrow \{G\} \cup \mathcal{G}$
5: **end for**
6: $G \leftarrow$ clusterize($\mathcal{G}$)
7: $\mathcal{P} \leftarrow$ DTW(G)
8: **if** obstacles() **then**
9:    $\mathcal{P} \leftarrow$ avoidancePaths($\mathcal{P}$)
10: **end if**
11: **return** $\mathcal{P}$

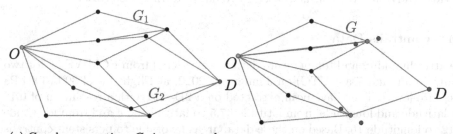

(a) Graphs generation: G_1 is generated with a small radius and G_2 with a long one.

(b) Graphs clusterization: points are merged to create new points in orange.

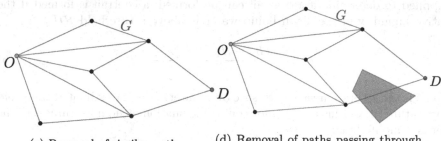

(c) Removal of similar paths

(d) Removal of paths passing through the obstacle

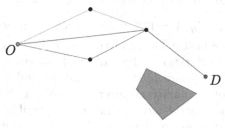

(e) Selection of avoidance paths

Fig. 8. Alternative trajectories generation process (Color figure online)

4   Results

In this paper, it is proposed to apply the alternative trajectories generation to the contrails avoidance problem. Contrail zones are not considered as "hard" obstacles that must be avoided for aircraft safety. It would be better to avoid them to reduce the non CO_2 effects of air traffic. However, such an avoidance maneuvering would release more CO_2. A compromise based on long term impact has to be found between both options. It seems that a mix between the two options would lead to the optimal solution. Contrail zone avoidance is a complex problem, it is the reason why we focus on avoiding them like they were hard obstacles. A contrail area can be vertically or horizontally avoided. The fuel consumption is lower for short lateral avoidance than for flight level change. Moreover, in operation, flight level change is rarely performed to avoid obstacles. In this study, we only consider lateral avoidance during the cruise.

4.1   Contrails Data

Relative humidity and temperature data are extracted from ECMWF [8] for two hours (6 am and 7 am UTC) on January 2, 2022, at Flight Level 300 (300 hPa pressure level). They have been extracted on a 2D-grid with a resolution of 0.1° on latitude and longitude, from latitude 37.5 to latitude 55.4 and from longitude −12 to longitude 16. Based on these data, areas favorable to persistent contrails are computed thanks to the following process, as usually done in the literature (see for instance [30]). First, on a given point, the *Schmidt-Appleman criterion* is applied to determine if a contrail can be formed: a contrail is formed if the relative humidity of the air in liquid water is above a threshold $RH_w \geq r_{min}$ where

$$r_{min} = \frac{G(T - T_c) + e_{sat}^{liq}(T_c)}{e_{sat}^{liq}(T)}, \tag{6}$$

$e_{sat}^{liq}(T)$ is the saturation vapor pressure over water, T_c is the estimated threshold temperature (in Celsius degrees) for contrail formation at liquid saturation. The later is computed via:

$$T_c = -46.46 + 9.43 \log(G - 0.053) + 0.72 \log^2(G - 0.053), \tag{7}$$

where $G = \frac{EI_{H_2O} C_p P}{\epsilon Q(1-\eta)}$, $EI_{H_2O} = 1.25$ is the water vapor emission index, $C_p = 1004 \ J.kg^{-1}.K^{-1}$ is the heat capacity of the air, P is the ambient pressure (in Pascals), $\epsilon = 0.6222$ is the ratio of the molecular masses of water and dry air, $Q = 43 \cdot 10^6 \ J.kg^{-1}$ is the specific heat of combustion, and $\eta = 0.3$ is the average propulsion efficiency of a commercial aircraft. Then, if the point is in an ice-supersaturated area, it is considered in persistent-contrail favorable area. In [30], the ice super saturated areas are determined thanks to the following criterion: $RH_i > 1$, where the relative humidity over the ice, noted RH_i is computed as follows:

$$RH_i = RH_w \cdot \frac{6.0612 \cdot \exp(\frac{18.102T}{249.52+T})}{6.1162 \cdot \exp(\frac{22.577T}{273.78+T})},\tag{8}$$

and where T is the ambient temperature in Celsius degrees.

Figure 9 presents the persistent contrails areas of January 2, 2020, at 7 am.

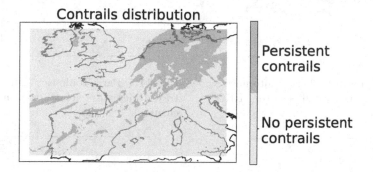

Fig. 9. Contrails data map

4.2 Alternative Trajectories Results

From this data, it is proposed to study two flight cases (London-Toulouse and Paris-Toulouse) to evaluate the method. In both cases, only the cruise phase is considered and the aircraft flies at FL300. Table 2 shows the parameters of the algorithm used for all tests. 15 graphs have been generated by the RRG algorithm.

Table 2. Algorithm parameters.

Parameters	η_{min}	η_{max}	n_g	α	β	$n_{samples}$
Values	0.5	2	15	0.75	3	50,000

Paris-Toulouse Case. As explained in Sect. 3, the first step is to generate several graphs. Figure 10 shows the alternative trajectories generated by the RRG with the parameters given in Table 2. In this case, 1,972 trajectories are generated. This number is too high and should be reduced. Then, the graphs are clusterized. Figure 11 shows the result of the clusterization. The number of paths remains the same but the number of nodes is significantly reduced.

Then, similar paths are removed by the similarity post-treatment. Figure 12 shows the result paths after this step. The resulting trajectories can be used

Fig. 10. Paris-Toulouse alternative trajectories generated by the RRG algorithm.

Fig. 11. Paris-Toulouse alternative trajectories after clusterization (140 clusters).

Fig. 12. Paris-Toulouse alternative trajectories after similarity post-treatment.

Fig. 13. Paris-Toulouse contrails avoidance trajectories at 6 am.

throughout the flight in case of unexpected events. It is proposed to study the use of these routes in the case of contrails avoidance.

Finally, in this case study, only contrails avoidance trajectories are kept. Figures 13 and 14 present the final paths for Toulouse-Paris at two different time scenarios. The orange path represents the shortest path from the origin to the destination. The blue paths are the alternatives. These figures show that the pilot has several options. He can first decide to follow the shortest path and then if an event occurs, he can follow a blue path just for the maneuver and then return to the optimal path. He can also choose to follow this route to the destination. Figure 14 also shows that the algorithm proposes obstacle avoidance from the right or from the left. However, it only offers one option if one maneuver is significantly longer than the other (See Fig. 13). Table 3 summarizes the number of paths at each step of the proposed algorithm. Table 3 presents also the computation time of each algorithm step. The generation of the alternative

Fig. 14.   Paris-Toulouse   contrails avoidance trajectories at 7 am.

Fig. 15.   London-Toulouse   contrails avoidance trajectories at 7 am.

trajectories takes 198.5 s, which is totally acceptable for a pre-flight calculation. The selection of avoidance trajectories is very fast and can be used during the flight. The simulation results show that the proposed algorithm can efficiently generate cruise alternative trajectories. Although the RRG algorithm generates a high number of paths, the KMeans and the post-processing reduce to a low but sufficient number to avoid complex obstacles.

To validate the results achieved by the methodology proposed in the paper. We compute the proportion of alternative paths connecting the Paris-Toulouse airports depending on their deviation from the shortest path (see Fig. 16). This figure also includes the paths that avoid obstacles for the scenario of Fig. 13. The more the alternative paths (light-blue bars) deviate from the shortest path the lesser they are. We can remark that most of the paths are close to the shortest path. Around 60% of alternative trajectories have a deviation of less than 4%. The figure shows that the obstacles can be avoided in different ways. For instance, the pilot can decide to follow the shortest avoidance path (deviation between 1% and 2%). However, he can also prefer to follow a longer trajectory to perform a safer maneuver to reduce the risk due to the uncertainties.

Table 3. Number of paths and computation time in seconds of each algorithm step.

	RRG	KMeans	Post	Avoidance	
				6 am	7 am
Number of paths	1972	1972	64	8	7
Computation Time (s)	191	1	6.5	0.019	

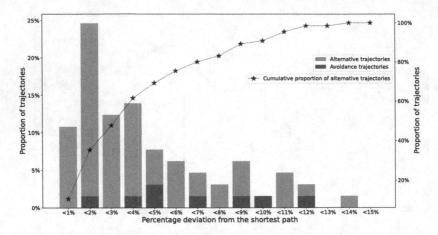

Fig. 16. Alternative and avoidance trajectories proportion depending on the deviation from the shortest path linking Paris and Toulouse. The avoidance trajectories are for the scenario of Fig. 13.

London-Toulouse Case. To complete this study, the London-Toulouse flight is tested. Figure 15 shows the alternative paths generated by the proposed algorithm for the London-Toulouse flight at 7 am. According to the results obtained, the method is promising. Indeed, for several case studies, the algorithm is able to generate multiple alternative trajectories. Moreover, these trajectories can be used to avoid obstacles and offer several options to pilots.

5   Conclusion

This paper addresses the automatic generation of alternative cruise trajectories to handle any type of unexpected event. In the first part of this paper, some methods to generate alternative paths are presented. Then, a solution algorithm is proposed, based on an adapted version of the RRG algorithm, K-means clusterization, and DTW similarity metric. Simulation results based on two different flights illustrate the proposed approach. According to the numerical results, this approach generates alternative trajectories with diversity and considers some aeronautical operational constraints. An analysis of the distribution of alternative paths shows that most of the trajectories generated by our method are close to the shortest trajectory. Moreover, the method proposes avoidance trajectories with different lengths. The proposed method can be used in different ways. For instance, it can be relevant in the case of the presence of persistent condensation trails. They can also be used as an alternative to the optimal flight plan. The proposed method seems promising, but for long-haul flights, a dynamic version with updated alternative trajectories would be necessary. Moreover, vertical alternative trajectories could be added to the framework. This study opens the way to the development of a complete flight system composed of an alternative cruise trajectory system and an emergency trajectory generation tool like the one developed in the SafeNcy project [6,25,26,29]. This tool would propose alternative cruise trajectories to avoid unexpected events during a flight and trajectories in case of an emergency. Each point of the generated graph would have a set of alternatives and one or more emergency trajectories. This system could enhance the safety of the flights. The pilot could thus react to any type of event, be it a simple weather event or an emergency. This kind of tool could reduce the workload of pilots and ATCs.

References

1. Akgün, V., Erkut, E., Batta, R.: On finding dissimilar paths. Eur. J. Oper. Res. **121**(2), 232–246 (2000)
2. Bellman, R.: On a routing problem. Q. Appl. Math. **16**(1), 87–90 (1958)
3. Bonin, L., Delahaye, D., Guitart, A., Feron, E., Prats, X.: Optimal path planning for soaring flight. In: Conference on Guidance Navigation and control, CEAS EuroGNC 2022, Berlin, Germany, May 2022. CEAS and AIAA (2022). https://hal-enac.archives-ouvertes.fr/hal-03619377
4. Chakravarty, A.: Four-dimensional fuel-optimal guidance in the presence of winds. J. Guid. Control. Dyn. **8**(1), 16–22 (1985)
5. Chondrogiannis, T., Bouros, P., Gamper, J., Leser, U.: Alternative routing: K-shortest paths with limited overlap. In: Proceedings of the 23rd SIGSPATIAL International Conference on Advances in Geographic Information Systems, SIGSPATIAL 2015, New York, NY, USA. Association for Computing Machinery (2015). https://doi.org/10.1145/2820783.2820858
6. Cordis and CleanSky: Safency - the safe emergency trajectory generator (2020). https://cordis.europa.eu/project/id/864771/fr
7. Dijkstra, E.W.: A note on two problems in connexion with graphs. Numer. Math. **1**(1), 269–271 (1959). https://doi.org/10.1007/BF01386390
8. ECMWF: ECMWF datasets (2020). https://www.ecmwf.int/en/forecasts/access-forecasts/access-archive-datasets
9. Fallast, A., Messnarz, B.: Automated trajectory generation and airport selection for an emergency landing procedure of a CS23 aircraft. CEAS Aeronaut. J. **8**(3), 481–492 (2017)
10. Gierens, K., Matthes, S., Rohs, S.: How well can persistent contrails be predicted? Aerospace **7**(12), 169 (2020)
11. Guitart, A., Delahaye, D., Feron, E.: An accelerated dual fast marching tree applied to emergency geometric trajectory generation. Aerospace **9**(4), 180 (2022)
12. Guitart, A., Delahaye, D., Camino, F.M., Feron, E.: Collaborative generation of local conflict free trajectories with weather hazards avoidance. IEEE Trans. Intell. Transp. Syst. **24**, 12831–12842 (2023). https://doi.org/10.1109/TITS.2023.3289191
13. Hu, X.-B., et al.: Finding the k shortest paths by ripple-spreading algorithms. Eng. Appl. Artif. Intell. **87**, 103229 (2020)
14. Irvine, E.A., Shine, K.P.: Ice supersaturation and the potential for contrail formation in a changing climate. Earth Syst. Dyn. **6**(2), 555–568 (2015)
15. Janson, L., Schmerling, E., Clark, A., Pavone, M.: Fast marching tree: a fast marching sampling-based method for optimal motion planning in many dimensions. arXiv arXiv:1306.3532, February 2015

16. Jardin, M.R., Bryson, A.E.: Neighboring optimal aircraft guidance in winds. J. Guid. Control. Dyn. **24**(4), 710–715 (2001)
17. Karaman, S., Frazzoli, E.: Incremental sampling-based algorithms for optimal motion planning. arXiv arXiv:1005.0416 (2010)
18. Karaman, S., Frazzoli, E.: Sampling-based algorithms for optimal motion planning. Int. J. Robot. Res. **30**(7), 846–894 (2011)
19. LaValle, S.M.: Rapidly-exploring random trees : a new tool for path planning. The annual research report (1998)
20. Lee, D., et al.: The contribution of global aviation to anthropogenic climate forcing for 2000 to 2018. Atmos. Environ. **244**, 117834 (2021)
21. Legrand, K., Puechmorel, S., Delahaye, D., Zhu, Y.: Robust aircraft optimal trajectory in the presence of wind. IEEE Aerosp. Electron. Syst. Mag. **33**(11), 30–38 (2018)
22. Ligny, L., Guitart, A., Delahaye, D., Sridhar, B.: Aircraft emergency trajectory design: a fast marching method on a triangular mesh. In: Fourteenth USA/Europe Air Traffic Management Research and Development Seminar, New-Orleans, United States (2021)
23. Liu, H., Jin, C., Yang, B., Zhou, A.: Finding top-k shortest paths with diversity. IEEE Trans. Knowl. Data Eng. **30**(3), 488–502 (2017)
24. Palopo, K., Windhorst, R.D., Suharwardy, S., Lee, H.-T.: Wind-optimal routing in the national airspace system. J. Aircr. **47**(5), 1584–1592 (2010)
25. Sáez, R., Khaledian, H., Prats, X.: Generation of emergency trajectories based on aircraft trajectory prediction. In: 2021 IEEE/AIAA 40th Digital Avionics Systems Conference (DASC), pp. 1–10. IEEE (2021)
26. Sáez, R., Khaledian, H., Prats, X., Guitart, A., Delahaye, D., Feron, E.: A fast and flexible emergency trajectory generator enhancing emergency geometric planning with aircraft dynamics. In: Fourteenth USA/Europe Air Traffic Management Research and Development Seminar, ATM 2021, New Orleans (virtual), United States, September 2021 (2021)
27. Sethian, J.A.: A fast marching level set method for monotonically advancing fronts. Proc. Natl. Acad. Sci. **93**(4), 1591–1595 (1996)
28. Sethian, J.A., Vladimirsky, A.: Ordered upwind methods for static Hamilton-Jacobi equations. Proc. Natl. Acad. Sci. **98**(20), 11069–11074 (2001)
29. Sáez, R., et al.: An automated emergency airport and off-airport landing site selector. In: 2022 IEEE/AIAA 41st Digital Avionics Systems Conference (DASC), pp. 1–10 (2022). https://doi.org/10.1109/DASC55683.2022.9925757
30. Soler, M., Zou, B., Hansen, M.: Flight trajectory design in the presence of contrails: application of a multiphase mixed-integer optimal control approach. Transp. Res. Part C Emerg. Technol. **48**, 172–194 (2014)
31. Talarico, L., Sörensen, K., Springael, J.: The k-dissimilar vehicle routing problem. Eur. J. Oper. Res. **244**(1), 129–140 (2015)
32. Yen, J.Y.: Finding the k shortest loopless paths in a network. Manage. Sci. **17**(11), 712–716 (1971)

Next Generation of Virtual Stops for Future Mobility Solutions

Louis Calvin Touko Tcheumadjeu(✉) and Johannes Rummel

German Aerospace Center (DLR), Institute of Transportation Systems,
Rutherfordstr. 2, 12489 Berlin, Germany
louis.toukotcheumadjeu@dlr.de

Abstract. The growing demand for mobility of people and goods poses major challenges for the inner-city transport infrastructure. At the same time, the increased volume of commuters increases the need for demand-oriented local public transportation (LPT) as well as more flexible connections to rural areas. In the long term, therefore, a shift in individual vehicle traffic toward intelligent, modern, low-emission and sustainable mobility solutions is necessary. Flexible, demand-oriented stops will be of increasing importance for new sustainable mobility solutions in the future.

In this paper, the concepts for new virtual stops as an integral part of the roadside infrastructure for future mobility solutions are presented. The paper gives the answer to these questions: which criteria does a public transport bus stop, on-street parking or parking bay have to meet so that it can act as a virtual stop or chosen by the end user like on-demand passenger of demand responsive transport? This paper also illustrates the most significant mobility uses cases involving virtual stops.

Keywords: next generation virtual stop · on-demand oriented stops · future mobility solution · stop recognition · stop management · stop selection criteria · stop placement criteria

1 Introduction

The demand for mobility of people and goods is growing due to the increasing number of large cities and global economic growth [1]. This poses major challenges for the inner-city transport infrastructure. At the same time, the increased volume of commuters increases the need for demand-oriented local public transportation (LPT) as well as more flexible connections to rural areas. If there will be no change in the mobility system, the emissions caused by the traffic will increase more and more. In the long term, therefore, a shift in individual vehicle traffic toward intelligent, modern, low-emission and sustainable mobility solutions is necessary [2].

The contribution presented in this paper describes the activities of the German mobility research project KoKoVi [3], founded by the German Federal Ministry for Digital and Transport. The project started in January 2022 with a duration of two years (2024).

© ICST Institute for Computer Sciences, Social Informatics and Telecommunications Engineering 2024
Published by Springer Nature Switzerland AG 2024. All Rights Reserved
A. L. Martins et al. (Eds.): INTSYS 2023, LNICST 540, pp. 51–65, 2024.
https://doi.org/10.1007/978-3-031-49379-9_3

The objective of this project is to connect traffic infrastructures and automated driving functions to central traffic nodes in order to develop building blocks for innovative and sustainable mobility solutions. New functions of automated networked vehicles and roadside infrastructure are being developed. This includes automated and connected driving functions that can use distribution functions for virtual on-demand stops in a complex urban traffic network and communicating with the traffic infrastructure. Flexible, demand-oriented stops will be of increasing importance for new sustainable mobility solutions in the future. Therefore, the concept of new virtual stops (VS) as an integral part of the traffic infrastructure is developed, implemented in road traffic and evaluated in the context of future mobility solutions.

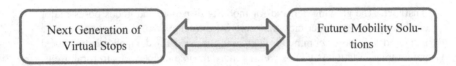

In this paper the focus is on the next generation of virtual stops and the future mobility solutions involving virtual on-demand stops.

2   Next Generation of Virtual Stops

As part of the project KoKoVi, a concept for a virtual stop was developed, implemented in road traffic and finally evaluated. In the following sections, the requirements for virtual stops are described. A distinction is made between legal, technical and user requirements.

2.1   Virtual and Physical Stops

In general, virtual stops are entry and exit points for on-demand services. Because they have no fixed travel times and more possible stopping points, on-demand services have greater flexibility than scheduled services. These stopping points do not have to be bus stops only, but can in principle be any place in the public street space where a stop is possible, or private areas, such as gas stations. The places in the public street space do not have to be structurally marked as a stop and are usually, in addition to bus stops, a place on the street suitable for stopping or a parking bay. Exactly which stops are used depends on the service offered and the demands placed on the stop. These stops are defined and stored in the background system (usually a database) and can be used as "virtual stops" for further services. In principle, any safe and feasible location in the road network can be defined as a "virtual" or "unconventional" stop. The possible location for a virtual stop can also be mapped to the "physical" existing stop, for example, a "conventional" public transport bus stop. The virtual bus stop can also be viewed as a special form of parking space.

Figure 1 shows possible realizations of virtual stops such as public transport bus stop, on-street stop or parking bay. In Germany, buses are not allowed to reverse in public spaces without further ado, so the only option is to stop along the road.

(a) VS as bus stop	(b) VS as on-street parking	(c) VS as parking bay

Fig. 1. Example of different categories of virtual stop (Google Maps).

2.2 Goals and Approach

The following two main goals are described in detail in the next sections.

- Goal 1: Criteria for the placement of a virtual stop in the public road network: What criteria does a public transport bus stop, on-street stop or a parking bay have to meet so that it can act as a virtual stop?
- Goal 2: Criteria for the selection of a virtual stop for mobility solutions: What criteria make the virtual stops comparable so that the preferred one can be selected by the mobility user or services?

Different categories are introduced in order to obtain as complete a picture as possible of the criteria for placing and selecting a virtual stop.

On the one hand, there are criteria that make it impossible to place or select a virtual stop. For example, a stopping ban is a general exclusion criterion for the placement of a virtual stop. On the other hand, there are criteria that are only relevant for special use cases, such as a barrier free access for a pram. Comparable criteria, such as walking distance from or to the virtual stop, are most important when selecting a virtual stop for a flexible mobility service.

2.3 Goal 1: Criteria for the Placement of a Virtual Stop in the Public Road Network

Research questions:

- Which general criteria does a stopping point have to meet in order to act as a virtual stop in the public road network?
- Which specific criteria should a stop meet in order to fulfil the needs of different user groups and stakeholders?

There are different strategies for placing virtual stops. A summary of three possible approaches can be found in [4]. The placements at street lamps, at intersections and at regular intervals (grid) are examined. Some criteria for the placement of virtual stops have already been named in [5]. However, these are mixed with attributes of virtual stops and are incomplete. A complete list of all relevant criteria will be provided in this chapter. The criteria for the placement of virtual stops are usually mandatory. Some are always relevant, such as the vehicle is allowed to stop, and others only for certain use cases, such as using autonomous vehicles or handling with users with large luggage.

2.3.1 Legal Requirements

The legal requirements describe the legal basis for "stopping" in road traffic, which takes place at virtual stops. In the legal sense, "stopping" is understood according to the German road traffic regulations (StVO) under §12 paragraph. 2 as the "intentional" interruption of the journey, i.e. the standstill of the vehicle, during which the driver remains in the vehicle and which does not last longer than 3 min, otherwise it is referred to as parking. In this context, stopping is generally not allowed under the legal conditions stated in Table 1. Some criteria may be time-dependent and thus only relevant in certain applications. All other criteria must always be fulfilled.

Table 1. Legal requirements for a stop as found in [4]

No	Criteria	Description
1	Absolute stopping prohibition	• Can be usually identified by the no stopping sign, also with time restrictions • On the road outside cities usually marked with a continuous lane boundary
2	Cycling infrastructure on the roadway	
3	Railroad crossing	• Also in front, if the vehicle hides the St. Andrew's cross
4	Entrance or exit lanes	
5	Fire department access road	• Usually marked with an appropriate sign
6	Taxi rank	• Usually marked with an appropriate sign
7	In the running space of rail vehicles	
8	Traffic roundabout	• Marked with an appropriate sign
9	In unclear road sections	
10	In the area of sharp curves	

2.3.2 Technical Requirements

Technical requirements for virtual stops consist of basic requirements of the stops, such as required dimensions of the stop to guarantee enough space for the shuttle/vehicle, and communication requirements of the dispatching system to guarantee the correct management of the stop (see Table 2).

If we talk about the basic requirements, it is important to meet the requirements of the shuttle to the virtual stop. This includes, as mentioned above, the dimension of the stop (total length and width), the corner points of the stop, the geo-coordinates, access restrictions, such as availability only on certain days or times or only for certain types of vehicles, and the type of stop (i.e. a public transport bus stop or a parking bay).

Table 2. Overview about the technical requirement of virtual stop.

No	Criteria	Description
1	Form of stop	Autonomous driving Manual driving
2	Type of stop	Bus stop, Shuttle stop Parking bay On-street stop
3	Dimension of the stop	Total length and width Corner point of the stop Geometry as shape
4	Availability of communication infrastructures on the stop	To guarantee the correct management of the stop e.g. Car2Infrastructure (C2I)
5	Location/position	Geo-coordinate
6	Location type	On-street virtual stop Off-street virtual stop
7	Parking Capacity	In terms of number of vehicles
8	Street name	The name or address of the street
9	Operating time	Information about the opening days and hours

2.3.3 Non-technical Requirements

The non-technical requirements for virtual stops are mainly user requirements. However, there are also requirements from the vehicles, the providers and the municipalities. The general criteria have been divided into nine categories and subdivided into further specifications. The category "accessibility" describes the unhindered access to the virtual stop under different circumstances. The category "security & safety" includes both subjective and objective requirements. For example, the presence of street lighting may contribute to a greater sense of safety and security for the user, but it may also reduce the risk of stumbling. "Accessibility" describes requirements on the way to or from the virtual stop for the user and the vehicle. For example, the vehicle must be able to reach and travel to the virtual stop, and for the user there must also be access to public transport if needed. "Convenience/Comfort" is more relevant to the selection of the virtual stop. "Uniqueness/findability" indicates how well the virtual stop can be found and identified by the user and the driver of the vehicle. E.g. points of interest (POIs) are suitable for this purpose. The category "costs" includes estimated parking fees at the time of the placement of the virtual stop which also include possible contracts that are concluded with the operators of parking facilities. Especially for electric vehicles, it is a good idea to integrate the charging infrastructure and bundle needed waiting times to reduce the costs. "Privacy" is not relevant to the placement of virtual stops. Sometimes it is necessary to include less attractive virtual stops in the system to achieve adequate "coverage". "Impact on traffic flow" may be relevant to the municipalities responsible for the traffic system. Excessive negative impact on traffic flow, e.g., due to high frequency, may result in the prohibition of certain potential virtual stops.

An overview of the specific requirements for the placement of virtual stops can be found in Table 3.

2.4 Goal 2: Criteria for the Selection of an Operative Virtual Stop for Mobility Solutions

Research question:

- What criteria must a virtual stop fulfil in order to meet the specific requirements of different users or vehicles?
- Which virtual stops can be used at the service time?
- What criteria make the virtual stops comparable so that the optimal one can be selected?

The criteria required to select a virtual stop should consist primarily of evaluative criteria. The mandatory criteria are either special needs of the user or time restrictions

Table 3. Overview of the criteria for the placement (Goal 1) or choose (Goal 2) of virtual stop.

No	Criteria	User	Vehicle	Provider	Municipality	Specification	Measurement	Description	Placement	Choose
1.a		☑				Disabled access [12]	Is available (yes or no)	• Can be very specific depending on the nature of the disability (e.g. walking impediment, visual impairment)	☑	☑
1.b	Barrier-free	☑				Space for loading/unloading luggage or strollers	Is available (yes or no)		☑	☑
1.c		☑				Direct access from/to the footway available	Is available (yes or no)	• There is no bike lane or grass verge	☑	☑
1.d			☑			Space to fold out the ramp of the vehicle	Is available (yes or no)	• Depends on the available ramp of the vehicle (lateral or at the back)	☑	☑
2.a		☑				Electrical lighting is available	Is available? (yes or no)	• When getting in and out of the vehicle	☑	☑
2.b		☑				Surveillance camera are available	Is available? (yes or no)		☑	☑
2.e	Safety	☑				Low traffic area	Is the virtual stop located at the low traffic area? (yes or no)	• E.g. Low traffic area consists of road with speed limit 30 km/h	☑	☑
2.f		☑				Pedestrian crossing is available	Is a pedestrian road crossing available? (yes or no)	• E.g. pedestrian road crossing	☑	☑
2.g		☑	☑			Compact road surface	Surface of the road allows a stable stop	Can be affected by: • Potholes • Inclination • Slippery ground • Material of the surface	☑	
2.h					☑	Increased risk of accidents with the vehicle [14]	Is the typical traffic flow disturbed? (yes or no)	E.g., caused by stop • At crossings • In the second row (next to parking vehicles)	☑	☑
3.a		☑				(Maximal) Distance (Length) of the footway / distance from the user actual position to the pickup virtual stop	Distance [in meter]	• Maximal Distance that the user has to travel from his actual position to location of the virtual stop • Measurement by pedestrian routing • Depending on the season, mobility and baggage or total travel time		☑
3.b		☑				(Maximal) travel time to the virtual stop	Time [in minute]	• The time that the passenger needs to reach the virtual stops		☑
3.c	Accessibility	☑				Complexity of the pedestrian route to the virtual stop (small detour)	Number of intersections / turns, curve, road category	• The necessary steps to find the way to the given stop. E.g., how often does the user have to turn, are there main roads or intersections that the user has to cross		☑
3.d		☑				Maximal duration of waiting time at the virtual bus stop until pickup	Time [in minute]	• The time that the passenger has to wait for the shuttle to arrive after arriving at the virtual stop • Define the maximum time a passenger should wait at the virtual stop until the vehicle arrives		☑
3.e		☑				Accessibility of virtual stop using public transport is possible	Number of train stations, tram stations, bus stops, and taxi stations at the virtual stop area	• Set the maximum value • Connection to the bus rail, tram, taxi transport services	☑	☑
3.f		☑				Pedestrian road crossing is possible	Is available at the virtual stop area? (yes or no)	•	☑	☑

(continued)

Table 3. (*continued*)

ID	Category				Criterion	Description	Notes		
3.g			☑		Vehicle has enough space to stop at the virtual stop	Vehicle fits into the virtual stop? (yes or no)	• Depends on the lengths of the used vehicles	☑	☑
3.h			☑		Vehicle has the right to reach the virtual stop	There are (currently) no restrictions such as taxi stand or one-way street which does not impede the driving on of the virtual stop (yes or no)	• Provider dependent contracts can affect these restrictions • Can depend on the characteristics of the vehicle as the weight	☑	☑
3.i			☑		Vehicle has the right to stop at the virtual stop	There are (currently) no restrictions specified by traffic regulations (yes or no)	• see **Table 1**	☑	☑
3.j			☑		Near to main roads	Time to access the superordinate road network [in minutes]	• Relevant for long trips especially in rural areas to reduce the detour	☑	☑
3.k			☑		Avoid typical areas of congestions	Time depending on the current traffic situation the vehicle can reach and/or leave the virtual stop [in minutes]	• Traffic situation can also be derived from historical data		☑
3.l			☑		Virtual stop is empty	The virtual stop can be used at the time of the request or an alternative stop is available (yes or no)	• The virtual stop can be shared with public transport • Virtual stop should be booked/blocked, if possible		
4.a	Convenience / comfort	☑			Shelter facilities are available	Is available at the virtual stop area? (yes or no)			☑
4.b		☑			Seats facilities are available	Is available at the virtual stop area? (yes or no)			☑
4.c		☑			Toilet is available	Is available at the virtual stop area? (yes or no)			☑
4.d		☑			Paid or free parking is available for own vehicles	Is available at the virtual stop area? (yes or no)	• Prefer low parking fees or free of charge		☑
4.e		☑			Low traffic area	Is available at the virtual stop area? (yes or no)		☑	
4.f				☑	High acceptance of the user	Are all criteria relevant for the user fulfilled? (yes or no/ how many?)			☑
5.a	Uniqueness / findability	☑			At intersection	Is near an intersection? (yes or no)	• The precise point of stop must be clear	☑	
5.b		☑	☑		POIs for identification of virtual stop available	Is near a POI? (yes or no)	• The street site must be clear	☑	
6.a	Costs		☑		Parking fees	Cost if the virtual stop is used [in EUR or similar]	• Contracts with the supplier of the parking place can reduce the costs	☑	☑
6.b				☑	Near charging infrastructure	Is charging currently needed? (yes or no)	• Reduce costs to combine charging with the stop or at least shorten the way to the charging infrastructure	☑	☑
6.c				☑	Short entire route	Is there another virtual stop that can be used near the current route? (yes or no)	• Use virtual stops near the current route • Prefer virtual stops of the current route ("common meeting points")		☑
7.a	Privacy / data protection	☑			Address not traceable	Is available at the virtual stop area? (yes or no)	• Stop at POI or minimum distance to address		☑
8.a	Coverage		☑		Density of the virtual stops within the service area	Is there at least one virtual stop near all potential requests? (yes or no)	• Important especially for public providers • Three different strategies of commercial providers are described in [Harmann et.al. [2]]	☑	
9.a	Impact on the traffic flow			☑	No negative impact on the traffic flow	Does a stop at the virtual stop causes a congestion? (yes or no)	Is influenced by: • The current traffic flow • Sufficient wide road • Main or side road • Stop on the lane or parking bay		

regarding the possible use of the virtual stop, such as enough space for the vehicle of the transport of disabled people to fold out the ramp used by the wheel-chair user, or temporary halting restrictions. A duplication of the criteria for the placement of a virtual stop is possible. In addition to the criteria described in Sect. 2.3.3, "privacy/data protection" can be relevant, if a door-to-door service is offered and thus includes private addresses that become traceable. "Convenience/comfort" includes the existence of infrastructure elements such as shelter or seats, but also low traffic. Some criteria are hard to evaluate and need more research to make them measurable, such as the perceived safety provoked by the illumination of the virtual stop.

An overview of the criteria for the selection or choice of the virtual stops in the public road network is also described in Table 3.

3 Future Mobility Services Related to the Virtual Stop

In the project KoKoVi the research activities are focused on the five mobility use cases described in Fig. 2. This section introduces these use cases and describes them in detail. These use cases are "Demand Responsive Transport (DRT)", "Autonomic

58   L. C. Touko Tcheumadjeu et al.

Identification", "Automatic Occupancy Status Detection", "Augmented Reality (AR) Recognition" and "Management Assignment" and use virtual stops in some form.

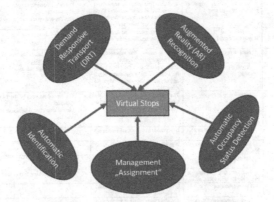

Fig. 2. An overview about mobility uses cases in the context of virtual stops.

The architecture of the KoKoVi sub-system, which covers the five use-cases above, is depicted in Fig. 3.

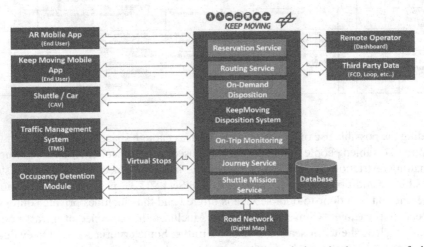

Fig. 3. KoKoVi sub-system architecture for future mobility solutions in the context of virtual stops.

The following actors and stakeholders are involved in the use cases (see Fig. 4)

1. <u>End-User (EU):</u> Who requests passenger transport from a disposition system via end-user device (e.g. mobile app) and allows himself to be transported by a shuttle
2. <u>End-User Device (EUD):</u> That transmits communication between the end user and the dispatching system. Two DLR end user devices are the Keep Moving app [6] and the augmented reality (AR) app.

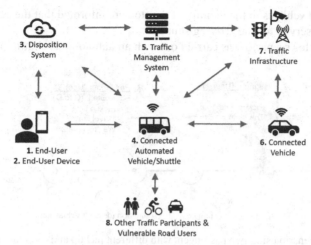

Fig. 4. Actors and stakeholders for the KoKoVi mobility use cases.

3. Dispatching/Disposition System (DS): That manages a shuttle fleet, receives the EU's passenger transport request from the EUD, instructs a shuttle with passenger transport and initiates the creation of virtual stops in the traffic management system. This is realized by the Keep Moving software from DLR [6].
4. Connected Automated Vehicle (CAD)/Shuttle (SH): That takes the order for passenger transport from the DS and transports the EUs from one virtual stop to the next (e.g. from pickup to drop-off virtual stop).
5. Traffic Management System (TMS): Its role is the management of virtual stops. Chosen by the DS it decides on the requests for virtual stops made by the disposition system and creates and /reserves/books virtual stops by informing connected traffic participants and, if available, also the road side infrastructure in the area of the planned virtual stops.
6. Connected Vehicle (CV): In the area near the virtual stops, who (if present) are informed of the stop and adjust their behavior accordingly.
7. Traffic Infrastructure (TI): In the area near the virtual stops, which (if present) is informed of the stop by roadside units and adapts its behavior accordingly.
8. Other Traffic Participants & Vulnerable Road Users (VRU): Play a role as obstacles, especially for autonomous shuttles.

3.1 Demand Responsive Transport (DRT)

Demand responsive transport (DRT) refers to a form of mobility in which routes and stopping points are not fixed from the outset, but are flexibly adapted to current mobility needs [7–9, 13, 15]. It supplements scheduled services in areas with lower mobility needs and will become economically relevant in the future especially in combination with autonomous shuttles. Figure 5 shows the storyboard of a DRT scenario where two passengers for a journey of the same shuttle are involved with two different pickup and drop off locations, which are implemented as virtual stops. The shuttle requests a DS to choose a virtual stop at the shuttle's destination. After the stop location is confirmed by the

TMS, automated vehicles in the vicinity of the stop are informed that the corresponding virtual stop is reserved for the arriving shuttle.

In KoKoVi, this scenario was carried out with an autonomous shuttle from DLR.

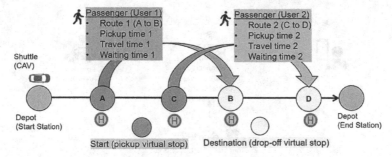

Fig. 5. DRT Scenario using two passengers with different pickup and drop-up virtual stops.

3.2 Automatic Identification, Detection and Mapping of Virtual Stops in the Public Road Network

Basically, a distinction can be made between the detection of possible virtual stops ("identification") and the determination of their occupancy status ("status determination"). Under certain circumstances, both can be done in one step, e.g. if the stop is identified for the first time, or if the identification should not be permanent. The following section provides an overview of existing technologies and procedures for the identification and detection of virtual stops.

Virtual stops can be regarded as a special form of parking space, as the basic conditions are very similar: the short-term or long-term parking of conventional vehicles in public traffic areas must be designed with minimal disruption to flowing traffic and other road users or participants, and for this reason takes place in designated (parking) areas. The same applies to virtual stops, therefore the following section describes procedures for identifying parking and stopping possibilities. The identification is achieved by different approaches of mapping.

In Germany, as in most other countries, the designation and management of parking and stopping zones, as well as prohibited zones, is a municipal task. These zones are also subject to constant change due to changing conditions, construction activity, transport policy initiatives, demographic change or a change in modal split (distribution of transport volume between different means of transport).

For the reasons mentioned above, parking or stopping zones are not yet a part of digital road maps, or only an incomplete one. There is a lack of both standards and scalable procedures for the area-wide and reliable mapping of parking and stopping facilities. A generally accepted data model could not be researched.

Digital map data on parking and stopping facilities offers a variety of benefits, including: 1. Higher transparency for city and traffic planners regarding the available parking space 2. Enabling new navigation functions in the vehicle, such as navigation to the parking lot, 3. Optimized route planning for delivery traffic and 4. Creation of breakpoints for (automated) on-demand vehicles.

The development of current databases for parking space data began with the introduction of digital maps and geographic information systems (GIS). Although maps with parking garages or very large parking areas, e.g., in front of companies, are already available today, these parking areas only account for a small proportion of all parking spaces. The far larger share is on-street parking. Public documentation on these parking spaces is currently only available in paper form from the individual city administrations.

Even though there are already some cities that digitize their plans, there is no uniform standard for this and also no central management system, so the information is only available on a city-by-city basis. Cross-city maps of parking and stopping facilities are nowadays only available digitally via the "crowdsourcing" platform OpenStreetMap or commercial providers.

OpenStreetMap (OSM): Today, OSM is the most comprehensive public digital map and the only GIS that contains significant amounts of parking information. The idea behind OSM is called "crowdsourcing" and describes the collaborative and voluntary collection of geographic information. This allows users to enrich OSM with additional geographic information. Among a variety of other geographic information, OSM also contains data about parking lots, including location, geometric shape, and, to varying degrees of completeness, meta-information. Through the OSM service, meta-information such as parking capacity, cost, opening hours or user group restrictions are made available. In Germany, just under 300,000 parking lot entries are mapped, with more than one million already recorded in OSM worldwide. About 50,000 parking lots contain additional meta information.

The first group of commercial solutions: In addition to OSM as an open data project, there are also a small number of commercial parking data providers. Companies such as INRIX [16], Streetline [17] or ParkingHQ [18] merge parking information from various sources such as car park operators, municipal traffic information systems or physical parking sensors into a single database for real time data. The problem here is that these platforms only contain data from managed parking areas, but not from parking spaces on the street or free parking spaces, which contain more than 85 percent of the city's parking infrastructure.

The second group of commercial solutions: is aware of this issue and is trying to solve it with a different way of collecting data: Companies like Parkopedia [19] rely on data contributed by their own user base. Users of Parkopedia's mobile app can enter parking spaces into the database with locations, opening hours, restrictions and prices. Therefore, Parkopedia's data collection is also able to obtain data for free on-street or off-street parking. The data collection model is thus similar to OSM, with the difference that Parkopedia makes the data commercially available for purchase rather than free. However, data volume, timeliness, and spatial coverage depend heavily on the size of Parkopedia's user base.

3.3 Automatic Occupancy Status Detection of Virtual Stops

As already explained, the detection of virtual stops refers to their time-dependent occupancy state and is in turn thematically very closely related to the state detection of parking spaces (determination of the occupancy state of a virtual stop ("state detection"). For this reason, the general state of the art for determining the occupancy status of parking spaces, especially in public spaces, will be discussed below.

If a vehicle leaves its parking space, this information is valuable for a person looking for a parking space, but also for other users of public parking and traffic space, such as delivery or on-demand vehicles. Nowadays, there are two approaches to detecting free parking spaces: via stationary sensors or crowdsensing systems, which are explained below.

Stationary detection systems: Stationary parking guidance and barrier systems are most commonly used for so-called off-street parking spaces such as parking garages. These systems consist of a mechanism for recording and counting the number of occupied parking spaces and a visualization that provides the user with information about the current occupancy. The measurement of the number of free parking spaces is usually carried out by cameras, ultrasonic or radar sensors, ticketing or barrier systems or ground sensors.

More advanced stationary systems also stream their information to a server, making it accessible to third-party services, such as mobile apps. Although these systems are quite accurate, they are expensive to install and maintain, and of course only cover a very limited portion of the total parking spaces in an area, as they are usually only operated by property owners.

In public spaces, the systems described are practically not used due to the lack of cost-effectiveness due to the high investment and maintenance costs. In conclusion, it can be said that stationary systems do not allow extensive coverage of entire cities or countries.

Distributed systems: On the other hand, crowd sensing or distributed systems try to use data from vehicles or users to track parking processes and inform other users about them. They are therefore not necessarily dependent on expensive hardware and, in addition, the costs incurred for hardware and connectivity are generally borne by the user. There are early attempts at mobile apps in which users enter free parking spaces on a map and thus inform other users about it. Due to the strong involvement of the driver and the fact that a critical mass of users was not reached, they could not achieve acceptable levels of accuracy. As a result, the systems did not offer sufficient added value. Even today's crowd sensing systems rely on a critical number of users, but they no longer require the manual entry of parking space. Nowadays, every mobile application can collect movement data in the background with user consent.

3.4 Augmented Reality for the Recognition of Virtual Stops

The automatic detection of a virtual stop as well as the reserved/booked vehicle arriving at the stop is useful and can help the mobility user to quickly find the virtual stop as a stop for the on-demand shuttle. Human machine interface (HMI) concepts using augmented reality (AR) technology for the interaction of mobile devices with virtual bus stops and

Fig. 6. DRT end user using prototype AR app for the localization of the virtual stop at the pick-up location (source: DLR).

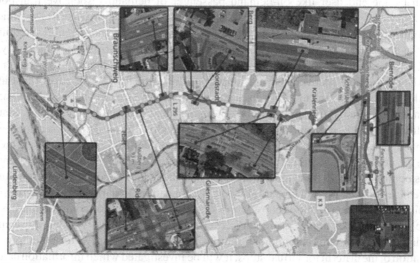

Fig. 7. Overview of the mobility corridor as a test field for the demonstration and management of virtual stops in Braunschweig, Germany. (Color figure online)

connected road users have proven to be very supportive for cooperative behavior. Using the AR application to automatically detect virtual stops and book a shuttle for on-demand traffic scenarios can help reduce the time to find the virtual stops and shuttle. Various research studies have been carried out in this area at DLR and other research institutions [10, 11]. Figure 6 shows an end user using an AR app developed by DLR to visualize the location of the virtual stop at the pickup position.

3.5 The Management and Assignment of Virtual Stops

The management of virtual stops for mobility purposes is complex and crucial to avoid conflict over the reservation and assignment of a virtual stop to a single vehicle (e.g., shuttle by the DRT) for a certain time duration. Traffic management can play the role of management of virtual stops in the city for different mobility solutions [4]. The project KoKoVi deals with the topic of the management of virtual stops. To test and demonstrate the mobility use cases related to the virtual stops in KoKoVi, a mobility corridor as a test field in Brunswick, Germany was defined and used. Figure 7 shows the mobility corridor and the location of some selected virtual stops (blue) and the roadside infrastructures like traffic light (green) and roadside unit (RSU) elements (yellow).

4 Conclusion and Outlook

In this paper, the concepts for new virtual stops as an integral part of the roadside infrastructure for future mobility solutions are presented. The paper gives the answer to these questions: which What criteria does a public transport bus stop, on-street parking stop or parking bay have to meet so that it can act as a virtual stop or will be chosen by the end user like on-demand passenger of demand responsive transport? for a request of an on-demand service? The aspects "legal requirements", "technical requirements" and "non-technical requirements" play a role. The non-technical requirements in particular were described in detail in the categories "barrier-free", "security & safety", "accessibility", "convenience/comfort", "uniqueness/findability", "costs", "privacy/data protection", "coverage" and "impact on the traffic flow". This paper illustrates also the most significant mobility uses cases where virtual stops are involved, such as demand responsive transport (DRT), automatic identification and occupancy status detection, automatic recognition using augmented reality for on-demand service users and management through effective assignment to the on-demand (autonomous) vehicle.

In the next step, the criteria for the placement and selection of virtual stops presented in this contribution will be evaluated in detail and the results according to the end user and vehicle expectation will be part of the next publication. In particular it is planned to combine several criteria into groups, which are always relevant for common use cases. These include, for example, mandatory criteria, criteria for users with large luggage, criteria for services with autonomous shuttles, etc. In order to strive for an automatic evaluation of the criteria for virtual stops, it will be investigated which information can be used from free sources like Open Street Map (OSM) and which criteria can be evaluated with it. In the best case, these criteria can be automatically queried for a selected area with a script. All research activities conducted in the scope of the German mobility project KoKoVi were founded by the German Federal Ministry for Digital and Transport.

References

1. ITF. ITF Transport Outlook (2019). OECD Publishing, Paris (2019). https://doi.org/10.1787/transp_outlook-en-2019-en
2. ITF ITF Transport Outlook 2023, OECD Publishing, Paris (2023). https://doi.org/10.1787/b6cc9ad5-en
3. German mobility research project KoKoVi (2023). https://verkehrsforschung.dlr.de/de/projekte/kokovi. Access 20 June 2023
4. Harmann, D., et al.: Methodological distribution of virtual stops for ride pooling. Transport. Res. Procedia **62**, 442–449 (2022)
5. Harmann, D., Yilmaz-Niewerth, S., Häbel, R., Vinke, V., Kögler, S., Friedrich, B.: Development of an evaluation system for virtual ridepooling stops: a case study. In: Antoniou, C., Busch, F., Rau, A., Hariharan, M. (eds) Proceedings of the 12th International Scientific Conference on Mobility and Transport. Lecture Notes in Mobility. Springer, Singapore (2023). https://doi.org/10.1007/978-981-19-8361-0_15

6. DLR Keep Moving Mobility Research Development Framework (2023). https://keepmoving. dlr.de. Accessed 30 June 2023
7. Armellini, M.G., Bieker-Walz, L.: Simulating demand responsive feeder transit services: a case study of Braunschweig. In: SUMO User Conference 2020: From Traffic Flow to Mobility Modeling, 26–28 October 2020 (2020). https://sumo.dlr.de/2020/SUMO2020_paper_8.pdf
8. Ryley, T.J., et al.: Investigating the contribution of Demand Responsive Transport to a sustainable local public transport system. Res. Transport. Econ. **48**, 364–372 (2014)
9. Bruzzone, F.: The combination of e-bike-sharing and demand-responsive transport systems in rural areas: a case study of Velenje. Res. Transport. Bus. Manag. **40**, 100570 (2021)
10. Hub, F., et al.: Supporting user experience of shared automated mobility on demand through novel virtual infrastructure: making the case for virtual stops. Int. J. Human-Comput. Stud. (2023). https://doi.org/10.1016/j.ijhcs.2023.103043. ISSN 1071-5819
11. Hub, F., et al.: Design and field test of a mobile augmented reality human-machine interface for virtual stops in shared automated mobility on-demand. Electronics (2022). https://doi.org/ 10.3390/electronics11172687. ISSN 2079–9292
12. Goralzik, A., König, A., Alčiauskaitė, L., et al.: Shared mobility services: an accessibility assessment from the perspective of people with disabilities. Eur. Transp. Res. Rev. **14**, 34 (2022). https://doi.org/10.1186/s12544-022-00559-w
13. Pettersson, F.: An international review of experiences from on-demand public transport services. K2 working paper 2019 (2019). ISBN: 978-91-985495-1-5
14. Cao, Y., Yang, Z.Z., Zuo, Z.Y.: The effect of curb parking on road capacity and traffic safety. Eur. Transp. Res. Rev. **9**, 4 (2017). https://doi.org/10.1007/s12544-016-0219-3
15. Lu, C., Maciejewski, M., Nagel, K.: Effective operation of demand-responsive transport (DRT): implementation and evaluation of various rebalancing strategies. In: 27th ITS World Congress, Hamburg, Germany, 11–15 October 2021 (2021)
16. Intelligent Mobility Solutions and Tools – INRIX (2023). https://inrix.com/products/
17. Streetline (2023). https://www.streetline.com/our-solutions/#demand
18. Parking HQ (2023). https://www.ilogs.com/en/industries/mobility-parking/
19. Parkopedia (2023). https://www.parkopedia.com/about-us/

Smart Cities and Blockchain

Points of Interest in Smart Cities and Visitor Behavior

Luís B. Elvas[1,2] (iD), Miguel Nunes[1] (iD), Bruno Francisco[1] (iD), Frederica Gonçalves[3] (iD), Ana Lucia Martins[4], and Joao Carlos Ferreira[1,2,4](✉) (iD)

[1] Instituto Universitário de Lisboa (ISCTE-IUL), ISTAR, Lisbon, Portugal
jcafa@iscte.pt
[2] Department of Logistics, Molde University College, 6410 Molde, Norway
[3] Universidade da Madeira, ESTG/ITI LARSyS, Funchal, Portugal
[4] Inov Inesc Inovação—Instituto de Novas Tecnologias, 1000-029 Lisbon, Portugal

Abstract. Smart cities leverage technology and data to enhance the quality of urban life, including the management of points of interest (POIs) and visitor experiences. This paper explores the relationship between POIs and visitor behavior in smart cities, examining the impact of technology-driven solutions on understanding, analyzing, and optimizing visitor experiences. It highlights the importance of data-driven approaches in identifying and managing POIs, enhancing visitor satisfaction, and driving economic growth. The paper reviews existing literature, discusses key concepts, and presents case studies to illustrate the role of POIs in smart cities and their influence on visitor behavior. Our major contribution is a data driven approach to extract useful information from real data to municipality decisions and understand the problem. It concludes with recommendations for future research and practical implications for city planners, policymakers, and tourism authorities.

Keywords: tourist behaviour · location data · data analytics · mobile phone sensing · Internet of Things · smart cities

1 Introduction

The significance of points of interest (POIs) in attracting visitors and driving economic growth cannot be overstated. POIs are key attractions and destinations within a city that draw the attention and interest of visitors. These can include tourist attractions, cultural landmarks, historical sites, entertainment venues, parks, shopping centres, and dining establishments. Here are some of the key reasons why POIs play a vital role in attracting visitors and fostering economic growth:

- Tourist Attraction: POIs are often the primary reason why visitors choose to travel to a particular city or destination. Iconic landmarks, natural wonders, and cultural sites have a unique appeal that entices tourists from around the world. These attractions create a sense of place and identity for the city, making it a must-visit destination.

A. L. Martins et al. (Eds.): INTSYS 2023, LNICST 540, pp. 69–91, 2024.
https://doi.org/10.1007/978-3-031-49379-9_4

- Increased Tourism Revenue: Visitors attracted to POIs contribute significantly to the local economy through spending on accommodation, transportation, dining, shopping, and entertainment. The revenue generated from tourism activities helps support local businesses, creates job opportunities, and drives economic growth in the hospitality, retail, and service sectors.
- Destination Competitiveness: Cities with well-developed and diverse POIs have a competitive advantage in the tourism industry. The presence of unique and compelling attractions differentiates the city from others, attracting a larger number of tourists and extending their length of stay. This, in turn, boosts the city's reputation as a desirable destination and enhances its overall competitiveness in the global tourism market.
- Urban Regeneration: Developing and promoting POIs can contribute to urban regeneration and revitalization efforts. Neglected or underutilized areas can be transformed into vibrant and attractive districts by focusing on the development of key POIs. This rejuvenation can attract new investments, businesses, and residents, leading to increased property values and overall urban improvement.
- Cultural Preservation and Heritage Conservation: Many POIs are of historical, cultural, or architectural significance. By attracting visitors to these sites, cities can raise awareness about their cultural heritage and promote preserving and conserving historical landmarks. This enhances the city's cultural identity and contributes to the sustainable development of the destination.
- Social and Community Benefits: Vibrant POIs often serve as gathering places and community hubs, fostering residents' pride, and belonging. These attractions can provide spaces for cultural events, festivals, and community activities, creating opportunities for social interaction, cultural exchange, and community cohesion.
- Supporting Ancillary Industries: The presence of POIs stimulates the growth of supporting industries, such as transportation, accommodation, retail, and food services. These industries benefit from the increased demand generated by visitors to the POIs. For example, hotels near popular attractions experience higher occupancy rates, and local businesses around POIs thrive due to increased foot traffic and customer engagement.

In summary, points of interest play a critical role in attracting visitors to a city and driving economic growth. They create unique experiences, contribute to tourism revenue, enhance destination competitiveness, promote cultural preservation, support urban regeneration, and provide social and community benefits. Strategic planning and management of POIs are essential for cities seeking to leverage their attractions as catalysts for sustainable economic development and overall urban well-being.

Municipalities must make data-driven decisions to effectively leverage the potential of Points of Interest (POIs). Here are some key reasons why data-driven decision-making is crucial: 1) Understanding Visitor Behaviour: Data collection and analysis provide insights into visitor behaviour, preferences, and patterns. By analysing data on visitor demographics, visitation patterns, and interaction with POIs, municipalities can gain a deeper understanding of what attracts visitors and how they engage with different attractions. This information helps in making informed decisions about marketing strategies, resource allocation, and infrastructure planning; 2) Optimizing Resource

Allocation: Data-driven insights enable municipalities to allocate resources effectively. By analysing visitor data, authorities can identify peak periods of activity, understand visitor flow between different POIs, and allocate resources such as transportation, staff, and amenities accordingly. This helps in optimizing the utilization of resources and improving the overall visitor experience; 3) Enhancing Visitor Experiences: Data-driven decision-making allows municipalities to personalize and enhance visitor experiences. By analysing data on visitor preferences, feedback, and behaviour, authorities can tailor their offerings and services to meet visitor expectations. This includes providing personalized recommendations, customized itineraries, and targeted promotions to enhance visitor satisfaction and engagement; 4) Planning Infrastructure and Services: Data analysis helps in planning and developing infrastructure and services around POIs. By examining data on visitor demand, transportation patterns, and accessibility, municipalities can make informed decisions about infrastructure improvements, public transportation routes, parking facilities, and the provision of amenities and services near POIs. This ensures a seamless and enjoyable experience for visitors; 5) Measuring Impact and ROI: Data-driven decision-making enables municipalities to measure the impact of their efforts and evaluate the return on investment (ROI). By analysing data on visitor numbers, spending patterns, and economic indicators, authorities can assess the economic impact of POIs on the local economy. This information helps justify investments, secure funding, and demonstrate the value of POIs to stakeholders and the community; and 6) Responding to Emerging Trends and Challenges: Data analysis allows municipalities to monitor emerging trends and challenges related to visitor behaviour and POIs. By continuously analysing data, authorities can identify changing visitor preferences, emerging attractions, and potential issues such as overcrowding or safety concerns. This helps in adapting strategies, implementing measures to address challenges, and staying responsive to the evolving needs of visitors.

By analysing visitor data, authorities can gain insights into visitor behaviour, optimize resource allocation, enhance visitor experiences, plan infrastructure, measure impact, and respond to emerging trends and challenges. This approach leads to more informed and effective decision-making, ultimately contributing to the success and sustainability of POIs and the city's overall development.

2 Literature Review

Tourism is one of the economic activities of strong relevance worldwide. According to the World Travel and Tourism Council [1], before the COVID-19 pandemic, its impact on the world GDP was 10.3%, and 1 in 4 new jobs were related to its development. According to the same source, it is also estimated that the revenue generated from international visitors was US$1.8 billion.

In Portugal, official data indicate that the wealth generated by tourism is equivalent to 8.8% of the GDP, and the sector represents 7.5% in total employment [2], with the Municipality of Lisbon being one of the main destinations for visitors, whether national or foreign. Tourism is, therefore, one of the main branches of the Portuguese economy.

The current scenario of competitiveness among organizations is characterized as a time when they need to be ahead of others in time to gain advantage in a continuous series of periods, so it is necessary to invest in constant innovation of their products and services [3].

Moreover, balancing the needs of residents with the expectations of visitors to tourist sites by providing them with high-quality experiences requires this population to be well characterized and managed [4].

The application of Big Data knowledge to the development of Business Intelligence systems applied to tourism stands out, in this sense, as a useful tool for the State and organizations to know this phenomenon and to better manage its economic and social performance in a timely manner.

In the specific case of this work, in which the goal is to analyze the movement of visitors in points of interest in the Municipality of Lisbon, several studies [3] show the importance and usefulness of geospatial analysis of large volumes of data for a better experience by the tourist, and for decision making by managers. In the case of Lisbon, some others have demonstrated how such decision support systems, based on analysis can become important information on the decision making [5–8].

Points of interest are, in the words of Gil et al. (2020), "regions of influence where citizens concentrate because of attractions or facilities and (…) places where the energy of the city is focused, and understanding the shape and size of POIs provides insights into how people experience the city" [9].

From a tourism perspective, it should be noted that the term tourist encompasses all visitors, which is why this term will be widely used in this study, including residents, day-trippers, as well as foreign visitors.

According to Harris & Howard (1996), as cited in Spangenberg (2013), "the focus here is on attractions, defined as the physical or cultural feature of a particular place that travellers or tourists perceive capable of satisfying one or more of their specific leisure-related demands. Such features may be environmental in nature (e.g., climate, culture, vegetation, or landscape), or they may be site-specific, such as a theatre performance, a museum, or a waterfall" [10].

Studies investigating human movement have a strong appeal for understanding this phenomenon, especially for the motivations that lie in its background [11]. They indicate that these movements are related to different activities (e.g., education, work, catering, etc.) in different urban environments.

Nearly a decade ago, in a study advocating the use of mobile device data for analysing people's movement [12], Zhang (2014) examined mobility patterns of users of such devices. Having noted the increasing use of devices such as smartphones, the author indicated that their data could be managed for application development and predictive modelling.

More recently, in a paper that indicated it was one of the first to adopt the Dictionary Learning method for characterizing human mobility patterns [13], Wu et al. (2017) indicated a step forward in this process, advocating that the large volume of data generated by mobile devices be handled in multiple collection centres due to the fact that we live in what they consider the era of data explosion.

It can be seen, therefore, that the use of large volumes of data from mobile devices, namely cell phones, has been asserting itself as a necessary tool for the analysis of people's movement behaviour with a focus on the most varied fields, such as urban planning, epidemiology, telecommunications, etc.

When discussing the importance of Big Data for the tourism industry, Shafiee & Ghatari (2017) state that big data leads to more efficient travel experiences in line with visitors' expectations, and also improves the levels of innovation, so necessary for this sector of the economy [14].

From this interest in innovation, studies have been developed around the analysis of visitor movement in tourist points of interest based on mobile devices. These points of interest (POI) correspond to larger areas or contiguous to tourist sites, such as monuments, museums, parks, buildings, etc.

Some recent studies deal with the development of intelligent systems for recommending POI to be visited based on the user's location and on characteristics of the site to be visited, such as distance, time spent travelling, evaluation given by other users, the desired category (e.g., museum, historical building, beach), etc. [15, 16].

In others, of particular interest for this work, human mobility in POIs is analysed from data visualization and modelling, in order to assist for the definition of urban planning strategies and investments for better exploitation of these territories [9–11, 17].

3 CRISP-DM

In developing this research work, the CRISP-DM (Cross Industry Standard Process for Data Mining) methodology [18] was followed to structure data to extract statistical and predictive information.

The efficiency of the method's application consists of the development in six stages: business understanding, data understanding, data preparation, modelling, evaluation, and deployment.

3.1 Business Understanding

POIs are places of agglomeration of people in each region characterized by their attractiveness and for being focuses of a great flow of visitors. How such mobility occurs is relevant for stakeholders to manage tourism-related problems.

Using big data from mobile devices used by visitors, the analysis of this problem becomes an indispensable tool for urban strategic planning in the tourism area.

Based on data from Vodafone mobile devices made available by CML, and aiming to provide an analysis tool, this work aims to evaluate the movement of visitors to certain areas of the city of Lisbon, differentiating their behaviour according to the winter and summer periods the day of the week the hours/periods of higher concentration in the POI the rainy days of the nationality.

This data is representative through an extrapolation of the market share of the other mobile operators and will be used for the behavioural study of visitors and their movement in the different POIs of the city.

This study will use a Python algorithm with a Jupiter Notebook interface for data analysis and transformation. The final statistics will be visualised using the Microsoft PowerBI tool. The predictive models will be developed using the Prophet algorithm.

3.2 Data Understanding

The base element of this work comes from a dataset made available by CML. This is composed of 12 monthly files, from September 2021 to August 2022, containing information about active cell phone terminals. The database sections the Lisbon Municipality in 200 m $\times$ 200 m^2 (grids) and indicates the number of active terminals in that zone, grouped every 5 terminals and in 5-min intervals, comprising the 24 h of each day. It contains all the data concerning the location of the POIs of local and roaming users, the latter with their nationality.

All files are composed of the same variables, and each dataset has the number of instances referenced. Each file contains a large volume of data that, to be processed together, would prevent processing on personal computers. Thus, the processing will be done on each monthly file for later grouping of the data to be treated.

To enrich the original information, data from the Portuguese Institute of Sea and Atmosphere (IPMA) will be used to collect the rainfall conditions in the studied period. These data contain the precipitation value at each hour of the day. To fill possible gaps in the IPMA data, the research will be complemented with data from the Time and Date website [20].

The available data present some gaps in the information:

– The IPMA database comprises a period of 5 months, from September 2021 to January 2022;
– The Vodafone dataset has a gap in the information for the month of February 2022 due to a "deliberate and malicious cyberattack" [21] suffered by the company on February 7 of that year.

Thus, due to lack or insufficiency of information, it was decided to limit the analysis to 6 months, divided into two 3-month periods to delimit two seasons: winter, from November 2021 to January 2022; and summer, from June to August 2022. The IPMA data complements the winter information with on-the-day precipitation. Of the total, 14,313,762 instances will be analysed, corresponding to approximately 58% of the available Vodafone data, with summer comprising 52%.

The data was also be augmented with another dataset made available by the faculty as part of this work: Wktcomplete. This dataset contains specific and relevant information about the city division grids, namely a name for the location, the parish and its georeferencing.

The data was also complemented with another dataset made available by the teaching team as part of this work: Wktcomplete. This dataset contains specific and relevant information about the city division grids, namely a name for the location, the parish and its georeferencing. This is geographic information.

To make the analysis more objective and targeted, we resorted to the study of visit recommendation websites to delimit the zones of the city to be analysed. In line with the recommendation of the websites Visit Lisbon [22], Turismo de Lisboa [23], O Guia da Cidade [24], Direção Geral do Património Cultural [25], LisbonLisboaPortugal [26] and Civitatis Lisbon [27] 4 zones of the city were selected for the analysis: Belém, Baixa/Chiado, Alfama/Castelo and Parque das Nações.

In the final dataset machine learning and forecasting algorithms will be applied for pattern detection and learning, developing a predictive model of visitors and their behavior.

3.3 Data Preparation

To optimize computational resources, data preparation began. We chose to keep the most relevant variables for the work: Grid_ID, Datetime, extract_month_3, extract_day_4, C1, C2, C9, C10 and D1.

Aiming to facilitate the analysis, it was decided to change the name of the columns to an easily identifiable nomenclature, namely:

- C1 → TN (National Terminals): active national terminals.
- C2 → TR (Terminals in Roaming): active roaming terminals.
- C9 → DN (National Data): national terminals with active data.
- C10 → DR (Roaming Data): roaming terminals with active data.

The datasets were analysed individually, month by month, and do not present duplicate lines. As for missing data, these were detected only in variable D1, which will be described in the item regarding the treatment of nationality.

After cleaning the dataset, the feature engineering process was started to add information for a better classification and understanding of the data. The dataset was enriched by creating new columns.

Day of the Week - To allow segmented analysis by day of the week, the date was used to create two nominal variables:

Weekday - Based on the date, the variable "Weekday" indicates the day of the week, Monday through Sunday.

Weekdays - Using the variable "Weekday" a new variable was created that classifies the days of the week into working days ("workday") or weekend days ("weekend").

3.3.1 Totalizers of the Number of Terminals

Given that the variables TN, TR, DN and DR comprise the number of active terminals and terminals with active data, national and roaming respectively, we created two variables that indicate the total of these variables, with the following information:

- "TT" - Total Terminals - indicates the total number of active terminals, obtained by adding the active national terminals and active roaming terminals (TN + TR);
- "DT" - Total Data - indicates the total number of terminals with active data, obtained by adding up the national terminals with active data and roaming terminals with active data (DN + DR)

Period - Aiming at an analysis that identifies the concentration of people at certain times of the day, it was decided to group the continuous variable of time into a categorical variable that comprises specific periods, as follows:

- Morning - comprised between 7 am and 11 am,
- Lunch - from 11 am to 3 pm,

- Evening - from 3 pm to 7 pm,
- Dinner - from 7 pm to 10 pm,
- Night - from 10 pm to midnight,
- Down - from midnight to 7 am.

Public Holiday - To analyse the impact of holidays on the affluence to POIs, the variable "Holiday" was introduced. The observations were identified with the respective holiday (national or municipal) according to the date. The others were identified with the nomenclature "na" to indicate "not applicable".

Parish and Place - To add easily recognizable information, the external database Wktcomplete.csv was used to create the variable "Parish". The relationship was made through the grid identifier and the name of the parish in which the respective grid cell is located is referred to.

Through the grid it was possible to identify, in the same source, the name/location of the grid (for example: Av. Brasília - Belém, Área ribeirinha Pedrouços or Feira Popular). This information was also added in a "Local" variable.

Precipitation - To identify behavior due to weather conditions, a binary variable was introduced to indicate the rainfall on the date.

This column was added using IPMA data. The values "0" and "1" are taken to indicate whether there was (1) or no (0) precipitation on that day.

The IPMA data was cleaned. For the imputation of missing data, the historical meteorological data for the Lisbon municipality available at the timeandate website [28] were used. In the total dataset considered there are 154837 instances with precipitation, which corresponds to 2.4% of the total for the winter period, comprising 13 days of a total of 92 days in the considered winter.

Data Selection - To maximize the efficiency of the statistics and presentations, it was decided to create a dataset limited to the zones object of the analysis, comprising Belém, Baixa/Chiado, Alfama/Castelo and Parque das Nações.

Once the information was limited, a detailed analysis of the variables targeted for analysis was carried out and possibilities for improvement were observed.

Location - With the goal of easy and immediate identification of the location, the nomenclatures identified in the "Location" variable were changed.

Zone - To provide a more comprehensive geographic visualization, a column was created with the information of the city zone where the "Location" is located. Thus, the categorical variable "Zone" was created, which now has the following nomenclatures: Belém, Alfama/Castelo, 'Baixa/Chiado and Pq Nações.

Station - Aiming at a quick sectioning of the data, it was decided to create the variable "Season" to identify the season of the year to which the data refers. The instances of the months of November, December, and January were identified as "winter" and the months of June, July, and August were identified as "summer".

nac1 (nationality) -Variable D1, representing the list of nationalities of the terminals, was disaggregated. It originated the variable "NAT1" to identify the country of origin of the respective terminal.

In this variable, nomenclature inconsistencies were identified, so a standardization was performed.

After analysing the missing data in this variable, it was found that they exist in only 59.6% of the total observations. Thus, it was decided to keep the whole dataset to obtain complete statistics on the number of active terminals, using this variable only for the analysis on the nationality of the visitors.

Country/Region - To facilitate the visualization of the geographic region, the variable "Country/Region" was created to group the terminals by region. The regions were selected according to the continental geographic location. In the case of Europe, it was divided between Europe-Shengen [29] and other European countries, thus allowing the identification of countries whose entry into Portugal does not require a visa.

4 Analysis of Results

To evaluate the behaviour of visitors in the selected zones, we started by visualizing the total number of active cell phones.

As shown in Fig. 1, the zones of the city with the highest number of terminals are, respectively, Baixa/Chiado, Parque das Nações, Alfama/Castelo and Belém. Referring to roaming visitors, one notices a slight difference in this trend. The areas with more active cell phones are Baixa/Chiado and Alfama/Castelo, followed by Parque das Nações and Belém. This difference can be explained by the business activity in the city, with the Baixa/Chiado and Parque das Nações areas indicating a higher concentration of offices.

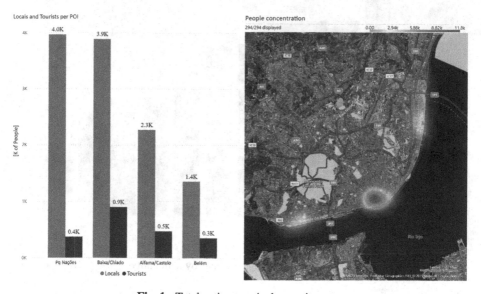

Fig. 1. Total active terminals per city zone

4.1 Concentration of Visitors by Nationality

The analysis of cell phones with active roaming allows us to identify the list of countries with more visitors.

The selection of the 10 countries with the highest number of terminals shows us that 8 belong to the European area, the others being from North and South America (Fig. 2).

Overall, the global trend of most visited zones is maintained in these 10 countries, with Baixa/Chiado and Alfama/Castelo showing the highest concentration of visitors (Fig. 3). For 7 of the 10 countries (France, United Kingdom, Brazil, Belgium, United States of America, Switzerland, and Ireland visit Parque das Nações more) the third most visited city area is Parque das Nações, while the Spanish, Italians and Germans have the highest concentration of visitors in Belém.

The analysis of the roaming terminals shows a higher prevalence of visitors in the summer period, with the Baixa/Chiado and Parque das Nações areas being more popular in the summer period, while Belém and Alfama/Castelo have a slightly higher demand in the winter period (Fig. 4 and Fig. 5).

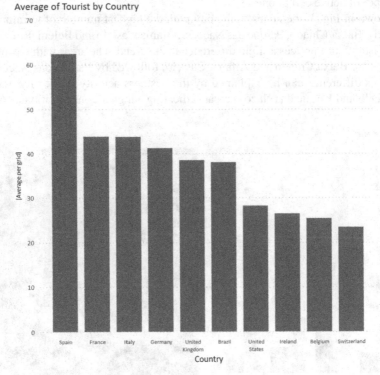

Fig. 2. Top 10 roaming terminals by nationality

The top 10 countries by season show that visitors from Italy and Switzerland have similar affluence of visits in summer and winter. Visitors from France, the United Kingdom, Brazil and Ireland are concentrated in the summer period. The United States and Belgium bring visitors mainly in the summer, and these two countries drop out of the top 10 list in number of visitors in the winter, see Fig. 6. Germany is the only country that brings more visitors in winter than in summer, increasing the influx by roughly 1.3%.

Average of Tourists per City Area

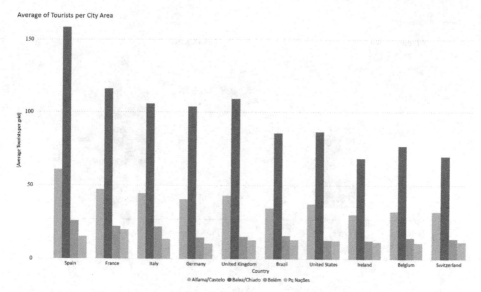

Fig. 3. Top 10 roaming terminals by nationality and city zone

Fig. 4. Overral Roaming Terminals

As shown in Figs. 7, 8, 9 and 10, visitors tend to concentrate in certain locations in the specific area.

In Belém, during the summer, there is a higher concentration of visitors in the area of the Jerónimos Monastery and the whole extension of the Praça do Império, followed by the garden area of the Belém Tower. In winter it is noted that on rainless days there

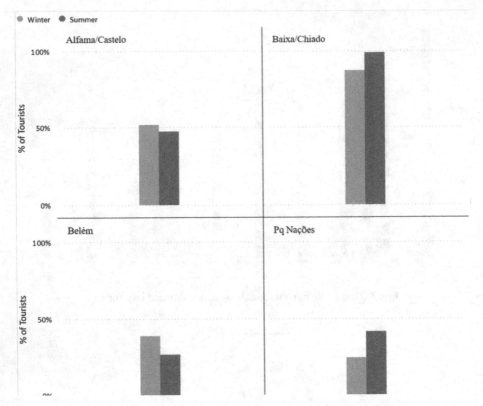

Fig. 5. Overall Roaming Terminal by year season and City area

is a greater concentration of visitors at the Monastery of Jerónimos and the Tower of Belém, while on rainy days there is an evident concentration at the Monastery.

In the Baixa/Chiado area, Praça Luís de Camões, Rossio and Rua Augusta are the areas that concentrate the highest number of visitors. On winter days when there is no rainfall the behavior of visitors is very similar to summer, and on rainy days there is less preference for the squares and a higher concentration near the local commerce is evident.

Baixa/Chiado – Summer Winter (no rain) Winter (rain)

In the summer visitors tend to concentrate near the Sé Patriarcal cathedral, coming from downtown. The second most visited place in this area is the Miradouro de Santa Luzia, followed by the Castelo de S. Jorge.

On winter days is also greater concentration of visitors in the vicinity of the Cathedral, and the Castle of St. George has more visitors on rainy days of winter than on days of the cold season when there is no precipitation.

When there is precipitation, the circulation of visitors in this area reduces by 70% to 80%, with Ireland and Denmark giving way to Austria and Finland in the top 10 list of visitors. In summer, visitors to Parque das Nações tend to concentrate on the Pavilion of Knowledge and the Altice Arena (Pavilhão Atlântico). On winter days when there is no

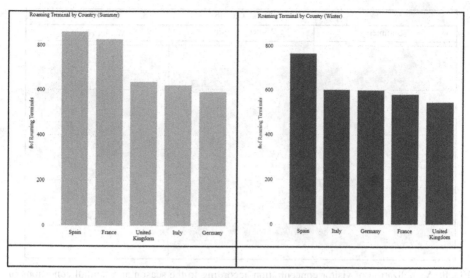

Fig. 6. Top 5 visitors by nationality/season

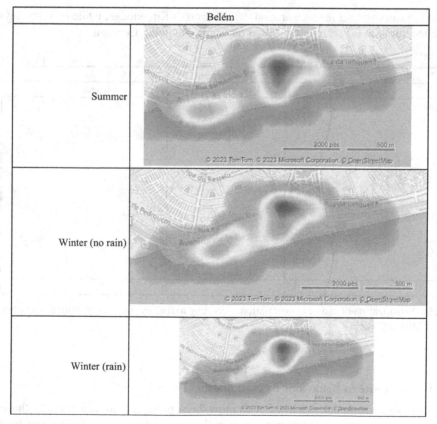

Fig. 7. Visualizing the concentration of visitors according to the season and rainfall conditions in the Belém.

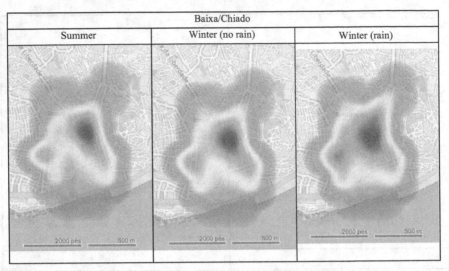

Fig. 8. Visualization of visitor concentration according to the season and rainfall conditions in the Baixa/Chiado area.

rainfall, visitors prefer the area around the Pavilion of Knowledge, while on rainy days, the concentration is higher in the Vasco da Gama Shopping Center area.

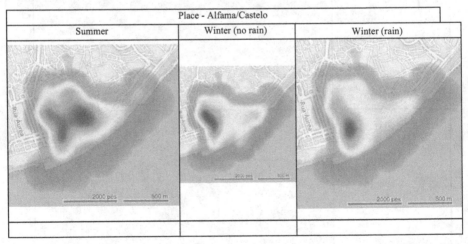

Fig. 9. Visualization of visitor concentration according to the season, season, rainfall conditions in the Alfama/Castelo

4.1.1 Difference in Behaviour by Nationality (Top 5)

The analysis by nationality shows that on rainy days (precipitation variable $= 1$), the top 5 foreign visitors tend to concentrate more in the Parque das Nações and Baixa/Chiado areas, to the detriment of the others (Fig. 11). The zone that suffers the largest decrease in affluence is Belém, with Alfama/Castelo losing slightly. This trend allows us to observe that the behaviour of all groups seems to be identical, regardless of nationality.

Place – Parque das Nações – Summer Winter (no rain) Winter (rain)

Place – Parque das Nações – Summer Winter (no rain) Winter (rain)

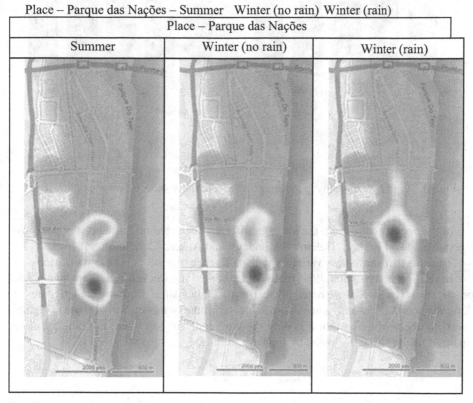

Place – Parque das Nações		
Summer	Winter (no rain)	Winter (rain)

Fig. 10. Visualization of visitor concentration according to season and precipitation season and rainfall conditions in the Parque das Nações area

4.2 Day of the Week

Figure 12 shows the turnout of roaming terminals on the different days of the week. It is important to reinforce that the percentage of visitors is significantly higher during weekends.

Regardless of the day of the week there are always more active roaming terminals in the Baixa/Chiado zone, followed by Alfama/Castelo. And as for Belém, only on weekends this zone is not the least visited, with Parque das Nações.

The peak of visitors in Belém is on Sundays, in Baixa/Chiado and Alfama/Castelo on Saturdays and in Parque das Nações on Mondays.

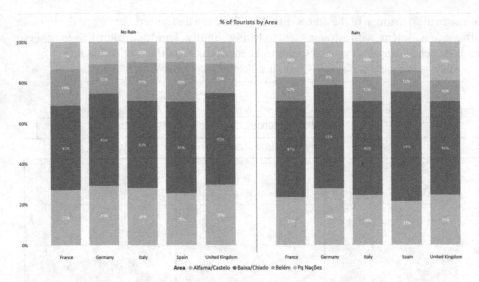

Fig. 11. Top 5 by nationality: comparing visitor behavior visitors behavior on rainy days

In the opposite direction, the lowest affluence is detected in Parque das Nações and Baixa/Chiado on Fridays, Belém on Mondays, and Alfama/Castelo on Sundays.

The area that shows less variation in the affluence of visitors is Alfama/Castelo.

In relation to the nationalities that visit Lisbon on the weekend vs. the whole week, practically no changes were noted in the Top 10. Only visitors from the United States of America appear in seventh when considering the whole week and Switzerland in eighth, reversing the positions when it is only the weekend. The top three, in both cases, are Spain in first position, followed by France and Italy.

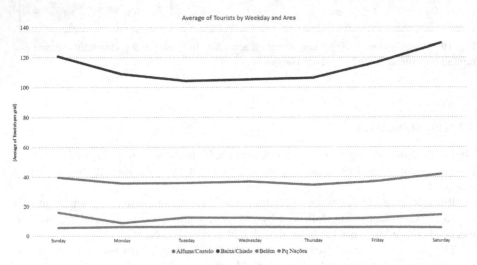

Fig. 12. Roaming terminal affluence in the city zones on the different days of the week

The analysis per daily period (Fig. 13) and per hour (Fig. 14) allows us to identify some trends:

- Visitors arrive in Bethlehem close to lunch time (from 11 am to 3 pm) and leave from there before dinner time (7 pm). It is the area with the lowest frequency of roaming terminals in the early morning period. Factors that contribute to this displacement may be related to the hotel supply and restaurant diversity in the area.
- Parque das Nações also has its peak of visitors at lunch time, decreasing this affluence as the end of the night approaches (1 h). It is an area of the city with a low frequency of roaming terminals during the early morning hours.
- Alfama/Castelo has a certain constancy in the volume of visitors. There is a balance in the affluence from lunch time, which starts around 11 am, until the end of the night, around 1 am. The period with the lowest incidence of roaming terminals is the early morning, even though it does not differ much from the other periods. It is also the area of the city whose affluence starts earlier in the morning.
- Baixa/Chiado, being the most frequented area by roaming visitors, has an increasing affluence since the morning, dropping only slightly at dawn. The affluence at dawn can be explained by the offer of entertainment establishments in the Chiado/Bairro Alto area.

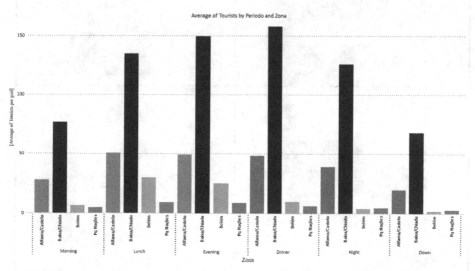

Fig. 13. Affluence of roaming terminals in the city zones the different periods of the day

Thus, the following visitor behaviors are evident:

- in Belém they flow fundamentally by lunch time and early afternoon.
- the movement in Parque das Nações starts late in the morning and gradually decreases until late in the evening.
- They arrive at Baixa/Chiado and Alfama/Castelo in the morning and keep the affluence high until the early morning.

The behaviour of visitors as a function of time was also analysed. In all the zones considered the value drops to less than half of the maximum value reached during the day in the period between midnight and 8 am. This factor may be related to visitors not sleeping in any of the zones considered.

Also, through these graphs we can consider that the number of roaming terminals always reaches its maximum value between 1 pm and 2 pm, except in the Baixa/Chiado area, which happens at 7 pm. The maximum number reached in the period between 1 pm and 2 pm may be related with the arrival time of several cruise ships in Lisbon, also with people who choose to make stopovers in Lisbon and with visitors who are staying in the surrounding area of the city like Cascais, Sintra and Oeiras.

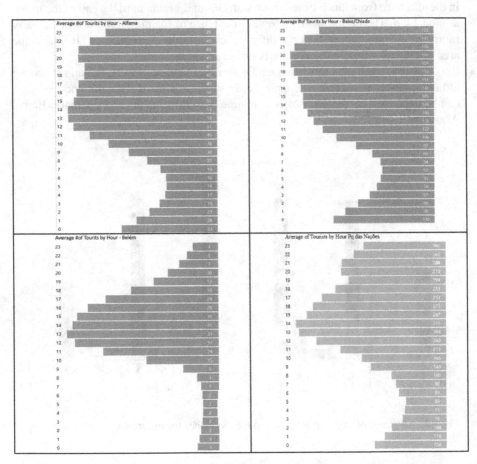

Fig. 14. Roaming terminals in the city zones city zones at different times of the day

Comparing the hours per zone on the days of the week, it can be concluded that:

– Alfama/Castelo shows practically no differences in the number of roaming terminals depending on the day of the week.

- Baixa/Chiado there are mostly differences during the afternoon to the end of the night, with on average approximately 10% more terminals in active roaming at the weekend during these hours.
- Belém, where the differences seem to be more significant after 10 am, increasing on average 25%.
- Parque das Nações has an opposite trend, with more data roaming during the week compared to the weekend. The maximum difference observed is at 2 PM, where during the week there are 309 roaming visitors compared to 225 with active roaming. It is also worth noting that at 2 pm the maximum number of visitors is reached in this zone.

5 Modelling and Evaluation

The generation of the prediction model was developed using Prophet, an open source software produced by Facebook [19]. This option is justified by the simpler and faster way of programming and for being visually more intuitive to reach conclusions or insights.

After re-analyzing the database, the DN, DR, and DT columns were eliminated because they are like the TN, TR, and TT columns, which represented optimization of memory space.

All observations with null values and less than five in the TT column were also eliminated, to take into consideration only information from instances with more than five active devices in total.

After verifying the almost irrelevant impact of the number of roaming devices on the total number of devices, it was decided to treat only the TT column as the prediction variable for the forecast model.

To facilitate visualization and to implement the prediction algorithm, the database was divided into two: "winter", which includes all the information from 11/01/2021 to 01/31/2022; and "summer", with observations dated between 06/01/2022 and 08/31/2022.

In the winter period, there is a tendency for a decrease in visitors in all POIs, except for the Baixa/Chiado POI, which registers an increase in visitors between the end of November and the beginning of December, probably due to Christmas shopping.

In the summer, there is a tendency of stability in the number of visitors in the POIs. However, one notices a downward movement in the week following the holidays of June 10th and 13th at the Baixa/Chiado POI, that is, between June 18th and 24th. This oscillation is not due to the lower amount of data.

The Prophet algorithm's prediction for the days of the week in the winter period shows that: in Belém, the number of visitors increases as the weekend approaches; in Baixa/Chiado, the number of visitors increases sharply between Thursday and Saturday, falling sharply on Sunday; in Alfama/Castelo, the largest number of visitors is found on Saturday, Tuesday and Wednesday; and in Parque das Nações, the largest flow of people is on weekdays, especially on Tuesday, which is justified by the fact that many workers who don't live in the area are allocated there.

For the summer period, and following the same forecasting approach, it is expected that: in Belém, the same trend as in the summer is observed, except for the decrease in visits on Wednesdays; differently from the winter, the movement of people in Baixa/Chiado

88   L. B. Elvas et al.

is higher on weekdays and Saturdays, falling sharply on Sundays; in Alfama/Castelo, visitors prefer Friday and Saturday, with the lowest movement being observed on Wednesdays and Thursdays; finally, in Parque das Nações, the same trend predicted for the winter is maintained.

The prediction model did not have the intended performance evaluation metrics, but the results of predicting values for the summer period are better than the winter, especially for the MAPE values that are between 0.07 and 0.18. This means an accuracy between 93% and 88%, respectively, in predicting the next 30 observations.

In Figs. 15, 16, 17 and 18 below, the graphs with the lines of observed versus predicted values in the summer season for the month of August can be observed.

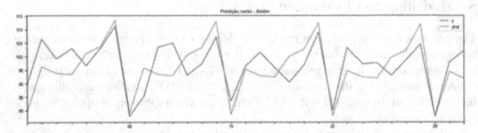

Fig. 15. Forecasting with observed and forecasted values for Belém POI in summer season

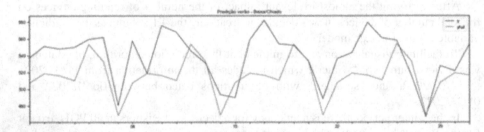

Fig. 16. Forecasting with observed and forecasted values for the POI of Baixa/Chiado in the summer season.

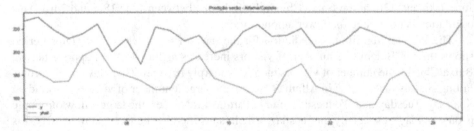

Fig. 17. Forecasting with observed and predicted values for the Alfama/Castelo POI in the summer season

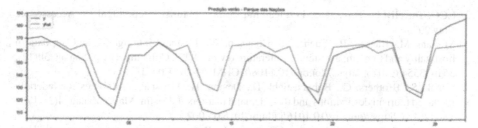

Fig. 18. Forecasting with observed and predicted values for the Parque das Nações POI in the summer season

We conclude that the results obtained with the data modelling using the Prophet software can help forecast and understand the evolution of the number of visitors at the analysed POI and its trend on the days of the week.

6   Conclusion

The paper concludes by summarizing the key findings and emphasizing the importance of understanding visitor behaviour within smart cities. It highlights the potential of utilizing visitor behaviour insights to optimize urban planning, enhance visitor experiences, and create sustainable and inclusive smart city environments.

In summary, this paper explores the concept of POIs in smart cities and investigates visitor behaviour patterns. By understanding visitor preferences, routing patterns, and interactions with POIs, policymakers, urban planners, and tourism stakeholders can make informed decisions to improve urban environments, optimize resource allocation, and deliver personalized visitor experiences in smart cities.

Summary of key findings and contributions.

Reiteration of the importance of POIs in smart cities and visitor behaviour.

Call for continued research and collaboration to advance POI management practices in smart cities.

Acknowledgment. We thank the Lisbon City Council for providing us with the data necessary for this study, namely Mr. António Costa (Lisbon City Council), Mrs. Helena Martins (Lisbon City Council) and Mrs. Paula Melicias (Lisbon City Council). We also thank IPMA for providing us with the data necessary to complement our study.

Funding. This work was supported by EEA Grants Blue Growth Programme (Call #5). Project PT-INNOVATION-0069 – Fish2Fork. This research also received funding from ERAMUS+ project NEMM with grant 101083048.

References

1. Travel & Tourism Economic Impact | World Travel & Tourism Council (WTTC). https://wttc.org/research/economic-impact. Accessed 22 May 2023

2. LCG. TravelBI by Turismo de Portugal. https://travelbi.turismodeportugal.pt/. Accessed 22 May 2023
3. Mariani, M., Baggio, R., Fuchs, M., Höepken, W.: Business intelligence and big data in hospitality and tourism: a systematic literature review. Int. J. Contemp. Hosp. Manag. **30**(12), 3514–3554 (2018). https://doi.org/10.1108/IJCHM-07-2017-0461
4. Supak, S., Brothers, G., Bohnenstiehl, D., Devine, H.: Geospatial analytics for federally managed tourism destinations and their demand markets. J. Destin. Mark. Manag. **4**(3), 173–186 (2015). https://doi.org/10.1016/j.jdmm.2015.05.002
5. Mesquitela, J., Elvas, L.B., Ferreira, J.C., Nunes, L.: Data analytics process over road accidents data—a case study of Lisbon city. ISPRS Int. J. Geo-Inf. **11**(2), Article no. 2 (2022). https://doi.org/10.3390/ijgi11020143
6. Elvas, L.B., Gonçalves, S.P., Ferreira, J.C., Madureira, A.: Data fusion and visualization towards city disaster management: Lisbon case study. EAI Endorsed Trans. Smart Cities **6**(18), e3–e3 (2022). https://doi.org/10.4108/eetsc.v6i18.1374
7. Elvas, L.B., Mataloto, B.M., Martins, A.L., Ferreira, J.C.: Disaster management in smart cities. Smart Cities **4**(2), Article no. 2 (2021). https://doi.org/10.3390/smartcities4020042
8. Elvas, L.B., Marreiros, C.F., Dinis, J.M., Pereira, M.C., Martins, A.L., Ferreira, J.C.: Data-driven approach for incident management in a smart city. Appl. Sci. **10**(22), Article no. 22 (2020). https://doi.org/10.3390/app10228281
9. Gil, E., Ahn, Y., Kwon, Y.: Tourist attraction and points of interest (POIs) using search engine data: case of Seoul. Sustainability **12**(17), Article no. 17 (2020). https://doi.org/10.3390/su12177060
10. Spangenberg, T.: Standardization, modeling and implementation of points of interest – a touristic perspective. Int. J. U- E- Serv. Sci. Technol. **6**, 59–70 (2013). https://doi.org/10.14257/ijunesst.2013.6.6.07
11. Zeng, W., Fu, C.-W., Müller Arisona, S., Schubiger, S., Burkhard, R., Ma, K.-L.: Visualizing the relationship between human mobility and points of interest. IEEE Trans. Intell. Transp. Syst. **18**(8), 2271–2284 (2017). https://doi.org/10.1109/TITS.2016.2639320
12. Zhang, Y.: User mobility from the view of cellular data networks. In: IEEE Conference on Computer Communications, IEEE INFOCOM 2014, pp. 1348–1356 (2014). https://doi.org/10.1109/INFOCOM.2014.6848068
13. Wu, T., Rustamov, R.M., Goodall, C.: Distributed learning of human mobility patterns from cellular network data. In: 2017 51st Annual Conference on Information Sciences and Systems (CISS), pp. 1–6 (2017). https://doi.org/10.1109/CISS.2017.7926085
14. Shafiee, S., Ghatari, A.R.: Big data in tourism industry. In: 2016 10th International Conference on e-Commerce in Developing Countries: with focus on e-Tourism (ECDC), pp. 1–7 (2016). https://doi.org/10.1109/ECDC.2016.7492979
15. Suakanto, S., Andreswari, R., Albasori, E.P.: SEMPIR: sequence multiple point of interest recommender system for overland tourism. In: 2021 International Conference on ICT for Smart Society (ICISS), pp. 1–7 (2021). https://doi.org/10.1109/ICISS53185.2021.9533194
16. Ajantha, D., Vijay, J., Sridhar, R.: A user-location vector based approach for personalised tourism and travel recommendation. In: 2017 International Conference on Big Data Analytics and Computational Intelligence (ICBDAC), pp. 440–446 (2017). https://doi.org/10.1109/ICBDACI.2017.8070880
17. Giglio, S., Bertacchini, F., Bilotta, E., Pantano, P.: Machine learning and points of interest: typical tourist Italian cities. Curr. Issues Tour. **23**(13), 1646–1658 (2020). https://doi.org/10.1080/13683500.2019.1637827
18. Wirth, R., Hipp, J.: CRISP-DM: towards a standard process model for data mining. In: Proceedings of the 4th International Conference on the Practical Applications of Knowledge Discovery and Data Mining (2000)

19. Prophet. http://facebook.github.io/prophet/. Accessed 22 May 2023
20. Current Local Time in Lisbon, Portugal (Lisboa). Consultado em 10 de abril de 20223. Disponível em https://www.timeanddate.com/worldclock/portugal/lisbon
21. Vodafone Portugal alvo de ciberataque. Press Release, 8 de fevereiro de 2022. Consultado em 03 de maio de 2023 (2022). Disponível em https://www.vodafone.pt/press-releases/2022/2/vodafone-portugal-alvo-de-ciberataque.html
22. 10 things to do and see in Lisbon. Visit Portugal. Consultado em 01 de abril de 2023. Disponível em https://www.visitportugal.com/en/destinos/lisboa-regiao/73773
23. Visit Lisboa. Turismo de Lisboa. Consultado em 01 de abril de 2023. Disponível em https://www.visitlisboa.com/pt-pt
24. O que visitar em Lisboa. O Guia da Cidade. Consultado em 01 de abril de 2023. Disponível em https://www.guiadacidade.pt/pt/discover-pois-lisboa-11
25. Indicadores TOP 100 - Registos de Património + Vistos. Direção Geral do Património Cultural. Consultado em 01 de abril de 2023. Disponível em http://www.monumentos.gov.pt/site/APP_PagesUser/SIPATop100.aspx?it=1
26. Lisbon Portugal Guide. LisbonLisboaPortugal.com. Consultado em 01 de abril de 2023. Disponível em https://lisbonlisboaportugal.com/index.html
27. Lisbon Travel Guide. Civitatis Lisbon. Consultado em 01 de abril de 2023. Disponível em https://www.lisbon.net/
28. Past Weather in Lisbon, Portugal. Consultado em 12 de março de 2023. Disponível em https://www.timeanddate.com/weather/portugal/lisbon/historic?month=12&year=2021
29. Europa sem fronteiras: O Espaço Schengen. Publicação da Comissão Europeia – Migração e Assuntos Internos. Consultado em 13 de abril de 2023 em (2019). https://doi.org/10.2837/71557, https://home-affairs.ec.europa.eu/system/files_en?file=2020-09

Blockchain-Based Solution for Charitable Supply Chains: Network Proposal Architecture for Portuguese Tax Consignment Program

Ulpan Tokkozhina[1,2,3]([envelope]) [ID], Ana Lucia Martins[1,2] [ID], and Joao C. Ferreira[2,3,4,5] [ID]

[1] Business Research Unit (BRU-IUL), Lisbon, Portugal
ulpan_tokkozhina@iscte-iul.pt
[2] Instituto Universitário de Lisboa (ISCTE-IUL), 1649-026 Lisbon, Portugal
[3] Inov Inesc Inovação/Inesc-ID, 1000-029 Lisbon, Portugal
[4] Information Sciences and Technologies and Architecture Research Centre (ISTAR-IUL),
Lisbon, Portugal
[5] Logistics, Molde University College, Molde, 6410 Molde, Norway

Abstract. This paper presents a blockchain-based solution for enhancing transparency, accountability, and efficiency in charitable supply chains, with a focus on the Portuguese Tax Consignment Program, but adaptively to other tax systems. Charitable organizations often face challenges in managing and tracking donations, leading to potential inefficiencies and distrust among stakeholders. Leveraging blockchain technology, this research proposes a network proposal architecture that enables secure and immutable recording of donation transactions, ensures proper allocation of funds, and fosters transparency in the charitable supply chain ecosystem.

Keywords: Blockchain · Charitable Supply Chains · Network Proposal Architecture

1 Introduction

The management of charitable supply chains involves multiple stakeholders, including donors, charitable organizations, and regulatory bodies. Charity initiatives coming from citizens reveal the level of social responsibility of population, therefore such initiatives sometimes require support of State as an intermediary and reliable third-party for safe transactions. However, the lack of transparency and accountability hampers the effectiveness and trustworthiness of these processes. One of the possibilities that State provides for citizens to support socially significant organizations and projects that align with their views and values is called the tax consignment or Personal Income Tax (IRS) consignment. This paper is focused on the example of IRS consignment of Portuguese Republic, which was introduced in 2001 and currently allows taxpayers to contribute to one of more than 4000 eligible nonprofit organizations (NPOs) at no cost [1]. Portuguese IRS consignment is a mechanism that gives taxpayers opportunity to donate 0.5% of

A. L. Martins et al. (Eds.): INTSYS 2023, LNICST 540, pp. 92–104, 2024.
https://doi.org/10.1007/978-3-031-49379-9_5

their tax owned to State to an entity of their choice [2] among the list of registered entities (e.g. NPOs involved in social, cultural, environmental, scientific, health, humanitarian and animal protection), for further convenience referred to as Beneficiary Entity (BE).

However, one of the crucial factors in any charitable initiative is public trust, because often there is only a minimal understanding of how exactly resources are allocated to organizations after citizens make donations [3]. Therefore, public trust building is a central issue that needs to be addressed to stimulate populations' interest in tax consignment programs. Issues, such as the lack of transparency and traceability of transactions might compromise the effectiveness of tax consignment and discourage taxpayers from participating in such initiatives. Questions like "Was the amount I consigned actually delivered to the chosen entity?", "What was the total amount that was assigned to a certain entity?", "How does the chosen entity spend the total consignment amount per year?", "What the NPO entity was able to improve in its sector?" are not easy to be answered, which once again can impact on taxpayers' willingness to participate in IRS consignment programs.

Thus, it is necessary to find solutions that may bring improvement to the tax consignment process and ensure greater security and transparency in transactions. One of the emerging technologies that is being discussed as a promising tool for transparency providing is blockchain technology (BCT). As defined by [4] BCT is a "digital, decentralized and distributed ledger in which transactions are logged and added in chronological order with the goal of creating permanent and tamper-proof records". With this definition, we may understand the potential that this technology holds for the transparency of charitable transactions, providing greater confidence to taxpayers and all stakeholders involved in the process.

This paper introduces the concept of utilizing blockchain technology to address these challenges, specifically in the context of the Portuguese Tax Consignment Program, which allows taxpayers to trace back the allocated percentage of their taxes to eligible NPO.

The purpose of this study is to investigate the ability of BCT to strengthen public trust in NPO-related transactions by providing an extensive level of transparency, traceability and efficiency. Therefore, the goal of this study is to consider the implementation of BCT on the example of Portuguese state tax consignment process through the introduction of comprehensive architecture of potential application.

The remaining of the paper is structured as following: second section contains literature review on the field, third section is describing the tax consignment program and explains the roles of main stakeholders, sections four proposes the architecture of BCT-based solution for the tax consignment program and the conceptual model of it, finally sections five and six discuss the BCT-based solution comparing it with the current process and provide paths for future research.

2 Literature Review

This section is aimed to build an understanding of the operations and the flow of resources in charitable initiatives, as well as the specifics of the BCT and improvements it can bring to charitable programs based on the example of existing applications.

2.1 Nonprofit Organizations' Supply Chains

Supply chain management (SCM) is usually used in a context of business and commercial processes, where the profit is an ultimate goal of stakeholders. However, SCM can also be applied in the context of NPOs, which also require a high level of performance, efficiency of processes and the speed of response. The authors in [5] suggest an adapted definition of such phenomena as the humanitarian supply chain management (HSCM), which characterizes "the systemic, strategic coordination of sourcing, procurement, storage and movement of physical relief goods and donations and the tactics across these functions within a particular humanitarian organization and across other actors within the humanitarian system, for the purposes of alleviating human suffering". Among the five main areas of focus for more efficient HSCM, [6] highlights the need of building trustful relationships across stakeholders and strengthening networks that may potentially extend the human resource pool available.

On the example of charity shops, [7] formulated the most common barriers that prevent populations' to be more involved in charitable initiatives, among which such issues as (1) the lack of information on how charity shops make use of donations; (2) the lack of familiarity and knowledge about the donation process; (3) the lack of awareness of the impact that donations make and other constraints can be highlighted.

When compared to commercial supply chain sector, HSCM is still an underdeveloped area, which requires more attention from scholars [8]. In order to facilitate the improvement of charity SCs and highlight the sustainability component of such, [9] suggest scholars to focus on the area of emerging technologies adoption and explore the potential that novel solutions hold for the elimination of information asymmetry and acceleration of the information flow across players. Like this, decentralized structure of the network would potentially add value to users that want to participate in charitable activities and ensure the receival of their donations in the selected organization. Thus, the next subsection is going to reveal the technological features of BCT to uncover the potential that it holds for the transparency of transactions in charitable area.

2.2 Technological Specifics of Blockchain Technology

Blockchain technology is a part of DLT (Distributed Ledger Technologies), which means that by default multiple copies of the ledger are held by different parties and are accessible in real-time, where data is added through consensus mechanism eliminating the need for a third party [10] and each transaction is represented by a data block with information, guaranteeing the security and integrity of the data (hash) [11, 12].

Like this, the main characteristics of BCT are decentralization, resistance to failures and cyberattacks, transparency and immutability of the recorded data, which enables the efficiency and trust in data for all ledger participants [10, 13]. Being immune to alteration, tampering or fraud entry [14], BCT-based networks allow verification of past entries at any time [15]. Although transparency is one of the main features of the technology, this does not mean that all data recorded on the network is necessarily visible to all participants. If required, it is possible to define different levels of access and permissions on the network, allowing only certain group of participants to have access to specific information, keeping the remaining information confidential. This is possible through encryption and authentication techniques, which ensure that only authorized users have access to confidential data [16], thus BCT-based solutions ensure both transparency and confidentiality, depending on the needs of each use case.

BCT-based solutions can be divided into three main types: public, private and hybrid/consortium networks. Public networks were first introduced for the use of Bitcoin cryptocurrency trade, these are open and fully decentralized networks that allow anyone to participate and make transactions without the need for prior permission [17]. Private networks are more compatible with business applications and are controlled by a single entity or group of entities and require permission to access. Hybrid or consortium networks combine elements of both public and private architectures, allowing some parts of the network to be public while others remain private, it usually involves multiple organizations working together in a controlled and secure environment.

2.3 Existing Use Cases of Blockchain Technology in NPO Area

Blockchain technology is discussed to be applicable in a broad spectrum of different sectors and industries such as finance, healthcare, supply chains, governance, food and agriculture etc.

The use of blockchain solutions to fund NPOs is being actively implemented as it allows reduction of costs associated with third-parties services, protection of donating individual's data and information, and increased efficiency in recipient organizations [18]. There are several existing use cases of BCT applications for management and tracking of donations, such as:

- **BitGive Foundation** - an NPO that is dedicated to BCT application for transparency of donations of social and environmental causes. Through the GiveTrack platform, donors can track the path of their money and see how it is being used by the recipient organization [19].
- **Giveth** - an organization that promotes a reward culture and is aimed to empower people that are willing to make donations. Giveth uses Web3 to disrupt and transform the way public goods are funded, helping NPOs to evolve and reach a new level of transparency [20].
- **Goteo** - BCT-based crowdfunding platform that is built upon a "win-win" model, where donors are rewarded with non-monetary rewards, such as exclusive access to events or products. The platform aims to fund projects that may bring positive social, cultural or environmental impact. It was one of the first BCT-based crowdfunding projects in Europe and since then has been a leader in social and financial innovation [21].
- **Blockchain Charity Foundation (BCF)** - is an initiative led by cryptocurrency organization Binance, it applies BCT to help address global charity and philanthropy problems. BCF aims to provide a secure and transparent platform for charitable donations around the world, applying BCT for donations tracking to ensure they reach the right charitable organizations. BCF's platform allows donors to see where their donations were used, as well as the results achieved by the charities they support [22].

Existing use cases once again prove that donation-related BCT projects are aimed at the improvement of transparency, traceability and efficiency of the donation process and transactions processing, guaranteeing that donations and contributions will get into the right organization safely and reliably.

3   Tax Consignment Process: From Taxpayers to Beneficiary Entities

This section aims to clarify the steps of the current process of tax consignment to BEs in Portugal, identifying challenges and constraints that needs to be addressed in future. Status quo is crucial to be understood and analyzed, as the limitations of the current process will identify where and how BCT may bring improvements.

3.1   Current Process

Tax consignment program in Portugal started in 2001, pursuing the aim of encouraging civil society participation in financing causes of public, cultural, environmental, and social interest, and thus contribute to the development of these areas for the good of country. Initially, the consignment was aimed exclusively towards religious institutions, private social solidarity institutions and public utility donations, but it has later been extended to other NPOs, including, but not limited to animal welfare, sustainability and environmental organizations etc.

Currently, in terms of tax consignment in Portugal, there are two main ways to consign part of the tax to a BE: through IRS consignment or through VAT consignment. As mentioned earlier, the IRS consignment allows taxpayers to donate 0.5% of the value of the tax they have already paid, or will pay, whereas, VAT consignment amount is deducted directly from the amount that the consumer would receive in terms of tax benefit. Both forms of tax consignment are completely voluntary. If the taxpayer does not indicate any NPO entity, or if the entity indicated does not meet the legal requirements, the value of the tax consignment goes to the State. Currently, there are 4,752 BEs registered on the Tax and Customs Authority (AT) website, which are authorized to receive the tax consignment in Portugal [23].

To be able to donate taxpayers need to indicate the entity they wish to donate to, access the AT website and indicate the Tax Identification Number (NIF) of the entity they wish to support, along with the option to consign IRS, VAT or both. After filing the IRS return, the tax consignment process is managed by the AT, which is responsible for receiving the consignations and performing transference to BEs through banking institutions.

The clearance of the consigned amounts is supervised by the AT's own internal inspection entities and external entities, such as the Court of Auditors (CA). These would be the entities responsible for the verification of the correct transfer amounts to BEs and controlling the process as a whole. AT does not publicly share such type of information, therefore according to newspapers [24], between 2014 and 2022, around 187 million euros were consigned to BEs through tax consignment program in Portugal. This once again proves that tax consignment program is an important source of funding for BEs in Portugal and that taxpayers' participation is increasing to support causes of public, cultural, environmental and social interest. However, the transparency and effectiveness of the tax consignment process is still an open issue, thus to involve and attract more citizens to participate in the program, there is a need for the assurance that the amounts consigned by taxpayers are properly delivered to the BEs of their choice, and are effectively contributed to further development and prosperity of the chosen sector.

3.2 Challenges and Potential Problems Identified

Although tax consignment is an important source of funding for Portuguese BEs, there are still some open issues and challenges that may compromise the effectiveness of the initiative, therefore discouraging taxpayers from participating in the process:

- **Bureaucracy** - The process of registering to become an accredited BE and obtaining authorization to receive the tax consignment can be bureaucratic and time-consuming for smaller NPOs;
- **Lack of awareness about the program** - The tax consignment process is only disclosed at the time of IRS submission, thus those individuals that were not aware about the possibility to consign or did not educate themselves about available options to donate might ignore the participation at all;
- **Complexity of choosing the right BE to donate** - Although there are more than 4,700 entities registered on the AT website, taxpayers often do not know how to find entities that are aligned with their visions and values;
- **Lack of transparency and traceability** - The current tax consignment process does not offer much transparency to taxpayers about the final destination of the consigned funds;
- **Difficulty in budget forecasting** - Entities that benefit from the tax consignment receive the consigned values referring to the previous year, thus makes budget forecasting difficult for those BEs which depend heavily on tax consignment funds.

As can be seen from the above-mentioned issues, it is necessary to build solutions that improve the process of tax consignment for both taxpayers and BEs, ensuring greater transparency, efficiency and traceability in transactions, where BCT emerges as a promising alternative to address these challenges and improve the process of tax consignment program.

4 Conceptual Design of Blockchain-Based Solution

The data flow diagram below (Fig. 1) represents a process that starts with the taxpayer's tax return, which is stored in the AT database. The AT then uses this database to create a smart contract that defines the transfer rules from the taxpayer to the BE. Before transferring the amount to the BCT-based ledger, the smart contract verifies the records and initiates steps that are predefined through the smart contract transaction automation. When funds are transferred by the AT in a token form to the BCT ledger, the smart contract is completed by automatically transferring the funds from taxpayer's wallet to the BE(s) of the choice, according to the rules predefined previously.

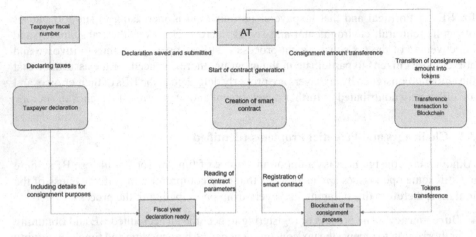

Fig. 1. Proposed data flow on a Blockchain network for tax consignment

The proposed BCT-based system guarantees the transparency of transfers of the taxpayers' consignments to the BEs, generating greater trust of taxpayers in the system itself and creating accountability in the further use of the donated funds. In terms of its architecture, the proposed BCT-based solution is conceptualized to be hybrid in order to ensure taxpayers' interests are safeguarded, at the same time providing the maximum possible transparency through open access to information. The anonymity of the taxpayer is a crucial point that needs to be considered, thus only the individual taxpayer, the AT and the CA can gain the visibility to such confidential data.

Considering the linear growth of the number of records and entries on the BCT ledger, the consensus mechanism of choice for this case is the Proof of Authority (PoA). This consensus mechanism considers that validators are trusted authorities, also called as deciding agents, thus their 'identities' are known to other players, which creates a "decentralized delegated centralization" environment [25]. For the State program, such as tax consignment, PoA is a consensus of fit, because here the knowledge about the trusted entity that is managing the funds allocation to BEs brings more security and confidence to all stakeholders involved, especially to citizens.

The role of validator nodes in the network are taken by State entities and other strategic partners in the blockchain ecosystem. These validators make their identity public, as their reputation and integrity of the process are critical to trust in the designed network. Through their active participation in the validation of transactions, validators help ensure the security and stability of the network, which is essential for its long-term growth and development. Such network architecture promotes and reinforces the legal mechanisms that support the original idea of tax consignment, which is the encouragement of civil society participation in socially significant projects.

4.1 Tax Consignment Process in the Blockchain Network

In order to achieve the objectives of creating a decentralized system, where all stakeholders have the possibility to contribute to the improvement of the solution it was chosen to apply the concept of Decentralized Autonomous Organization (DAO). DAO can be characterized as a network, where it is guaranteed that all active parties of the process have influence on the designation and success of the blockchain system. Since this paper suggests the architecture of a solution for a State program, any decision to change the rules of the proposed network must be framed in accordance with the Portuguese legal context.

The process starts with the taxpayer filing the tax return, and upon the finalization of the tax return process the taxpayer has the possibility to choose an BE to which he/she wants to consign part of the income tax. Once the tax declaration is completed and validated by the AT, a smart contract is created and the following steps are further taking place on a BCT-powered network:

1. The smart contract is created and registered on the network;
2. The donated amount is made available in a token form and is transferred to the taxpayer's address;
3. Further, this donated amount will be automatically transferred from the taxpayer's address to the selected BE's address, thus allowing to keep track of the funds transference;
4. When the funds are received by the BE, it is free to decide when to withdraw them, removing them from the tokenized network and converting them into monetary values.

To initiate the entrance to the blockchain network, it is necessary that the taxpayer consigns part of the tax to be donated to a BE, and that this declaration is further validated by the AT. If so, the AT creates a smart contract that will be placed on the BCT network and will allow the taxpayer to visualize the track of dedicated donations until they get to the chosen BE.

4.2 Smart Contract

The nature of a smart contract is an automated and digitalized version of a contract in the physical world, where an agreement between several parties exists and where several conditions need to be met in order to confirm and trigger the execution of a smart contract. The major difference between a classic physical business contract and a smart contract is that the smart contract is purely digital and automates the execution of the rules and conditions pre-defined in the contract [26], which is designed to be autonomous, immutable and secure without the need to rely on third-parties and intermediaries [27].

In the proposed architecture, smart contract is applied to automatically execute and deposit the donated amounts consigned by each taxpayer, they further validate that the BE meet the necessary legal requirements to receive the designated funds, and finally safely and transparently transfer the funds to the BEs' portfolios. Since such process can be carried out without the need for human intervention, it is expected to be more efficient, secure and unbiased. Any changes to the rules and pre-defined conditions of this contract must be first communicated and agreed upon the defined governance parameters.

After submission of each taxpayer declaration, its verification and subsequent validation by the AT, a smart contract is created and stored in the BCT network. Once the AT is able to generate tokens in exchange for monetary funds that are placed in reserve, smart contract will deposit tokens at the taxpayer's address. After confirming the deposit, smart contract will transfer the tokens from taxpayer's wallet to the chosen BE. The whole process is automated based on the rules contained in the smart contract coding and registered in the blockchain by the AT. The sequence diagram below (Fig. 2) demonstrates the execution of the smart contract as per described process.

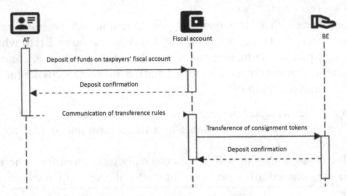

Fig. 2. Smart contract execution process

4.3 Tokenization of Assets on Blockchain

This network is based upon the transference of an asset that translates into the amount of tax consignment assigned to a BE by the taxpayer and further facilitated by the AT. The design of this system, is supported by the State, therefore it guarantees the conversion of the dedicated amount of money into a token and vice versa.

The proposed design of the system guarantees stabilized value of the token within the network, since there is no mechanism for either reducing or increasing them. State entity will be the actor that is responsible for the reserve of monetary values that are corresponding to the number of tokens within the network.

The decision to create an asset that transits the network was made in order to be able to leverage the creation of an ecosystem that increases the use cases within the same environment and generates synergies that can leverage the positive contribution to the fulfillment of the mandate of the BEs that are one of the key parts of the ecosystem. Under this proposal, the token is suggested to be named "Solidarity Currency" to signify the values and goals of the described solution.

4.4 Incentive Mechanisms for Blockchain-based Network Participation

Due to its hybrid typology, any entity or individual that is granted access by the State, can participate in the maintenance of this network and contribute to its success. Although the State is the guarantor of the proper functioning of this network, it is important that the network stays open and transparent to remaining actors of the process.

There may be several incentive mechanisms for participants of the platform (specially taxpayers and BEs):

- **Reputational** – for taxpayers it creates the way to increase positive experience with the tax consignment process by contributing in a novel and more involving architecture of the network;
- **Access to data in a direct way** – for State entities the novel decentralized way of accessing the data and information in the real time will likely increase the efficiency of the process;
- **Ability to trace back or forward** - for both taxpayers and BEs the transparency provided through BCT allows the traceability of all transactions, where BEs will be guaranteed to receive the exact amount of donations, and taxpayers will be able to verify such allocation of donations.

Depending on the strategic path given to this application and the spread of its adoption, other forms of incentives can be created to move more towards a decentralized network.

4.5 Availability of Transparent Data and the Importance of the User-Friendly Interface

One of the key features of BCT is its decentralized nature and the ability for any participant in the network to read all of the transactions that are in the ledger. However, it is important to keep in mind that even though BCT creates a greater level of transparency, its novelty and complexity can make it difficult for the general public to interpret the data.

Fig. 3. User-friendly interface proposal for the tax consignment tracking

In this sense, it is essential that the competent entities disseminate the tax consignment data with interfaces and tools that allow presenting the data in a clear, intuitive and accessible way, such as graphs, tables, maps and other visual resources that facilitate the understanding of the data. In addition, it is important that information about the meaning and importance of the donated data will be accessible and available to taxpayers, so that they will visualize the relevance of tax consignment and the impact of their choice on societal benefits. Exemplary proposal of an interface can be seen in Fig. 3.

5 Discussion

The current process of tax consignment is characterized by being highly dependent on the AT, since it is the entity that manages the process from the submission of the taxpayer's taxes until the transfer of the consigned amount to the BEs that benefit from this system. During this whole process, both of the parties (taxpayers and BEs) do not have any information about amounts that were funded, how much BEs will receive, or even when they will receive it [1]. This lack of transparency, associated with the long periods of time between the submission and dedication of the taxes to the BEs by taxpayers, until the final transference and receival of funds by BEs, damages the reputation and credibility of the AT and public institutions in general, and creates difficulties for the BEs that rely on such funds and are not able to allocate capital or plan actions in a concrete way. On the taxpayers' side, there is currently no way to directly validate that the amount that was consigned by them, if it actually reached the chosen NPO.

The proposed BCT-based network brings solutions to all of the abovementioned challenges, as it creates traceability of the transactions and therefore provides more trust towards the tax consignment process. This type of proposed solution is able to generate an active development of the BCT-based network, as all stakeholders will have their own motivations in moving towards a more transparent network. The main challenges of the implementation of such solution are twofold: (1) currently there is still a lack of clear and specific legal regulations regarding BCT-based networks, especially applied to State programs; (2) the lack of awareness and knowledge of the BCT itself might create hesitancy in cooperation between various entities, which may further translate into higher costs and greater complexity.

6 Conclusions and Future Research

The use of BCT for tax consignment process has several advantages over the current situation, such as transparency and security of donated funds, build of trust towards the program, elimination of intermediaries, and guaranteed accountability. With the implementation of the proposed solution, taxpayers will be able to verify that their dedicated part of tax is safely designated to chosen BE, thus increasing confidence in the donation and encouraging participation in solidarity actions and socially significant projects.

This paper focused on a simplified concept of tokenization and the value transfer between the taxpayer and BE through a State entity. Other ideas for tax consignment that might be explore in future would also add value to the solution proposed in this paper. The most interesting directions for future:

- Allowing the transfer of tokens between BEs will allow an increased cooperation between NPOs;

- Allowing the purchase of tokens for direct donations to BEs will extend the scope of donation to anyone who wishes to donate funds, without limiting it to taxpayers only;
- Development of the solution to allow BEs to register projects they want to develop and to give the taxpayer/donor the ability to clearly see and track where their funds have gone within the network. Such functionality could additionally allow the registration of invoices or cost statements to ensure the trustworthiness of the projects within the network;
- Involvement of the CAs as external auditors of the process, in order to use the BCT-based network as a tool for its supervisory function. The use of smart contracts will also help validate that the BEs have met the legal and statutory requirements, i.e. were in a position to be granted to receive the tax consignment;
- Future extension of the platform to other NPOs that are not accredited as BEs for tax consignment.

We hope that this paper will serve as a comprehensive basis for the BCT-based solution for charitable supply chains, which opens new frontiers for the applications of State programs and involvement of citizens in socially significant activities.

Acknowledgement. This work was supported by EEA Grants Blue Growth Programme (Call #5), Project PT-INNOVATION-0069 – Fish2Fork. We thank Master students of ISCTE-IUL Doroteia Serrão, Nuno Santos and Pedro Nascimento for their collaboration and valuable inputs in the development of the study. We also express our gratitude to reviewers for their valuable feedback that allowed further improvement of this chapter.

References

1. Ascension, R.: Associação Salvador arranca com campanha de consignação de IRS: Comunicação tardia dos resultados é um entrave. https://eco.sapo.pt/2023/03/21/associacao-salvador-arranca-com-campanha-de-consignacao-de-irs-comunicacao-tardia-dos-resultados-e-um-entrave/. Accessed 31 July 2023
2. Dias, K.: Personal Income Tax Consignment in Portugal in 2023 - what is it and why should you do it?. https://www.coverflex.com/en-pt/blog/personal-income-tax-consignment-in-portugal-in-2023-what-is-it-and-why-should-you-do-it#:~:text=What%20is%20IRS%20consignment%3F,NGOs%2C%20according%20to%20Law%20n. Accessed 31 July 2023
3. Yang, C., Northcott, D.: How do charity regulators build public trust? Financ. Accountability Manag. 37(4), 367–384 (2021)
4. Treiblmaier, H.: The impact of the blockchain on the supply chain: a theory-based research framework and a call for action. Supply Chain Manag. Int. J. 23(6), 545–559 (2018)
5. Altay, N., Heaslip, G., Kovács, G., Spens, K., Tatham, P., Vaillancourt, A.: Innovation in humanitarian logistics and supply chain management: a systematic review. Ann. Oper. Res. (2023)
6. de Camargo Fiorini, P., Chiappetta Jabbour, C.J., Lopes de Sousa Jabbour, A.B., Ramsden, G.: The human side of humanitarian supply chains: a research agenda and systematization framework. Ann. Oper. Res. 319(1), 911–936 (2022)
7. Guo, H., Xu, X.: Exploring the barriers that influence intention to donate and role of the charity shop within the multi-tier supply chain. J. Hum. Logist. Supply Chain Manag. 11(3), 522–549 (2021)

8. Abidi, H., De Leeuw, S., Klumpp, M.: Humanitarian supply chain performance management: a systematic literature review. Supply Chain Manag. Int. J. (2014)
9. Xu, X., Chung, S.H., Lo, C.K., Yeung, A.C.: Sustainable supply chain management with NGOs, NPOs, and charity organizations: a systematic review and research agenda. Transp. Res. Part E: Logist. Transp. Rev. **164**, 102822 (2022)
10. Deshpande, A., Stewart, K., Lepetit, L., Gunashekar, S.: Distributed ledger technologies/blockchain: challenges, opportunities and the prospects for standards. Overview report The British Standards Institution (BSI) **40**, 40 (2017)
11. Chenthara, S., Ahmed, K., Wang, H., Whittaker, F., Chen, Z.: Healthchain: a novel framework on privacy preservation of electronic health records using blockchain technology. PLoS ONE **15**(12), e0243043 (2020)
12. Zhai, S., Yang, Y., Li, J., Qiu, C., Zhao, J.: Research on the application of cryptography on the blockchain. In: Journal of Physics: Conference Series, vol. 1168, no. 3, p. 032077. IOP Publishing (2019)
13. Ayoade, G., Karande, V., Khan, L., Hamlen, K.: Decentralized IoT data management using blockchain and trusted execution environment. In: 2018 IEEE International Conference on Information Reuse and Integration (IRI), pp. 15–22. IEEE (2018)
14. Ajao, L.A., Agajo, J., Adedokun, E.A., Karngong, L.: Crypto hash algorithm-based blockchain technology for managing decentralized ledger database in oil and gas industry. J **2**(3), 300–325 (2019)
15. Ko, T., Lee, J., Ryu, D.: Blockchain technology and manufacturing industry: real-time transparency and cost savings. Sustainability **10**(11), 4274 (2018)
16. Zhou, B., Li, H., Xu, L.: An authentication scheme using identity-based encryption & blockchain. In: 2018 IEEE Symposium on Computers and Communications (ISCC), pp. 00556–00561. IEEE (2018)
17. Nakamoto, S.: Bitcoin whitepaper (2008). https://bitcoin.org/bitcoin.pdf. Accessed 31 July 2023
18. Shin, E.J., Kang, H.G., Bae, K.: A study on the sustainable development of NPOs with blockchain technology. Sustainability **12**(15), 6158 (2020)
19. About Us | BitGive Foundation. https://www.bitgivefoundation.org/about-us/. Accessed 31 July 2023
20. Giveth: Welcome to the Future of Giving. https://giveth.io/. Accessed 31 July 2023
21. Goteo.org: Crowdfunding the commons. https://pt.goteo.org/. Accessed 31 July 2023
22. Binance Charity. https://www.binance.charity/. Accessed 31 July 2023
23. Benefício fiscal da consignação de quota do IRS. https://info.portaldasfinancas.gov.pt/pt/apoio_contribuinte/IRS/Pages/IRS_entidades_beneficiarias_consignacao.aspx. Accessed 31 July 2023
24. ECO, Consignação do IRS deu 91 milhões às instituições desde 2014. https://eco.sapo.pt/2020/04/22/consignacao-do-irs-deu-91-milhoes-as-instituicoes-desde-2014/. Accessed 31 July 2023
25. Manolache, M.A., Manolache, S., Tapus, N.: Decision making using the blockchain proof of authority consensus. Procedia Comput. Sci. **199**, 580–588 (2022)
26. Saini, K., Roy, A., Chelliah, P.R., Patel, T.: Blockchain 2.0: a smart contract. In: 2021 International Conference on Computational Performance Evaluation, ComPE, pp. 524–528 (2021)
27. Ma, R., Yang, X., Gao, F.: Discussion on smart contract under blockchains technology. In: 2022 International Conference on Industrial IoT, Big Data and Supply Chain, IIoTBDSC, pp. 338–342 (2022)

Mining Tourists' Movement Patterns in a City

Luís B. Elvas[1,2](✉) ⬤, Miguel Nunes[1] ⬤, José Augusto Afonso[3,4] ⬤,
Berit Irene Helgheim[2] ⬤, and Bruno Francisco[1] ⬤

[1] Instituto Universitário de Lisboa (ISCTE-IUL), ISTAR, Lisboa, Portugal
luis.elvas@iscte.pt
[2] Department of Logistics, Molde University College, 6410 Molde, Norway
[3] CMEMS–UMinho, University of Minho, 4800-058 Guimarães, Portugal
[4] LABBELS –Associate Laboratory, Braga/Guimarães, Portugal

Abstract. Although tourists generate a large amount of data (known as "big data") when they visit cities, little is known about their spatial behavior. One of the most significant issues that has recently gained attention is mobile phone usage and user behavior tracking. A spatial and temporal data visualization approach was established with the purpose of finding tourists' footprints. This work provides a platform for combining multiple data sources into one and transforming information into knowledge. Using Python, we created a method to build visualization dashboards aiming to provide insights about tourists' movements and concentrations in a city using information from mobile operators. This approach can be replicated to other smart cities with data available. Weather and major events, for instance, have an impact on the movements of tourists. The outputs from this work provide useful information for tourism professionals to understand tourists' preferences and improve the visitors' experience. Management authorities may also use these outputs to increase security based on tourists' concentration and movements. A case study in Lisbon with 4 months data is presented, but the proposed approach can also be used in other cities based on data availability. Results from this case study demonstrate how tourists tend to gather around a set of parishes during a specific time of the day during the months under study, as well as how unusual circumstances, namely international events, impact their overall spatial behavior.

Keywords: tourist behaviour · location data · data analytics · mobile phone sensing · Internet of Things · smart cities

1 Introduction

A network of actual, physical things that are linked to the Internet is known as the Internet of Things (IoT) [1]. These things are able to gather and exchange information about themselves and their environment. These data can be used to monitor and manage the objects, as well as to understand and improve the systems they are part of. The IoT has the potential to transform the way we live and work and make our lives more convenient and

A. L. Martins et al. (Eds.): INTSYS 2023, LNICST 540, pp. 105–125, 2024.
https://doi.org/10.1007/978-3-031-49379-9_6

comfortable. The IoT can be used to collect big data, which can be used to understand trends and patterns. It can also be used to improve the efficiency of systems and to make better decisions. The physical objects of the IoT can range from wireless sensor network [2] devices specifically designed for an application to more general objects such as vehicles [3] and mobile devices. The use of mobile devices to collect useful data is also called mobile phone sensing [4]. The data that may be collected using mobile devices includes location data, data from other internal sensors (e.g., accelerometers, microphone, etc.), and data from wearable devices (e.g., a Bluetooth Low Energy heart rate monitor).

In the context of smart cities, related work includes exploring the application of data-driven approaches and visualization techniques in order to support decision makers in urban settings by providing valuable insights and tools for them. Research have been conducted in order to study areas like disaster management [5, 6], incident management [7], road accidents [8] and city-wide data analytics. The findings highlight the potential benefits of leveraging data and advanced analytics to enhance urban planning, enhance road safety, and develop effective strategies for disaster and incident management. Ultimately there's been a contribution to emphasizing the importance of data-driven approaches in empowering decision-makers to create more efficient, sustainable, and resilient urban environments.

This paper proposes an approach for understanding tourist mobility and its patterns, using mobile phone location data, which allows to analyse people's mobility quickly and accurately in a city. This information can be useful to decision makers of tourism infrastructure and marketing, as well as to negotiate with local businesses and tourism-related organizations to ensure that the economic benefits of tourism are shared fairly among all stakeholders. In addition, tracking tourist movement patterns can help cities to better manage their resources and plan for the future. By understanding how tourists are using the city, city planners can anticipate the demand for certain services and amenities, such as public transportation, accommodations, and visitor centres, and allocate resources accordingly. They can also identify areas of the city that may be experiencing overcrowding or congestion due to high levels of tourist traffic and develop strategies to mitigate the impact. Tracking tourist mobility can also help cities to better understand and address the environmental impact of tourism. By analysing location data, city planners can identify areas of the city where tourists are likely to generate the most waste or pollution and develop strategies to minimize these impacts.

The main contributions of this paper are: (1) provide platform that can merge multiple data sources into one, transforming information into knowledge; (2) provide a data visualization tool that enables all the stakeholders to interpret data in a more efficient way; (3) build a decision support system that allows users to make data-driven decisions based on a visualization component.

After a year of 2020 marked by a severe pandemic scenario in which Portugal registered a sharp drop in international tourism, there was a recovery in international tourism starting in the second half of 2021 [9]. This trend continued in the first two months of 2022, with a 769.2% increase in guests from abroad in February 2022 compared to February 2021.

To get a better understanding of how international tourists move in a city, we collaborated with the Lisbon City Council, who provided us with location data (roaming and non-roaming) from a mobile carrier company–Vodafone, in the city of Lisbon, from September 2021 to January 2022. We also collected weather data from the Portuguese Sea and Atmosphere Institute (IPMA), a national meteorological organization, in the same timeline and in the same city. In this study, we considered people using mobile phones in roaming as possible tourists. Based on the raw data, this work analyses the spatial-temporal behaviour of Lisbon tourists with the following goals:

- Being aware of the key tourist attractions, restaurants, and accommodations;
- Finding the main concentration points and how they changed during the study period;
- Recognizing how variations in weather affect tourists' mobility patterns;
- Identifying peculiar mobility patterns in international events taking place in Portugal during the study's months.

The remainder of this paper is structured as follows: Literature Review is presented in Sect. 2. Section 3 introduces the methodology that we have used, as well as all the methods used in this work. Then, in Sect. 4 we present the results of our work and finally, Sect. 5 presents the conclusions.

2   Literature Review

In order to assess the relevancy of our study, we have conducted a literature review of the last 5 years, where we have used a PRISMA (Preferred Reporting Items for Systematic Reviews and Meta-Analysis) [10] as our methodology for answering the following research question (RQ): What is the state of the art on tourists' behaviour analysis and tourism mobility analysis in smart cities?

The database used for the search was Scopus, and the study took place between May 8 and 12, 2022; all the findings had to be publications published within the past five years and written in English. Based on the data synthesis and analysis results mentioned above, a qualitative evaluation was conducted.

The Scopus database was thoroughly searched for published work on topic related with the concept "data analysis" or "behaviour analysis", the target population "smart cities" or "cellular network" or "tourist" or "roaming" and within the "mobility" context of the study. All keywords were searched using wildcards (such as "#" and "*"), which are used to match variations of the keywords, allowing us to perform a better search. The search query was built by intercepting all the columns, that is Concept AND Population AND Context, as depicted in Table 1. All the limitations have been applied. This query resulted in 44 documents, from which 16 papers were retrieved after a manual procedure was completed to determine major subjects on their research questions and define the outcomes. Year, region, RQ topic, and a brief description were all factors in our study systematization.

The trend line in Fig. 1 shows that the issue we are examining is growing in popularity, demonstrating its importance.

Figure 2 presents the percentage of documents on each topic. This figure shows that most of the documents focus on behaviour analysis and/or used mobile phones/information and communications technology (ICT) infrastructures.

Table 1. Search keywords and numbers of documents.

Concept	Population	Context	Limitations
data analysis	smart cities	mobility	2018–2022
behavio#r analysis	cellular network		
	touris*		
	roaming		Only journal papers, articles and reviews
44 documents			

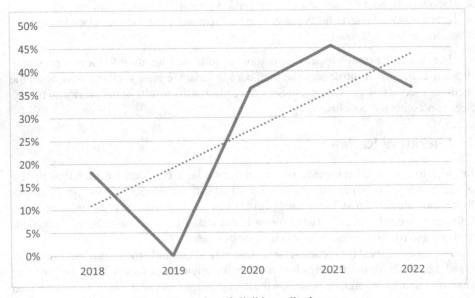

Fig. 1. Evolution of eligible studies by year.

The research work presented in this paper is also based on both concepts, since we not only investigate people's behaviour using the communication infrastructure of a mobile phone operator in the city of Lisbon, but we also analyse it, in order to comprehend it and build a strategy to meet their demands.

After reading all of the publications, it was clear that the amount of behavioural research on tourist mobility has expanded dramatically in recent years all over the world.

Authors from [11] present a method for estimating origin–destination (O–D) matrices using passively obtained cellular network signalling data from millions of anonymous mobile phone users in the Rhône–Alpes region of France, enhancing and revolutionizing the field of travel demand and traffic flow modelling.

Still on the subject, the authors of study [12] can identify pedestrian hotspots and provide future traffic signal and street layout information to make the city more pedestrian-friendly, as well as apply the knowledge gained to other data sets, such as bicycle traffic, to guide city infrastructure initiatives.

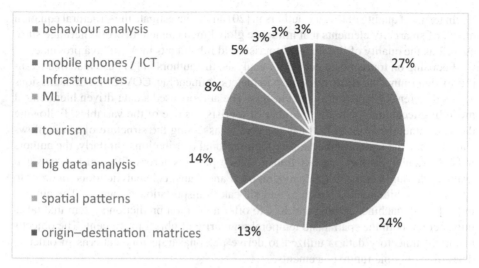

Fig. 2. Research topics on the state of the art

In a similar vein, but focusing on behaviour analysis, study [13] identifies a number of metrics for determining whether a person on the move is stationary, walking, or riding in a motorized private or public vehicle, with the goal of providing city users with personalized assistance messages for, among other things, sustainable mobility, health, and/or a better and more enjoyable life. This work was applied to the cities of Tuscany and Florence. The authors in [14] study and compare the density of users in Shanghai city using Weibo geolocation data and univariate and bivariate density estimation approaches, such as point density and kernel density estimation (KDE), where the main findings are based on characteristics of users' spatial behaviour, such as the centre of activity based on check-ins, and the feasibility of using check-in data to explain the relationship between users and their social media accounts. Continuing in this vein, the research in [15], based on long-term mobile phone data (from 2007 to 2012) of Beijing participants, gives a means to visualise individual mobility patterns.

The authors in [16] aim to provide a taxonomy of 5G Core Network (CN) mobility prediction frameworks, from data gathering to model provisioning, while taking into account the 3GPP architecture and interfaces. The authors provide two critical use cases in 5G CNs, in which the benefits of mobility predictions are assessed using information from real networks, whereas study [17] focuses on building a mobile sequential recommendation system to assist auto services (e.g., taxi drivers).

On the subject of behavioural analysis, the authors in [18] present an urban travel behaviour model and assesses its feasibility for creating a greener, cleaner environment for future generations, whereas the study in [19], based on a trip survey from the São Paulo metropolitan area, one of the world's busiest traffic locations, supplements a current bundling approach to enable multi-attribute trail datasets for the visual study of urban mobility, aiding in the identification and analysis of urban mobility.

In terms of quality of life, the authors in [20] aim to investigate the structural equation model of smart city elements that influence global management of world heritage sites, as well as the quality of life for Thai tourists and inhabitants in Ayutthaya province.

Focusing on tourism and behaviour analysis, the authors in [21] use machine learning to determine the most relevant parameters influencing COVID-19 transmissions across different Chinese cities and clusters. The authors used a data-driven hierarchical modelling technique, with the "number of tourists" as one of the variables. Following the same line, the work in [22] has the goal of assessing the structure of tourist flows and examine the variables that impact their regional distribution. Similarly, the authors in [23] examine distinct intercity transportation patterns across different holidays and evaluate driving factors utilizing geographical and statistical analytic tools, in order to optimize city hierarchical structure and allocate transportation resources. The authors in [24] used machine learning and ICT to offer a position prediction system that takes into account both the spatial and temporal regularity of object movement. The object's historical trajectory data is utilized to derive personal trajectory patterns in order to determine possible future placements.

Using Airbnb data, the authors in [25] examine how visitors use local public transit in connection to the locations they visit. They employ a big data analysis of the factors influencing tourists' mobility behaviour and use of public transportation in various tourist sites to assess the attractiveness profile of 25 prominent tourist attractions throughout the world.

In [26], the authors present novel techniques for studying pedestrian mobility aspects over the whole road network using ICT and study the influence of visitor flows on the quality of life of locals and maintaining cultural resources. This study was performed in the city of Venice.

After reading all these publications, it was clear that the amount of behavioural research on tourist mobility has expanded dramatically in recent years all over the world. However, no study explores the use of mobile phone location data to create spatial or temporal graphs considering the correlation with rainy weather conditions and big events.

3 Methodology

The development of this study was conducted by the Cross Industry Standard Process for Data Mining (CRISP-DM) methodological approach, which is a common approach for creating data mining projects to lower costs, boost dependability, and manageability, making the data mining process more effective [27]. However, for this study, given the data in question and our main goals, we opted for a different version of this methodology consisting of 4 phases, as shown in Fig. 3: 1) Data Understanding; 2) Data Preparation; 3) Data Integration; and 4) Data Visualisation.

The data was provided by a mobile operator in Lisbon, worked in Python and visualised in Microsoft Power BI.

Fig. 3. Development methodology used in this paper.

3.1 Data Understanding

In order to fully understand the potential of our data and how we could optimize the added value of this study, we meticulously investigated each variable once we had collected the data for our study.

As stated previously, our main goal was understanding mobility patterns in tourists. To achieve that, the Lisbon City Council provided some data related to the mobility of people (roaming and non-roaming) in the city of Lisbon based on anonymized mobile phone data supplied by Vodafone, a British multinational telecommunications company. The data, which were collected from people who have Vodafone as a mobile carrier, was anonymized through the removal of all data related to personal information. To provide a more accurately reflection of the mobility of all the people who circulated in Lisbon between September 2021 and January 2022, Vodafone extrapolated the data, resulting in the dataset we have used (Vodafone dataset). This extrapolation was based on market share of the three operators available in Lisbon.

To get more accurate insights on the mobility of international tourists and how weather conditions change their mobility patterns, we reached out to the Portuguese Sea and Atmosphere Institute (IPMA) and requested data on the weather conditions in Lisbon between the months of September 2021 and February 2022. Therefore, there are two different datasets (Vodafone dataset and IPMA dataset), so they are addressed separately.

The dataset provided by Vodafone was divided into several files in CSV format separated by months. From this data, we selected 14 variables (see Table 2) and 126 443 863 records in total. As for the number of observations per month, Table 3.

Table 2. Metadata from used variables from the Vodafone dataset.

ID	Variable Name	Variable Description	Variable Type
0	Grid_ID	Number of grid cells–There are 3743 squares of 200 by 200 m in order to cover the metropolitan area of Lisbon	Nominal
1	Datetime	Time and date of occurrence	Datetime
2	C1	Number of distinct mobile phone terminals counted on each grid cell–Measured every 5 min	Numeric
3	C2	Number of distinct terminals in roaming counted on each grid cell during the 5 min period–Measured every 5 min	Numeric

(continued)

Table 2. (continued)

ID	Variable Name	Variable Description	Variable Type
4	C3	Number of distinct terminals that remained in the grid cell counted at the end of each 5 min period	Numeric
5	C4	Number of distinct terminals in roaming that remained in the grid cell counted at the end of each 5 min period	Numeric
6	C5	Number of distinct terminals entering the grid cell	Numeric
7	C6	Terminals leaving the grid cell– These are the distinct terminals that left the grid cell; the calculation is made using the previous 5-min interval as reference, also considering the crossings of the grid in the same interval	Numeric
8	C7	Number of entries of distinct terminals, in roaming, in the grid cell	Numeric
9	C8	Number of exits of distinct terminals, in roaming, in the grid cell	Numeric
10	C9	Total number of distinct terminals with active data connection in the grid cell–Measurement every 5 min	Numeric
11	C10	Total number of distinct terminals, in roaming, with active data connection in the grid cell–Measurement every 5 min	Numeric
12	C11	Number of voices calls originating from the grid cell	Numeric
13	C12	Number of devices that for 5 min enter the 11 street sections considered for analysis; for this purpose, a section of track is considered to be a route with a few km which begins outside and ends inside the Municipality of Lisbon	Numeric

Table 3. Number of observations per month (Vodafone dataset).

Month	Observation Numbers
September 2021	17 233 318
October 2021	32 627 337
November 2021	21 619 292
December 2021	33 121 658
January 2021	33 344 624

3.2 Data Preparation

After acquiring a better understanding of the data, we moved to the second phase, which consists of four subphases: data selection, data cleaning, resource selection and data integration. Originally, the Vodafone dataset was spread over several files in CSV format, each month consisting of four to nine files with the same format. To handle the data more efficiently on personal computers and to proceed with preparation of the data, we decided to merge the CSV files by months, rather than compiling all the files provided into one file. Later, we did the same to the IPMA dataset, which was divided by months.

Vodafone Dataset

Location data was obtained based on the radio waves that are sent and received by the telecommunications base station. The mobile network operators immediately save this data in their log files or memory, in this case Vodafone. When a mobile phone is registered in a country but used in another one, its user can be seen as a potential tourist, and the corresponding information, such as the country of origin and location coordinates, are registered as mobile roaming.

In the data selection subphase, the information provided by Vodafone was aggregated over 3743 squares of 200 by 200 m, with no values of less than 10 devices reported, and collected in 5-min periods. The data becomes available after a processing period of approximately 45 min. This information is very important to study the mobility of tourists.

In the data cleaning subphase, we discarded missing values and removed duplicate rows.

In the resource selection subphase, one of the first things we did was selecting the variables which were not of interest to our goal and removing them from the dataset. Thus, the original dataset identified in Table 2, was reduced to only a few variables of interest for our objectives. Subsequently, we created a new dataset with only the mobility data of people in roaming (foreign tourists) from the Vodafone dataset. This was achieved by keeping only the variables related to people in roaming.

As the goal of our work focuses on the mobility of people, it was also important to have information about holidays and weekdays/weekends in our dataset. To do this we have built a function to identify which days there was a holiday. Only holidays on weekdays have been marked, since at the weekend they do not have much impact on mobility in general.

To check some events during the different times of the day, a column with distinct time intervals was also created.

We coupled a grid dataset to the Vodafone dataset to have information about the parish and latitudes and longitudes of each Grid_ID. From the merge of these datasets, it was possible to build new columns to facilitate posterior data analysis and visualisation in Microsoft Power BI. A column with zones of Lisbon was then created, in which the 24 parishes of Lisbon were grouped into 5 distinct zones according to the administrative reorganization of the parishes in 2012, namely [28]:

- North Zone (Green Zone) - Santa Clara, Lumiar, Carnide, São Domingos de Benfica, Benfica;
- Western Zone (Yellow Zone) - Alcântara, Ajuda, Belém;
- Center Zone (Orange Zone) - Campolide, Alvalade, Avenidas Novas, Santo António, Arroios, Areeiro;
- Historic Downtown Area (Purple Zone) - Campo de Ourique, Estrela, Misericórdia, Santa Maria Maior, São Vicente, Penha de França;

• Eastern Zone (Blue Zone) - Beato, Marvila, Olivais, Parque das Nações.

From the variable that represents the TOP10 of country of origin of equipment (mobile phone), by order of representativeness, a split was applied in order to separate the countries that belonged to that column by distinct columns: TOP1 to TOP10, and then decreasing from TOP10 to only TOP3 of representativeness of the countries in that location, so that instead of creating 10 additional columns, only 3 columns were created, making data manipulation more efficient.

To facilitate the visualisation of the mobility of tourists through the city of Lisbon, the countries were grouped by territorial zones, except the main nationalities of tourists in Portugal: Spain, France, Germany and United Kingdom [29]. Three new columns were then created (zonasnacionalidade1, zonasnacionalidade2 and zonasnacionalidade3), which represent the TOP1, TOP2 and TOP3, respectively, of different nationality groups.

IPMA Dataset

IPMA is the national meteorological, seismic, sea and atmospheric organization of Portugal. It generates data about the weather conditions in real time. These data were then grouped into datasets to be studied and analysed by professionals qualified to know the weather and its variations, to aid in prediction models, e.g., time series. In this case, the IPMA data were used to complement the main Vodafone dataset, due to their importance in understanding the mobility pattern of tourists.

To clean this dataset, we discarded missing values, removed duplicate rows, and deleted all rows which had an observation with the number -99 (Error Code). After that, we moved to the resource selection subphase, where we eliminated the variables that were not of interest to our goal and the variables that had no variance. Thus, the original dataset was reduced to only a few variables of interest (see Table 4), the most relevant ones being humidity, wind intensity, accumulated precipitation, and temperature.

Table 4. Remaining variables (IPMA Dataset).

ID	Variable Name	Variable Description	Variable Type
0	Day	Day of observation	Datetime
1	Hour	Hour of observation	Numeric
2	Month	Month of observation	Numeric
3	Month_txt	Month of observation in text format	Nominal
4	Station	Station where the data was collected from	Nominal
5	Position	Coordinates of the Station	Coordinates
6	Humidity	Relative Humidity in %	Numeric

(*continued*)

Table 4. (*continued*)

ID	Variable Name	Variable Description	Variable Type
7	Humidity_txt	Categorized version of the variable Humidity	Categorical
8	WindIntensity	Wind intensity Index used by IPMA	Ordinal
9	WindIntensity_txt	Categorized version of the variable WindIntensity	Categorical
10	WindIntensityKm	Wind Intensity in km/h	Numeric
11	PrecAccumulated	Accumulated Precipitation in mm	Numeric
12	PrecAccumulated_txt	Categorized version of the variable PrecAccumulated	Categorical
13	Temperature	Temperature in °C	Numeric
14	Temperature_txt	Categorized version of the variable Temperature	Categorical

3.3   Data Integration

We have created new columns that were the categorical version of our numeric variables of interest (see Table 5), basing our categories in the metadata from IPMA and the measuring system of each variable, i.e., name and measurement unit, and created a text version of the month variable to aid in the visualisation.

Table 5. New categorical variables (IPMA dataset).

Variable Name	Categories	Scale
Humidity_txt	No humidity	0–5 (%)
	Low humidity	6–20 (%)
	Moderate humidity	21–60 (%)
	High humidity	61–100 (%)
WindIntensity_txt (Index used by IPMA from 0 to 12)	No wind	0–1
	Low wind	1–4
	Moderate Wind	4–7
	Intense wind	7–12
AccPrecipitation_txt	No rain	0–5 (%)
	Low rain	6–20 (%)
	Moderate rain	21–60 (%)
	Abundant rain	61–100 (%)
Temperature_txt	Very Cold	− 5–0 (°C)
	Cold	1–20 (°C)
	Pleasant	21–28 (°C)
	Warm	29–40 (°C)

4   Results

In this stage, we represented the data in graphical form, as graphs and charts let us explore and learn more about it, providing a quick way to see trends and patterns in the mobility of the tourists and to focus on the most important points [30]. Good data visualisation also makes it easier to communicate our ideas and insights to other people [30]. With Power BI we represented each parish and used the data available to visualise the movement of tourists and to identify major patterns.

4.1   Overview

As shown in Fig. 4, of the four months under review, October had the biggest peaks of tourists. Therefore, this month was selected for an analysis of the spatial distribution of tourists in the various periods of the day, as shown in the next figures.

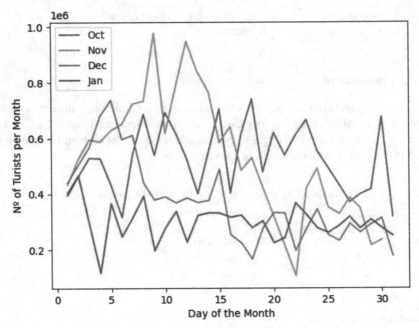

Fig. 4. Tourists in Lisbon by day, in millions, during the months of October 2021 to January 2022.

Figure 5 presents an analysis of the parishes frequented by tourists at lunchtime and afternoon. As shown in the figure, in the lunch hour period, the parishes that tourists frequent the most are Belém, Alvalade and Parque das Nações, whereas in the afternoon and evening periods, the most visited parishes are Belém, Alvalade and Avenidas Novas; finally, during the early morning hours the most frequented parishes are Avenidas Novas, Belém and Arroios (see Fig. 5b)). This is aligned with the suggested places to eat available from tourist literature, such as TripAdvisor [31].

Figure 6 presents an analysis of the nationalities of the tourists that frequented the Lisbon parishes at two different periods: night and dawn.

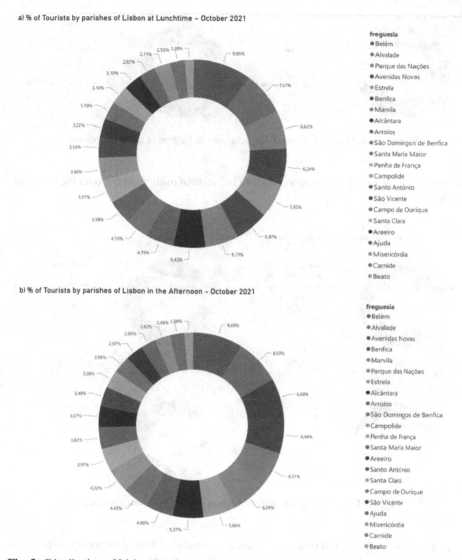

a) % of Tourists by parishes of Lisbon at Lunchtime - October 2021

freguesia
- Belém
- Alvalade
- Parque das Nações
- Avenidas Novas
- Estrela
- Benfica
- Marvila
- Alcântara
- Arroios
- São Domingos de Benfica
- Santa Maria Maior
- Penha de França
- Campolide
- Santo António
- São Vicente
- Campo de Ourique
- Santa Clara
- Areeiro
- Ajuda
- Misericórdia
- Carnide
- Beato

b) % of Tourists by parishes of Lisbon in the Afternoon - October 2021

freguesia
- Belém
- Alvalade
- Avenidas Novas
- Benfica
- Marvila
- Parque das Nações
- Estrela
- Alcântara
- Arroios
- São Domingos de Benfica
- Campolide
- Penha de França
- Santa Maria Maior
- Areeiro
- Santo António
- Santa Clara
- Campo de Ourique
- São Vicente
- Ajuda
- Misericórdia
- Carnide
- Beato

Fig. 5. Distribution of Lisbon tourists by parishes at lunchtime and afternoon in October 2021.

4.2 Case 1–Mobility Patterns in Different Weather

One interesting case is the influence of tourists' movements based on weather conditions and the destinations they choose to visit when it is raining or sunny. When we looked at the tourist's nationalities, we discovered that during the months of October, November, and December the most common nationality in Lisbon was Spanish, followed by South American, French and Irish and English (see Fig. 7). In January 2022 the nationalities remained with similar representations except for the South American nationality, which

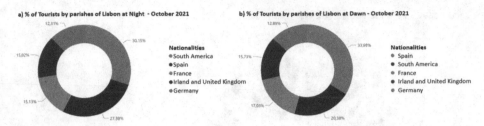

Fig. 6. Distribution of tourists' nationalities in Lisbon at night and dawn.

had the most representation in Lisbon with an increase of more than 6% over the previous month (see Fig. 7d).

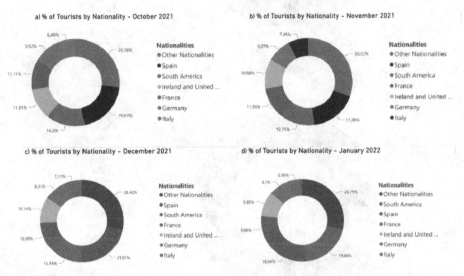

Fig. 7. Tourists by nationality in Lisbon in October–January 2022.

In Fig. 8 we represented tourists' movements on sunny and rainy weeks. When it is raining, tourists tend to concentrate in certain places (the historic downtown area, the airport, near Carnide, where we found a lot of hostels and apartments for rent, and in the Eastern zone). Tourists tend to stick to monuments, their places of stay and shopping centres on rainy days (see Fig. 8a)). When it is sunny, rather than concentrating in some places, tourists tend to spread out more and visit more areas than just the "hotspots" (see Fig. 8b)). The effects of the weather on the mobility of tourists are clearly visible in these results.

4.3 Case 2–The Effect of Big Events: Web Summit

The Web Summit is an annual technology conference held in Lisbon, Portugal, and the biggest in Europe [32]. In 2021, while still under the effects of the COVID-19 pandemic,

Fig. 8. Tourists' mobility on a rainy week in December (a)) vs a sunny week in October (b)). These heat maps about tourists' location go from deep blue (high concentration of tourists) to light blue (low concentration). (color figure online)

the event gathered over 40,000 visitors. This influx of people allowed us to visualise the impact that the event had in the area where it was held (FIL–Lisbon International Fair).

To analyse this, we mapped the movement of roaming users and considered those who were staying in the same grid for more than 5 min when the event was taking place, putting those results side by side with the remaining days of the month. On the Web Summit period (1st–4th November 2021), we were able to register an average of 2852 tourists at any given time in the event area, compared to the 262 for the rest of the month of November (5th–30th November 2021). It's a 987% increase in tourist activity, Fig. 9.

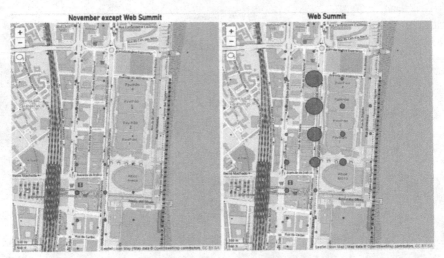

Fig. 9. Comparison of tourist distribution outside of Web Summit (left) and during the Web Summit (right).

4.4   Case 3–Big Events Monitor Process–Case of a Football Game Day

Football tourists are those who travel to attend a football event, usually a game. The proposed method enables for real-time surveillance of tourist movements around the city. Since the UEFA Champions League games create big movements of people from around the world, we tracked 4 major games in Lisbon.

From the four games (UEFA Champion League in Lisbon, Benfica-Barcelona, Benfica-Bayern Munich, Sporting-Besiktas and Sporting-Dortmund) we monitored, we chose the one that brought more tourists from a less common nationality (Turkey) to Lisbon during the course of the study. This aspect allowed us to monitor the football fans' movements a lot more effectively and clearly than if we had a considerable number of tourists just visiting the city in general.

As can be seen in Fig. 10 a), we were able to identify the time of arrival of the football fans at Lisbon airport at 9 am on the day of the match (marked in the figure).

During the day, these tourists went mainly to the historic downtown area, arriving there as 2 pm, as shown in Fig. 10b). Then at the game time, we identify around 5000 tourists from Turkey at the Sporting stadium, as shown in Fig. 10c). After the game, since there are no flights, they returned to the historic downtown area (Fig. 10d)), and in the next day, around 9 am, they went back to the airport to depart from Lisbon (Fig. 10e)). This case highlights the importance of this analysis for parishes to understand tourists' movements and to better manage big events.

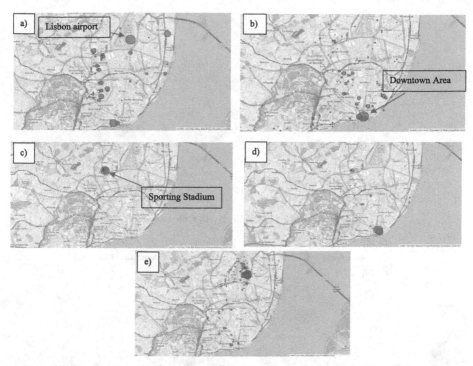

Fig. 10. Turkish tourist's movements during the football match in Lisbon, a) to d) represents the match day and e) the day after when they left the country.

Also for authorities can be useful to monitor football away fans activity to prevent confrontations between them and the local fans. Unfortunately a common event.

4.5 Case 4–The Effect of Events–Shopping Activity

Shopping activity can be monitored using the communication antennas that cover a shopping mall. The number of tourist visitors is useful information for authorities and store owners. Visit patterns and abnormal behaviour during promotion days (e.g., during Black Friday) are examples of useful information that can be extracted from the data. We can check where tourists shop more and see if the promotions influence their behaviour. The data collected shows this influence, and it is possible to witness this behaviour based on the nationality. Figure 11 and Fig. 12 show this effect and the main places where tourists' shop. Promotions increase concentration in shopping areas, even for tourists.

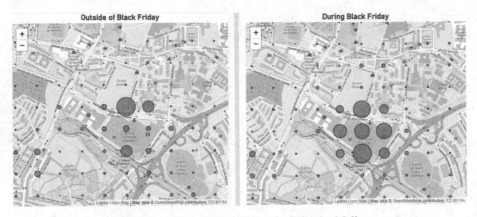

Fig. 11. Effect of Black Friday in Colombo Mall.

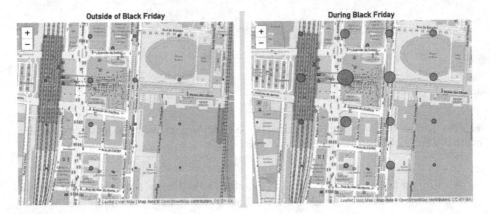

Fig. 12. Effect of Black Friday in Vasco da Gama Mall.

5 Conclusions

This work presented an analysis of Lisbon tourists' mobility patterns, allowing decision makers to perform better and more efficient decisions considering the dashboards. Mobile operators' availability on the market enables the representation of a city's population. The approach described in this paper can be replicated to other cities using similar mobile phone location data. From the provided data visualisation, it is possible to see that tourists visit the central, historic downtown district and travel to the interesting coastal regions.

Our strategy began with data cleaning and processing created in Python, followed by data visualisation created in Microsoft Power BI in the form of maps and dashboards. It is possible to replicate this in other locations, and it is a useful tool for city management authorities to comprehend tourist concentrations and movements and modify facilities and processes.

The research presented in this paper provides comprehension of tourist patterns and movements as they relate to events, weather, and nationality. Results demonstrate that tourists are deterred from exploring the city attractions by the rain. They frequently stay in "hotspots" like the city's centre and historic downtown, where they may visit attractions like museums and shopping centres or simply relax in the comfort of their accommodations. When it's sunny, tourists behave differently, spreading out more throughout the city and stopping in more places. Major international events draw a lot of tourists to the host city and particularly the neighbourhood.

Public policy must consider the spatial spread of urban tourism. In locations with a high concentration of tourists, local authorities should take measures to improve the tourist experience, such as setting up new tourist information centres, constructing pedestrian-only lanes, extending walkways, or expanding the availability of public spaces with free Wi-Fi hotspots. The real time insight supplied by current developed work may enable local authorities to understand the peoples' movements to improve both the visitors and the local inhabitants experience, as well as to generate security alerts in case of harmful concentrations in major events.

Another critical topic is the modelling of tourist behaviour, which might be done in future research with a time-series analysis. This research can also be improved by including an anonymous ID in the data to track actual human mobility patterns, allowing researchers to determine the most frequently utilized city entrances and exits, design decongestion tactics, and understand the affluence of people at bus terminals. This study could be improved by having more months of data to compare tourist mobility and patterns by season.

Acknowledgment. We thank the Lisbon City Council for providing us with the data necessary for this study, namely Mr. António Costa (Lisbon City Council), Mrs. Helena Martins (Lisbon City Council) and Mrs. Paula Melicias (Lisbon City Council). We also thank IPMA for providing us with the data necessary to complement our study.

Author Contributions. C.C. conducted all data mining processes and the system development; L.B.E. wrote the state of the art; C.C. performed all the management interface and contributed to the writing of the article; A.L.M contributed with the writing and review; J.C.F. coordinated the research and contributed to the article's writing; J.A.A contributed with the writing on review and editing. All authors have read and agreed to the published version of the manuscript.

Funding. This work was supported by EEA Grants Blue Growth Programme (Call #5). Project PT-INNOVATION-0069–Fish2Fork. This research also received funding from ERAMUS+ project NEMM with grant 101083048.

References

1. Al-Fuqaha, A., Guizani, M., Mohammadi, M., Aledhari, M., Ayyash, M.: Internet of Things: a survey on enabling technologies, protocols, and applications. IEEE Commun. Surv. Tutor. **17**(4), 2347–2376 (2015). https://doi.org/10.1109/COMST.2015.2444095
2. Jino Ramson, S.R., Moni, D.J.: Applications of wireless sensor networks — A survey. in 2017 International Conference on Innovations in Electrical, Electronics, Instrumentation and Media Technology (ICEEIMT), pp. 325–329 (2017). https://doi.org/10.1109/ICIEEIMT.2017.811 6858

3. Gerla, M., Kleinrock, L.: Vehicular networks and the future of the mobile internet. Comput. Netw. **55**(2), 457–469 (2011). https://doi.org/10.1016/j.comnet.2010.10.015

4. Khan, W.Z., Xiang, Y., Aalsalem, M.Y., Arshad, Q.: Mobile phone sensing systems: a survey. IEEE Commun. Surv. Tutor. **15**(1), 402–427 (2013). https://doi.org/10.1109/SURV.2012.031 412.00077

5. Elvas, L.B., Gonçalves, S.P., Ferreira, J.C., Madureira, A.: Data fusion and visualization towards city disaster management: Lisbon case study. EAI Endorsed Trans. Smart Cities **6**(18), e3–e3 (2022). https://doi.org/10.4108/eetsc.v6i18.1374

6. Elvas, L.B., Mataloto, B.M., Martins, A.L., Ferreira, J.C.: Disaster management in smart cities. Smart Cities **4**(2), 819–839 (2021). https://doi.org/10.3390/smartcities4020042

7. Elvas, L.B., Marreiros, C.F., Dinis, J.M., Pereira, M.C., Martins, A.L., Ferreira, J.C.: Data-driven approach for incident management in a smart city. Appl. Sci. Switz. **10**(22), 1–18 (2020). https://doi.org/10.3390/app10228281

8. Mesquitela, J., Elvas, L.B., Ferreira, J.C., Nunes, L.: Data analytics process over road accidents data—a case study of Lisbon city. ISPRS Int. J. Geo-Inf. **11**(2), 143 (2022). https://doi.org/ 10.3390/ijgi11020143

9. LCG, Toursim numbers in Portugal (2022). https://travelbi.turismodeportugal.pt/turismo-em-portugal/turismo-em-numeros-marco-2022/. Accessed May 13 2022

10. Moher, D., Liberati, A., Tetzlaff, J., Altman, D.G.: Preferred reporting items for systematic reviews and meta-analyses: the PRISMA statement. BMJ **339**, b2535 (2009). https://doi.org/ 10.1136/bmj.b2535

11. Fekih, M., Bellemans, T., Smoreda, Z., Bonnel, P., Furno, A., Galland, S.: A data-driven approach for origin–destination matrix construction from cellular network signalling data: a case study of Lyon region (France). Transportation **48**(4), 1671–1702 (2021). https://doi.org/ 10.1007/s11116-020-10108-w

12. Carter, E., Adam, P., Tsakis, D., Shaw, S., Watson, R., Ryan, P.: Enhancing pedestrian mobility in smart cities using big data. J. Manag. Anal. **7**(2), 173–188 (2020). https://doi.org/10.1080/ 23270012.2020.1741039

13. Badii, C., Difino, A., Nesi, P., Paoli, I., Paolucci, M.: Classification of users' transportation modalities from mobiles in real operating conditions. Multimed. Tools Appl. **81**(1), 115–140 (2022). https://doi.org/10.1007/s11042-021-10993-y

14. Ali Haidery, S., Ullah, H., Khan, N.U., Fatima, K., Rizvi, S.S., Kwon, S.J.: Role of big data in the development of smart city by analyzing the density of residents in shanghai. Electronics **9**(5), 837 (2020). https://doi.org/10.3390/electronics9050837

15. Li, C., Hu, J., Dai, Z., Fan, Z., Wu, Z.: Understanding individual mobility pattern and portrait depiction based on mobile phone data. ISPRS Int. J. Geo-Inf. **9**(11), 666 (2020). https://doi. org/10.3390/ijgi9110666

16. Jeong, J., et al.: Mobility prediction for 5G core networks. IEEE Commun. Stand. Mag. **5**(1), 56–61 (2021). https://doi.org/10.1109/MCOMSTD.001.2000046

17. Guo, P., Xiao, K., Ye, Z., Zhu, W.: Route optimization via environment-aware deep network and reinforcement learning. ACM Trans. Intell. Syst. Technol. (TIST) **12**(6), 1–21 (2021). https://doi.org/10.1145/3461645

18. Leow, N.X., Krishnaswamy, J.: Smart cities need environmental consciousness and more social responsibilities as an outcome of COVID-19–reflections from urban road commuters. Foresight **24**(2), 276–296 (2022). https://doi.org/10.1108/FS-02-2021-0035

19. Martins, T.G., Lago, N., Santana, E.F., Telea, A., Kon, F., de Souza, H.A.: Using bundling to visualize multivariate urban mobility structure patterns in the São Paulo metropolitan area. J. Internet Serv. Appl. **12**, 1–32 (2021). https://doi.org/10.1186/s13174-021-00136-9

20. Keawsomnuk, P.: A structural equation model of factors relating to smart cities that affect the management of the world heritage site as well as the quality of life of tourists and villagers in Ayutthaya, Thailand. Humanit. Arts Soc. Sci. Stud. **21**(1), 35–42 (2021). https://doi.org/10.14456/hasss.2021.4
21. Cheshmehzangi, A., et al.: A hierarchical study for urban statistical indicators on the prevalence of COVID-19 in Chinese city clusters based on multiple linear regression (MLR) and polynomial best subset regression (PBSR) analysis. Sci. Rep. **12**(1), 1964 (2022). https://doi.org/10.1038/s41598-022-05859-8
22. Šauer, M., Vystoupil, J., Novotná, M., Widawski, K.: Central European tourist flows: intraregional patterns and their implications. Morav. Geogr. Rep. **29**(4), 278–291 (2021). https://doi.org/10.2478/mgr-2021-0020
23. Lao, X., Deng, X., Gu, H., Yang, J., Yu, H., Xu, Z.: Comparing intercity mobility patterns among different holidays in china: a big data analysis. Appl. Spat. Anal. Policy (2022). https://doi.org/10.1007/s12061-021-09433-z
24. Li, X., et al.: Position prediction system based on spatio-temporal regularity of object mobility. Inf. Syst. **75**, 43–55 (2018). https://doi.org/10.1016/j.is.2018.02.004
25. Türk, U., Östh, J., Kourtit, K., Nijkamp, P.: The path of least resistance explaining tourist mobility patterns in destination areas using Airbnb data. J. Transp. Geogr. **94**, 103130 (2021). https://doi.org/10.1016/j.jtrangeo.2021.103130
26. Mizzi, C., et al.: Unraveling pedestrian mobility on a road network using ICTs data during great tourist events. EPJ Data Sci. **7**(1), 44 (2018). https://doi.org/10.1140/epjds/s13688-018-0168-2
27. Wirth, R., Hipp, J.: CRISP-DM: Towards a standard process model for data mining, p. 11
28. "Lisbon Administrative Reform - First Quarterly Monitoring Report." https://www.am-lisboa.pt/451600/1/008910,000505/index.htm. Accessed Oct 27 2022
29. INE, "Tourism Statistics - 2020." https://www.ine.pt/xportal/xmain?xpid=INE&xpgid=ine_publicacoes&PUBLICACOESpub_boui=280866098&PUBLICACOESmodo=2. Accessed Oct 21 2022
30. Healy, K.: Data Visualization: A Practical Introduction. Princeton University Press, Princeton (2018)
31. "Tripadvisor," *Tripadvisor*. https://www.tripadvisor.pt/. Accessed Aug 09 2022
32. "Web Summit: Lisbon hosting the largest tech event in the world - Portugal - Portuguese American Journal." https://portuguese-american-journal.com/web-summit-lisbon-hosting-the-largest-tech-event-in-the-world-portugal/.Accessed May 13 2022

City Mobility and Night Life Monitor

Luís B. Elvas[1,2](✉) (iD), Miguel Nunes[1] (iD), Bruno Francisco[1] (iD),
and Nuno Domingues[3] (iD)

[1] Instituto Universitário de Lisboa (ISCTE-IUL), ISTAR, Lisbon, Portugal
`luis.elvas@iscte.pt`
[2] Department of Logistics, Molde University College, 6410 Molde, Norway
[3] ISEL-ADEM, Rua Conselheiro Emídio Navarro, 1, 1959-007 Lisbon, Portugal

Abstract. This paper presents an Internet of Things (IoT) system designed to collect and analyse information regarding the travel patterns and movements of individuals in densely populated locations, in the context of smart cities. People's movements are retrieved from coarse-grained aggregated cellular network data without collecting sensitive information from mobile devices and users. These data were provided by a Portuguese cellular operator to the Lisbon City Council to characterize people movements in the city. In this sense, the mobile phones act as useful sensor devices for collecting rich spatiotemporal information about human movement patterns. The purpose of this research work is to create a machine learning-based data-driven approach that is able to receive anonymised data from telecommunication operators to provide a big picture about citizen mobility in the city and to identify patterns based on the collected data, in order to provide relevant information for city planning and events coordination. Some of the main applications of the proposed system are the coordination of big events and the management and control of commuting traffic.

Keywords: machine learning · big data · mobility patterns · IoT · smart cities

1 Introduction

In contemporary cultures, the fast growth of information and communication technologies (ICTs) has produced abundant resources for spatio-temporal data mining and knowledge discovery. Understanding aggregated urban mobility patterns based on mobile phone statistics, such as identifying activity hotspots and clusters, is one important topic for municipality city management.

With the advent of powerful smartphones and creative mobile apps, the data volume generated by these tools has exploded. Due to the potential value contained within these enormous datasets, it is vital to be able to correctly and efficiently monitor and analyze these data. In this sense, several methods have been developed for comprehending associated patterns.

A. L. Martins et al. (Eds.): INTSYS 2023, LNICST 540, pp. 126–150, 2024.
https://doi.org/10.1007/978-3-031-49379-9_7

In the context of smart cities, work has been done to investigate the application of data-driven methodologies and visualization techniques in order to support decision-makers in urban settings by giving them useful information and tools. Studies on topics like incident management [1], traffic accidents [2], disaster management [3, 4], and city-wide data analytics have all been done. The results show the potential advantages of using data and sophisticated analytics to improve urban planning, increase traffic safety, and create efficient plans for disaster and event management. In the end, emphasis has been placed on the value of data-driven strategies in enabling decision-makers to build urban environments that are more effective, sustainable, and resilient.Different uses for the collected smartphone data include the recognition of mobility path patterns, traffic planning, route prediction and city-wide sensing applications. Previous research on the application of these data emphasizes their significant potential for analyzing minute differences in human mobility. However, high-level mobility information and low-level location data are often disconnected. Consequently, it is necessary to provide suitable methods for dealing with low-level location data to allow gaining valuable insights regarding the mobility patterns of users.

Mobile phones present unique qualities that entice academics and enterprises to leverage their data. The research conducted in the past has led to the development of several mobile sensing techniques that rely on position tracing or mobile positioning, which involves tracking the location coordinates of mobile phones. Numerous location-based services (LBSs) incorporate geographical information systems (GISs), based on global navigation satellite systems (GNSSs), such as the Global Positioning System (GPS), and the Internet. These LBSs record the movement, flows, and location of individuals in order to recommend social activities or provide tailored advertising.

Mobile phone location tracking may be classified as either active or passive. In the former the device position is identified, for example, using the proximity to radio-waves (cell ID tracking) and the triangulation of signals from multiple sources, such as with GPS. The latter resorts to billing data that are saved as a result of routine procedures. This solution requires the capacity for distance-based charging. Mobile phone calls and SMSs sent or received produce records including cell IDs, enabling the approximate position of the phone to be established. By receiving and analyzing this kind of location data supplied by mobile networks, mobile operators may subsequently build more effective monitoring tactics.

The remainder of this paper is structured as follows: State of the art is presented in Sect. 2. Section 3 introduce the methodology that we have used, as well as all the methods used in this work. Finally, Sect. 4 presents the conclusions.

2 State of the Art

2.1 Search Strategy and Inclusion Criteria

A systematic literature review was made by following PRISMA (Preferred Reporting Items for Systematic Reviews and Meta-Analysis) Methodology [5], and with the research question (RQ) "What is the state of the art on the behaviour and mobility analysis on smart cities?".

The database searched was Scopus and the research was conducted between 8 and 12 of May, 2022; all the results had to be articles published on the last five years and written in English. Grey literature, reviews, conference papers, workshops, books, and editorials were excluded, as well as works not related to the domain.

The search strategy was based on queries made with different research focuses of. This method allowed for the observation of the number of existing articles, considering the concept and context, and the population under study. The initial selection of papers was done using the title and abstract, and, in some cases in which that information was insufficient, the full document was analyzed.

2.2 Data Extraction and Synthesis

The review data were managed and stored using Zotero and Microsoft Excel. These data were title, author, year, journal, subject area, keywords and abstract. For data synthesis and analysis, a qualitative assessment was conducted based on the results presented above. The Scopus database was searched systematically regarding the published literature work related with the purpose of "Data Analysis" or "Behavior Analysis", with the target scenario of "Smart cities" or "Cellular network", and within the "Mobility" context for the study.

2.3 Results

The number of documents obtained using the defined keywords is presented in Table 1. The query was made in the Scopus database with the same restrictions and filters.

Table 1. Documents obtained using the selection criteria.

Concept	Population	Context	Limitations
Data Analysis Behaviour Analysis	smart cities cellular network	Mobility	2018–2012
453.106 Documents	35.965 Documents	642.769 Documents	Only journal papers, articles, and reviews
923			
17 Documents			

From this we can see that when the query was made using the keywords from all columns, it returned 17 documents. After performing a manual process towards the identification of significant subjects from research questions and identifying the outcomes, 10 documents were obtained. Our research systematization considered year, area, RQ topic and a small description.

2.4 Study Characteristics

From Fig. 1 we can notice from the trend line that there is a growth on the topic that we are studying, revealing his relevance.

Emphasizing also the relevance of the theme in our area, it's possible to confirm on Fig. 2 that the subject area where more studies are concentrated is precisely Computer Science.

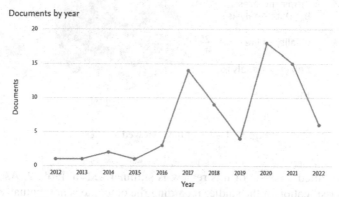

Fig. 1. Evolution of the number of documents per year.

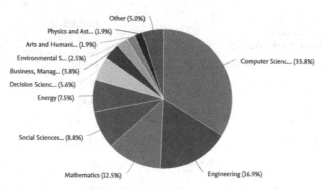

Fig. 2. Classification of the document in subject areas.

Considering that the main goal of this paper is to analyse the user behaviour and mobility in smart cities, a list of the main topics discussed on each of the 10 reviewed articles is illustrated on Fig. 3, where it is noticeable the focus on use of mobile phones and behaviour analysis. Notice that some articles cover multiple topics.

From Fig. 3, we can see that most of the studies focus on mobile phones/information and communications technology (ICT) infrastructures and/or on behaviour analysis. The pertinence of our study falls in between these two themes, because we not only use data from the cellular operators' ICT infrastructure for the city of Lisbon to study people's behaviour, but we also perform a behaviour analysis to understand and help on planning the measures to meet the needs of the citizens.

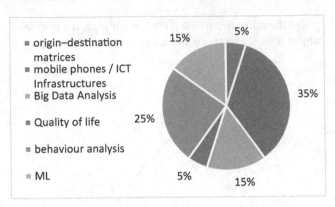

Fig. 3. Topics of the reviewed articles.

A more detailed analysis of this review is summarized in Table 2. As mentioned before, the classification of the studies regarding the outcome is not mutually exclusive, given that these were attributed due to presence/absence in the study.

Table 2. Main topics of reviewed articles.

Topic	Reference
(1) Origin–destination matrices	[6]
(2) Mobile phones / ICT infrastructures	[6–12]
(3) Big data analysis	[6, 8, 12]
(4) Quality of life	[13]
(5) Behaviour analysis	[7, 10, 12, 14, 15]
(6) Machine Learning	[7, 9, 11]

From the topic of mobile phones, authors from [6] offer a technique for estimating origin–destination (O–D) matrices using passively obtained cellular network signalling data from millions of anonymous mobile phone users in the Rhône–Alpes region of France, enhancing and revolutionizing the field of travel demand and traffic flow modelling. Still on this topic, authors on study [8] identify pedestrian hotspots and provide future traffic signal and street layout information to make the city more pedestrian friendly, allowing also the use of this obtained knowledge to other datasets, such as bicycle traffic, to guide city infrastructure initiatives.

From the same topic of mobile phones, but focusing on behaviour analysis, the study in [7], which was applied to Tuscany and Florence, identifies a number of metrics for determining whether a person on the move is stationary, walking, or riding in a motorized private or public vehicle, with the goal of providing city users with personalized assistance messages for sustainable mobility, health, and/or a better and more enjoyable life, among other things.

On this chapter Still on the combination of topics 2 and 5, the goal of [10] is to study and compare the density of users in Shanghai city using Weibo geolocation data and univariate and bivariate density estimation approaches, such as point density and kernel density estimation (KDE), where the main findings concern the characteristics of users' spatial behaviour, such as the center of activity, based on check-ins, the feasibility of using check-in data to explain the relationship between users and social media, and the presentation of clear results for regulatory or managing authorities in urban planning. Continuing in these two topics, study [12], based on long-term mobile phone data (from 2007 to 2012) of volunteers from Beijing, presents a way to illustrate individual movement patterns.

Blending topic 2 with machine learning, study [9] intends to give a taxonomy of 5G Cellular Network mobility prediction frameworks, from data gathering to model providing, while taking into account the 3GPP architecture and interfaces.; and we The authors provide two critical use cases in 5G Cellular Networks (CNs), in which the benefits of mobility predictions are assessed using information from real networks. On the other hand, study [11] focuses on building a mobile sequential recommendation system to help auto service companies to increase their profits (e.g., taxi drivers).

On the subject of behavioural analysis, study [14] provides an urban travel behaviour model and evaluates its feasibility for creating a greener environment for future generations. Study [15], based on a trip survey from the São Paulo metropolitan area, which is one of the world's busiest traffic locations, supplement a current bundling approach to enable multi-attribute trail datasets for the visual study of urban mobility, helping to identify and analyse distinct mobility patterns for various data variables, such as peak hours, socioeconomic strata, and transportation modes, according to the findings.

Regarding quality of life, The aim from study [13] is to look at the structural equation model of smart city factors that impact worldwide management of world heritage sites, as well as the quality of life, for Thai visitors and residents in the Ayutthaya province.

3 Methodology

This project follows the Cross-Industry Standard Process for Data Mining (CRISP-DM) Methodology. CRISP-DM is a well-known and commonly utilized methodology for successful data mining operations. CRISP-DM provides a complete framework that leads data mining practitioners through the full data mining process, from identifying business objectives through delivering the findings. The approach is divided into six key phases: Business Understanding, Data Understanding, Data Preparation, Modelling, Evaluation and Deployment. Each phase includes a collection of goals and activities that guarantee that data mining initiatives are approached in a methodical and iterative manner. CRISP-DM highlights the significance of understanding the business context and aligning data mining goals with organizational objectives, which increases the likelihood of success in extracting meaningful insights and actionable information from data. Organizations may improve their decision-making processes, optimize resource allocation, and promote innovation by using the CRISP-DM technique [16].

3.1 Business Understanding

The main goal behind the exploration of this dataset is to identify and explore patterns, behaviors and reactions in the population related to the measures taken by the government to lift the restrictions that were imposed to deal with the COVID-19 pandemic. Some of our focus points were studying and exploring the adherence of the population to some activities that were not so usual in the last couple of years, such as the comeback of the nightlife, going to work or going to school.

To create value from the collected data, the following objectives were defined:

- To study and correlate the changes that have occurred in nightlife in periods with different pandemic restrictions. To do this, the movements that occur during night time hours in different establishments and areas with regular nightlife were analysed. Heat maps were constructed, in which the differences in the movement of the population in certain periods can be observed.
- To study the evolution of mobility in Parque das Nações, a redeveloped area of Lisbon which was the site of the 1998 Lisbon World Exposition (Expo '98), during the different months of the pandemic. This area was selected for being composed of business and leisure zones and for containing the only active vaccination centre in the city of Lisbon during the months of study. With this approach it will be possible to study eventual patterns and isolate their causes. After mapping the zone, it was necessary to collect data on factors such as events that occurred in the area, government measures on teleworking and hybrid regimes and vaccination to study population movements in more detail.

3.2 Maintaining the Integrity of the Specifications

The dataset under analysis consists of data provided by Vodafone that contain information about the cellular connections (segmented in a total of 3743 different squares or grid cells of 200 by 200 m) established between mobile devices and base station towers in Lisbon, between September 2021 and January 2022 for every 5 min. It is formed by 3 different types of files. The main files, which contain more information, are composed by 27 different variables. Those variables provide different information about the devices that were detected in every 200 square meter area around the city during those 4 months. The other file types consist of information about the coordinates of every 200-square meter area and the coordinates of 11 selected roads that connect the city to other areas and that help to explore the entrances and the exits of the city during these months.

Each month was splitted into multiple datasets, where each of these datasets contained information about a set of grid cells, divided into 29 columns (Table 3).

After a brief exploratory analysis, it was found that there were several missing data, such as weeks without any records or even missing grid cells. In other words, there was no information about some areas of Lisbon.

Due to the high volume of data, it was necessary to download the data in stages, to ensure that the data were not corrupted during the process and to check one by one if everything was complete. After all this analysis we proceeded with the data cleaning and data procedures.

Table 3. Description of each variable present in the main files.

Variable	Description
Grid_ID	Identification of the grid cell number
Datetime	Date and Time
extract_year_2	Year
extract_month_3	Month
extract_day_4	Day
C1	Number of distinct terminals in the grid, during the 5 min
C2	Number of distinct terminals, roaming, in the grid, during the 5 min
C3	Number of distinct terminals remaining in the grid at the end of each 5 min period
C4	Number of distinct terminals remaining in the grid, roaming, at the end of each 5 min
C5	Number of distinct terminals entries in the grid
C6	The number of distinct terminals exits in the grid
C7	Number of distinct terminal entries in the grid, roaming
C8	Number of distinct terminals exits in the grid, roaming
C9	Number of distinct terminals with an active data connection, in the grid cell, during the 5 min
C10	Number of distinct terminals with an active data connection, roaming, in the grid cell, during the 5 min
C11	Number of voice calls originating from the grid
C12	Number of entries into Lisbon along the 11 main roads
C13	Number of exits into Lisbon along the 11 main roads
D1	Top 10 home countries of terminal equipment roaming
E1	Number of voice calls terminated in the grid
E2	The average downstream rhythm of the grid
E3	The average upstream rhythm of the grid
E4	Peak downstream rhythm of the grid
E5	Peak upstream rhythm of the grid
E6	Top 10 apps (semicolon separated)
E7	Duration of the minimum stay within the grid
E8	Duration of the average stay within the grid
E9	Duration of the maximum stay within the grid
E10	Number of devices performing grid connection sharing during the 5 min period

3.3   Data Preparation

To give a uniform treatment to all the datasets of the analysis, a general Python script was created so that it was possible to apply to all datasets the same process of data cleaning and treatment.

In the first stage of this process, the existence of missing values and duplicate values was verified. It was found that variables "D1" and "E6" always contained more than 50% of missing data. However, the elimination of these rows implied a big loss, so it was decided to eliminate the columns with these variables. There were also many duplicated values, so we eliminated them.

Since each dataset contained millions of observations and our machines are not powerful enough to handle such a large amount of data, we decided to eliminate the irrelevant variables for our analysis, together with the two variables mentioned in the previous paragraph.

It was also verified that the variable "Datetime" was not in the correct format. Consequently, the value recorded in each entry of that variable was broken down into three new variables:

- Date - represents the date on which the device had its registration effected in a day/month/year format;
- Time - represents the time of day on which the record was made in an Hour: Minutes format;
- Hour - selects the time recorded in the "Time" variable to facilitate its use and optimise potential hourly analysis in Microsoft Power BI.

Subsequently, a new variable, called "Weekday", was created using the Pandas library, which was able to represent the day of the week where the record occurred, from the "Date" variable. After this treatment and cleaning phase, all datasets were joined.

In a second phase, to meet the defined objectives and because it would not be computationally feasible to work with all records in the database, the different periods, times and areas of the city of Lisbon that were to be analysed were separated. In this case, the analysis of the zones of Bairro Alto, Santos-o-Velho e Docas were restricted, from 2 am to 4 am on Thursdays, Fridays and Saturdays to analyse the impact of COVID-19 restrictions on nightlife. For the analysis of the mobility in the urban centre of Parque das Nações, we restricted the grid squares to this area. Both analyses comprise all the months under study.

With these two areas, we managed to have a study that covers both the movements of people during the day and the early hours of nightlife. However, to ensure that the right grid cells are chosen, we mapped both areas by going to the locations in person and using tools such as Google Earth or Google Maps. The reason for this decision was that there was a time discrepancy between the records present in these tools and what currently exists at the sites, which required a few weeks of exploration to delimit the areas for study.

After all the mapping was completed, we were faced with another challenge: each of the grid cells where there are records covers an area of 40 000 square meters and there are several types of buildings and/or activities that are covered. For this reason, to avoid an inaccurate and fallacious analysis, we classified each of the cells used in a category that represented the predominantly registered activity.

Since the longitude and latitude are important for the visualisation of the results, it was necessary to add these two variables to the datasets, since they were in different datasets. Finally, as the elimination of irrelevant variables was not enough to reduce the size of the data, it was decided to create samples of the datasets with 20% of the total size so that it would be possible to visualise them.

3.4 Visualization

The Impact of COVID-19 on Nightlife

One of the main objectives of this research was to understand how the measures imposed by the Portuguese government to control the COVID-19 pandemic affected Lisbon's nightlife. For this purpose, this first study started in September 2021 and ended in December 2021. During this period, there were some relevant changes in the measures imposed to control the pandemic. At the start of the study, during September, nightclubs and bars were closed to avoid the propagation of the COVID-19 virus. On the 1st of October, these places were allowed to reopen upon presentation, by the customers, of a digital certificate proving that they had been vaccinated against COVID-19 or otherwise that a test proving the customer was not infected had been performed. This measure lasted until December 24th, when new measures have been imposed making it obligatory for these places to stay closed.

Based on these measures, two distinct periods were selected for analysis: 1) the month of September, in which the measures imposed still prevented nightlife venues from opening; 2) the following three months (October, November and December), in which the nightclubs and bars were allowed to reopen. Within these periods, the areas that were selected for analysis were very popular Lisbon's nightlife areas: the Urban Beach nightclub and the Bairro Alto area, which has several bars that stay open until very late.

Firstly, the research was directed to the study of how movements occurred in the space near the Urban Beach nightclub in September (Fig. 4). It was possible to realize that during the night, the movement reached the minimum daily values, which corroborated the existing limitations on the opening and operation of nightlife spaces.

Urban Beach's Hourly Average Circulation - September

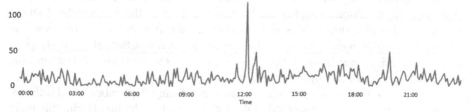

Fig. 4. Evolution of mobility in Urban Beach by hours, in September 2021.

It was also analysed how the movements in this nightclub occurred over the weeks (Fig. 5). During the periods between Friday and Sunday - which are the days when there are typically more events - these movements were low, which suggests that is a direct consequence of the measures implemented by the government to control the pandemic of COVID-19 that were in force during this month.

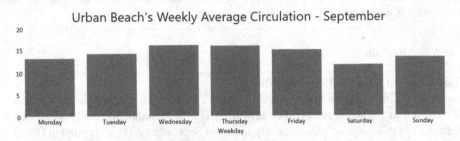

Fig. 5. Evolution of mobility in Urban Beach by weekday.

To continue this analysis and for comparison purposes, a graph was reproduced (Fig. 6), comprising the period between October and December. This graph aimed to get a better understanding of how the fluctuations of movements occurred throughout the hours. For this period, the results were practically opposite to those obtained for September. The period in which the busiest movements are registered in the Urban Beach nightclub is during the late-night period, revealing that the measures imposed by the Government to lift the restrictions had an effect that had immediate repercussions.

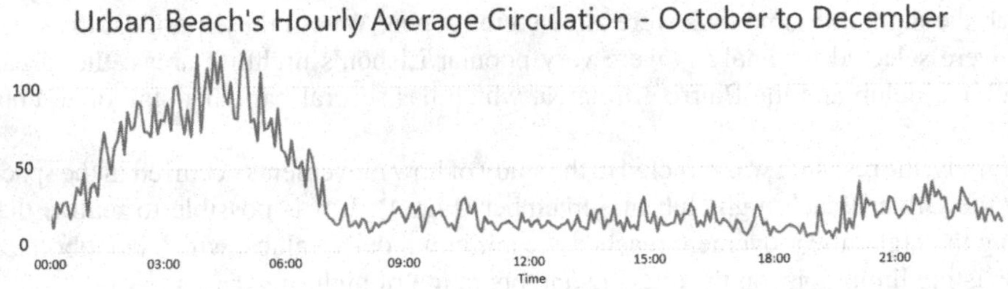

Fig. 6. Evolution of mobility in Urban Beach by hour, between October and December 2021.

For comparison purposes with the graph reproduced in Fig. 5, a visualization (Fig. 7) of the frequency with which people visited Urban Beach during the weeks in the observed months was also reproduced. This visualization made it possible to see that with the implemented deconfinement measures the pattern changed substantially, with the periods between Friday and Sunday becoming especially representative concerning the frequency of visits that the nightclub received.

As for Bairro Alto, it was possible to notice that during September it had different patterns from those that were verified in the Urban Beach nightclub. During the night periods, there was already some affluence of people in this area (Fig. 8), which resulted from several gatherings and parties that were illegally held during this period.

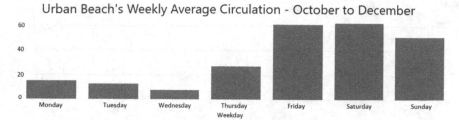

Fig. 7. Evolution of mobility in Urban Beach by weekday, between October and December 2021.

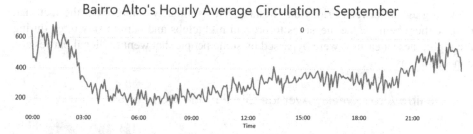

Fig. 8. Evolution of mobility in Bairro Alto by hours, in September 2021.

The weekly evolution of people's concentration at Bairro Alto (Fig. 9) was also under study. It was noticed that movement reaches its peak between Friday and Sunday, days that correspond to the periods when people are resting from their jobs and/or studies.

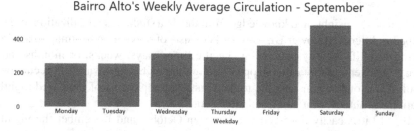

Fig. 9. Evolution of mobility in Bairro Alto by weekday, in September 2021.

For comparative purposes, it was visualized how the concentrations of people at Bairro Alto occur between October and December during 24h periods (Fig. 10) and how they vary throughout the week (Fig. 11).

Given the hourly variations, it was possible to verify that they exhibited very similar behaviour to September's, reaching the peaks of people circulation in the late-night period, with emphasis on the even higher average number of people that were registered in this zone during the period in question.

Finally, analysing the flow of people variations throughout the week it was again verified a similar trend to the one obtained in September, with the peaks of circulation

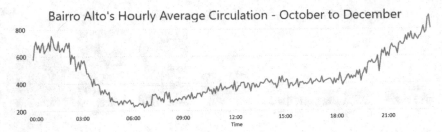

Fig. 10. Evolution of mobility in Bairro Alto by hour, between October and December 2021.

occurring again between Friday and Sunday. This similarity comes from the fact that, despite there being some measures to prevent nightclubs and bars to stay open during the night, these measures were bypassed by some people that went to illegal parties and concentrations.

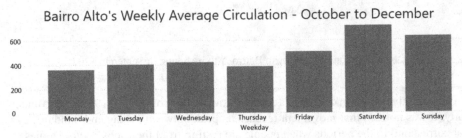

Fig. 11. Evolution of mobility in Bairro Alto by weekday, between October and December 2021.

To gain better insights and knowledge from the data studied, a visualization tool was developed in Microsoft Power BI. This tool consists of a dynamic heatmap that allows observing nightlife activity patterns at specific times, days, weeks, or months and to observe the movement flows that happen through the nights in town. With recursion to this tool, it was once again possible to demonstrate the patterns of increased nightlife circulation and activity that happened after September.

In Fig. 12 it is easily observed that between October and December the nightlife activity gained a new focus that is located near Avenida 24 de Julho, an area where there are several nightlife establishments such as bars, discos and restaurants. This recovery is due, once again, to the deconfinement measure that allowed bars and discos to reopen to the public and operate during the early hours of the morning.

In addition to this pattern, it was possible to see (in Fig. 13) that between 2 AM and 4 AM the concentration of people in areas near the river (again, where several discos and bars are located) tended to increase considerably.

Finally, it was also analysed the set of days - between December 24th and January 9th - on which a period of containment dictated the closure of discos and bars. Through an analysis of the visualization in Fig. 14, it is possible to see that the pattern of behaviour and nocturnal activity changes again in this set of days when compared with the general set of days under study. On this set of days, the riverside areas of the city show a lower

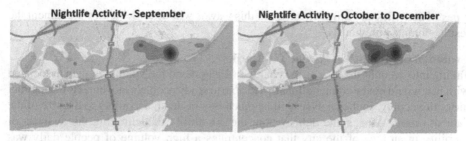

Fig. 12. Heatmap of evolution of mobility in nightlife activity in Lisbon (Sep x Oct-Dec).

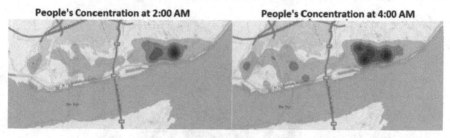

Fig. 13. Heatmap of evolution of mobility in nightlife activity in Lisbon (2 AM x 4 AM).

degree of concentration of people which increases considerably on the days following this period.

Fig. 14. Heatmap of evolution of mobility in nightlife activity in Lisbon.

Despite the conclusions drawn, it is undeniable that they are not enough to explain all the impacts of the COVID-19 pandemic on the mobility of the inhabitants of the county of Lisbon. For this reason, it was considered necessary to study with the same level of detail the movements of the population, during the day, in an area concentrating on other types of activities and infrastructures. In this way, it will be possible to complement the results obtained previously.

Evolution of Mobility in Parque Das Nações

Taking into account the size of the county of Lisbon and the volume of data associated with it, it would not be computationally feasible to study people's movements throughout the entire county, so the analysis will be much less in-depth according to the size of the database used. After some deliberation, the possibility of delimiting the analysis of mobility in an area of the city that concentrates a high volume of people daily was considered. This creative process led to the selection of a representative area of the parish of Parque das Nações which is illustrated in red on Fig. 15.

Fig. 15. Representative area – Parque das Nações (red zone). (Color figure online)

After the well-known International Exhibition - Expo in 1998, this area of the municipality of Lisbon, where various infrastructures associated with industrial activity used to be concentrated, such as refineries and rubbish dumps, underwent intense urban rehabilitation, gaining new prominence and becoming one of the busiest areas of the municipality.

The construction of the Gare do Oriente and the Vasco da Gama bridge played a very important role in the rehabilitation of this area since it started to connect this area of the municipality to the metro, train and bus networks, as well as making the connection to the other side of the river. An extremely high-quality urban space was created, with plenty of services and the integration of the latest technologies in the infrastructures. As a result, the number of companies that have their offices in this area has been growing over the last few years. On the other hand, the new residential buildings that have been built are among the most coveted by the Portuguese due to their proximity to diversified support services such as commerce and restaurants, schools and public and leisure spaces of high quality, and also cultural spaces such as the Pavilhão do Conhecimento.

Within the parish of Parque das Nações, the cells corresponding to the coastal area and the main streets from the Lisbon Oceanarium to the pavilions of the Lisbon International Fair were selected. The criterion for the delimitation of the study area was made through data analysis and explorations made presently by the group members in several weeks, thus ensuring that only areas with relevant infrastructures and significant movements were selected.

In this way, it was possible to make a very detailed mapping of the area that could facilitate the subsequent analysis of the mobility of the population. As each cell corresponds to an area of 200 by 200 m, resulting in an area large enough to cover several infrastructures. During the analysis of the site, it was possible to see that some residential buildings concentrated commercial or catering activities on the ground floors, which could alter our visualisation of the results.

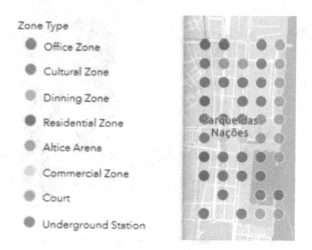

Fig. 16. Parque das Nações divided by zones.

Taking these factors into consideration, a variable was created that classifies each cell studied according to the type of activity that is predominant within the delimited area. After a few days of work on site the area presented on Fig. 16 was mapped.

After completion of the data mapping and classification process, we proceeded to analyse the data regarding the effects of the measures taken by the government to combat the COVID-19 pandemic on people's mobility.

In a first stage, it was studied how the different "zones" previously created could help in the analysis of the mobility of the population. The number of devices was counted, during the 5 months under study, according to the type of zone in order to understand how each "zone" contributes to the concentration of people.

The impossibility of counting the devices in each "cell" only once meant that an alternative method had to be used to reduce as much as possible the margin of error in the visualizations that would be made. For this reason, the value recorded in each cell during a day is equal to the sum of all devices counted in the 5-min periods in which data collection occurred, divided by the 24 h that make up the day. In this way, an estimated value of the number of devices that have been counted is obtained that is closer to reality.

This approach is not perfect, however after several meetings with the Municipality of Lisbon, an agreement was reached. It was recognised that, with the limited resources available to us, this would be the best option to obtain results that would meet their expectations, assuming each device corresponds to one person.

Once all these treatment processes were completed, the data were analysed in greater depth. First, the number of devices counted per month from September 2021 to January 2022 was analysed to understand how the number of devices varied as the pandemic developed (Fig. 17).

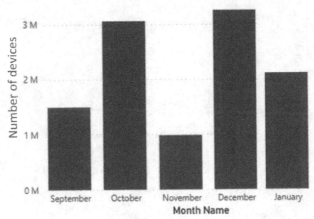

Fig. 17. Number of Devices counted per month.

By analysing Fig. 18, it was possible to see that there is an uneven distribution in the number of devices counted over the months. Although a lower value in the number of devices was expected in January 2022 due to the teleworking and confinement measures announced in that month by the government, the values for September and November were subject to further analysis.

Taking into account the study variables present in the database, the variation in the number of devices counted over each month was analysed, with special attention to September and November (Fig. 17 and Fig. 18).

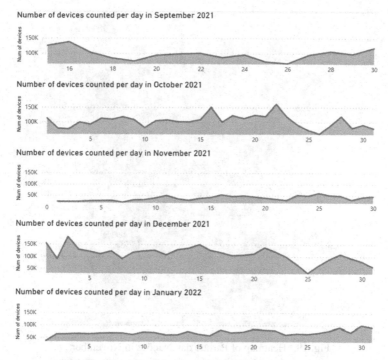

Fig. 18. Number of devices counted by day, per month.

Using the visual elements created in Microsoft Power BI it was possible to verify that, in September, devices were only accounted for from the second half of the month. This reduction in the time window can be pointed out as the main cause of the discrepancy between the values recorded in that month and the following one.

However, the reduced number of devices counted in November cannot be justified by the previous reason as devices were counted during the whole month. Even so, the values remained suspicious as during that time of the year several events were organised at Parque das Nações, some of which were of an international nature, such as the Web Summit, which attracts thousands of companies and start-ups to this part of the county every year.

In order to ascertain the true cause of the November values, the concentration of devices in each of the cells during that month was analysed to check the possibility of a problem having occurred in some parts of the study area, Fig. 19.

Considering the results obtained in the previous heatmap it was verified that most of the cells in Parque das Nações did not exist, which prevented the counting of devices. The municipality of Lisbon is composed by 3999 cells and during the month of November data was only collected in the first 3000 cells.

This situation was discussed with the Lisbon City Council who explained that the data existed, however, at the time the project was carried out, the data was corrupted, and it was not possible to present a deadline for it to be treated and delivered for study. After some conversations, and taking into consideration the problems raised previously,

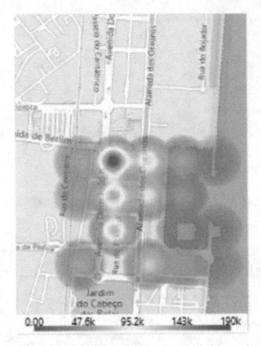

Fig. 19. Heatmap of Parque das Nações in November.

it was agreed that the study of mobility in Parque das Nações would be more focused in the months of October, December and January.

During the month of October, the only measure declared by the Directorate General of Health that would have some impact on the mobility of the Portuguese was the end of the limitations for people in closed spaces or events and the conclusion of the mandatory status of telework (Resolution of the Council of Ministers no. 135-A/2021). For this reason, more movements were recorded at Parque das Nações, given that several companies were able to choose between the permanent face-to-face regime and the hybrid regime, having more employees in their offices.

As a result of these measures, 3 055 047 people were counted during that month (Fig. 20). Taking into consideration the previous graph, it is possible to verify that most of the people that went to Parque das Nações during that month were employees from the several companies that are based in that office zone.

The second highest number of people was recorded in the residential zone, since in addition to residents, people passing through establishments located on the ground floors of residential buildings were also counted. A practical example are the cafes and small shops that during the day attract some people who are not exclusively residents in that area.

With the lifting of restrictions on the limit of people in enclosed spaces and the holding of fairs and exhibitions in spaces such as the Feira Internacional de Lisboa and Pavilhão do Conhecimento, the cultural zones counted more people than the Vasco da Gama shopping centre.

Total devices counted by Zone Type in October

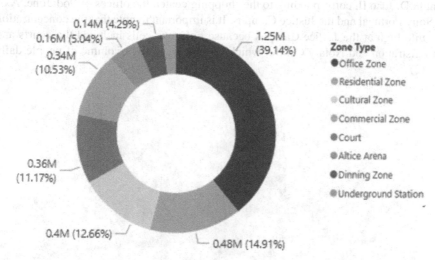

0.14M (4.29%)
0.16M (5.04%)
0.34M (10.53%)
1.25M (39.14%)
0.36M (11.17%)
0.4M (12.66%)
0.48M (14.91%)

Zone Type
- Office Zone
- Residential Zone
- Cultural Zone
- Commercial Zone
- Court
- Altice Arena
- Dinning Zone
- Underground Station

Fig. 20. Total Devices counted divided by zone in October.

During the analysis of the number of devices counted throughout the month it was verified if there was any pattern according to the type of zone a peculiar pattern was detected. When isolating the area corresponding to the Parque das Nações Restaurant Zone it is possible to verify the existence of a peak in the number of devices between days 21 and 22, followed by a significant drop until day 26 where the value rises again substantially (Fig. 21).

These fluctuations are the result of different days on which workers are paid, the civil service generally receives their salary on the 20th of the month and private companies usually pay their employees between the 24th and 26th. It is possible to conclude that on the days before workers are paid, fewer people go out to eat in restaurants, but after receiving their salary on the following days, they try to do so.

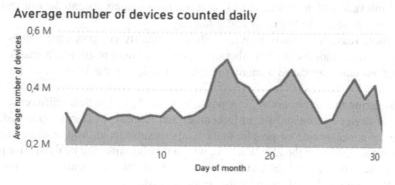

Average number of devices counted daily

0,6 M

0,4 M

0,2 M

Average number of devices

10   20   30

Day of month

Fig. 21. Daily Count of devices.

As a complement to the previous results, a heatmap of that month was created in which it was possible to detect that the cells that registered more people were located in Avenida D. João II, corresponding to the shopping center, the offices of Vodafone, Axians, Sony Portugal and the Justice Campus. It is important to note that the concentration was quite high at the Justice Campus because only two cells included the courts and the Registration and Notary Centre, which concentrate a high volume of people daily (Fig. 22).

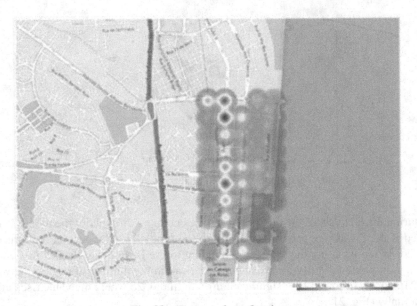

Fig. 22. Heatmap from October.

During the month of November to the beginning of December the number of cases of COVID-19 suffered a very significant increase to the point that the Directorate General of Health had to take more demanding measures. Among the various measures, it was highlighted the obligation to present a negative test to enter some spaces, the need to have the full vaccination certificate to visit restaurants and events and the obligation of teleworking between 25 December and 9 January.

For these reasons an analysis was made that directly compares the values registered between the months of December and January as more restrictive measures were implemented that may cause a more significant impact on the mobility of people in Lisbon.

Considering the graphs above, it is possible to verify a significant difference in the number of devices accounted for in December and January. In December, in addition to a greater concentration of people, there is also a substantial drop in the number of devices accounted for on the 25th (Fig. 23), which may be explained by the festive period celebrated on this day. Like the October analysis, the highest concentration of people is in the office zone, followed again by the residential zone.

Total Devices Counted by Zone Type in December 2021

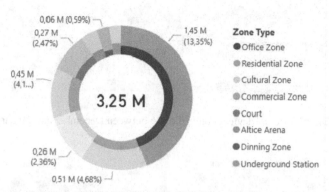

Total Devices Counted by Zone Type in January 2022

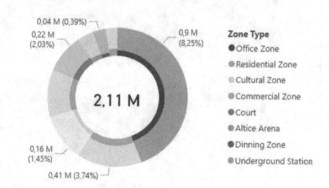

Fig. 23. Total Devices by zone Type between December and January.

After the 9th of January, there is a slight increase of devices accounted for until the end of the month. This result can be explained by the sales period that started on the 10th and by the easing of measures that took place throughout the month.

After observing the December heatmap (Fig. 25) and considering the analysis of the number of devices counted throughout the month (Fig. 24), there was a large affluence in the Vasco da Gama Shopping Centre area. This result was expected, since in the weeks before Christmas, the flow of people increases substantially in shopping areas for the festive season.

In the meetings that took place with the Lisbon City Council to monitor the project, the various results were presented through the Microsoft Power BI business analysis service, since it allows the provision of interactive visualizations with a simple interface. Throughout these meetings, this entity showed interest in this tool because it made it possible to filter data quickly. The question was raised whether it would be possible to implement this type of analysis on other types of data, using the same initial treatment. To answer this problem, a visualization tool with interactive dashboards was developed. This

Number of Devices counted per day in December 2021

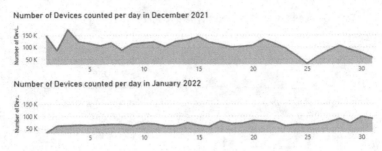

Number of Devices counted per day in January 2022

Fig. 24. Number of devices counted daily between December and January.

Expo December 2021 Heatmap

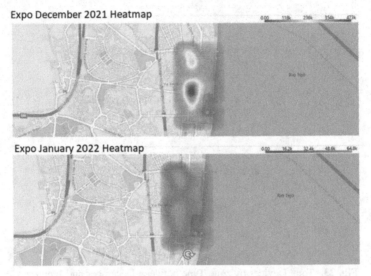

Expo January 2022 Heatmap

Fig. 25. Heatmaps from December and January.

allows staff, even if they have no experience with this software, to navigate intuitively and gain insights into large concentrations of people, as well as explore nightlife activity in the city.

4   Conclusions

Smart city planners and destination managers need to comprehend how people travel from one site to another. Possibilities for the development of relevant, evidence-based insights for decision-makers have been provided by the abundance of data supplied by social networking platforms. While prior research have offered observational data analysis techniques for social media data, there is still a need for method development - especially for capturing the movement patterns and behavioral aspects of individuals.

This research that outlines a novel way for analyzing people's activities, behaviors, and movements for monitoring and planning reasons. Our strategy employs information from mobile operators that establish a partnership with local municipality in Lisbon providing anomized data and we create a process to work with these data towards big pictures visualization process using Microsoft Power BI. This visualization allows city municipality identify big persons concentration, explore night life activity that is always a problem in a city and provide useful information how people move.

Funding. This work was supported by EEA Grants Blue Growth Programme (Call #5). Project PT-INNOVATION-0069–Fish2Fork. This research also received funding from ERAMUS+ project NEMM with grant 101083048.

References

1. Elvas, L.B., Marreiros, C.F., Dinis, J.M., Pereira, M.C., Martins, A.L., Ferreira, J.C.: Data-driven approach for incident management in a smart city. Appl. Sci. Switz. **10**(22), 1–18 (2020). https://doi.org/10.3390/app10228281
2. Mesquitela, J., Elvas, L.B., Ferreira, J.C., Nunes, L.: Data analytics process over road accidents data—a case study of Lisbon City. ISPRS Int. J. Geo-Inf. **11**(2), 143 (2022). https://doi.org/10.3390/ijgi11020143
3. Elvas, L.B., Mataloto, B.M., Martins, A.L., Ferreira, J.C.: Disaster management in smart cities. Smart Cities 4(2), Art. no. 2 (2021). https://doi.org/10.3390/smartcities4020042
4. Elvas, L.B., Gonçalves, S.P., Ferreira, J.C., Madureira, A.: Data fusion and visualization towards city disaster management: Lisbon case study. EAI Endorsed Trans. Smart Cities **6**(18), e3–e3 (2022). https://doi.org/10.4108/eetsc.v6i18.1374
5. Moher, D., Liberati, A., Tetzlaff, J., Altman, D.G.: Preferred reporting items for systematic reviews and meta-analyses: the PRISMA statement. BMJ **339**, b2535 (2009). https://doi.org/10.1136/bmj.b2535
6. Fekih, M., Bellemans, T., Smoreda, Z., Bonnel, P., Furno, A., Galland, S.: A data-driven approach for origin–destination matrix construction from cellular network signalling data: a case study of Lyon region (France). Transportation **48**(4), 1671–1702 (2021). https://doi.org/10.1007/s11116-020-10108-w
7. Badii, C., Difino, A., Nesi, P., Paoli, I., Paolucci, M.: Classification of users' transportation modalities from mobiles in real operating conditions. Multimed. Tools Appl. **81**(1), 115–140 (2022). https://doi.org/10.1007/s11042-021-10993-y
8. Carter, E., Adam, P., Tsakis, D., Shaw, S., Watson, R., Ryan, P.: Enhancing pedestrian mobility in smart cities using big data. J. Manag. Anal. **7**(2), 173–188 (2020). https://doi.org/10.1080/23270012.2020.1741039
9. Jeong, J., et al.: Mobility prediction for 5G core networks. IEEE Commun. Stand. Mag. **5**(1), 56–61 (2021). https://doi.org/10.1109/MCOMSTD.001.2000046
10. Ali Haidery, S., Ullah, H., Khan, N.U., Fatima, K., Rizvi, S.S., Kwon, S.J.: Role of big data in the development of smart city by analyzing the density of residents in shanghai. Electron. Switz. **9**(5), 837 (2020). https://doi.org/10.3390/electronics9050837
11. Guo, P., Xiao, K., Ye, Z., Zhu, W.: Route optimization via environment-aware deep network and reinforcement learning. ACM Trans. Intell. Syst. Technol. **12**(6), 1–21 (2021). https://doi.org/10.1145/3461645
12. Li, C., Hu, J., Dai, Z., Fan Z., Wu, Z.: Understanding individual mobility pattern and portrait depiction based on mobile phone data. ISPRS Int. J. Geo-Inf. 9(11), 666 (2020). https://doi.org/10.3390/ijgi9110666

13. Keawsomnuk, P.: A structural equation model of factors relating to smart cities that affect the management of the world heritage site as well as the quality of life of tourists and villagers in Ayutthaya, Thailand. Humanit. Arts Soc. Sci. Stud. **21**(1), 35–42 (2021). https://doi.org/10.14456/hasss.2021.4
14. Leow, N.X., Krishnaswamy, J.: Smart cities need environmental consciousness and more social responsibilities as an outcome of COVID-19 – reflections from urban road commuters. Foresight **24**(2), 276–296 (2022). https://doi.org/10.1108/FS-02-2021-0035
15. Martins, T.G., Lago, N., Santana, E.F., Telea, A., Kon, F., de Souza, H.A.: Using bundling to visualize multivariate urban mobility structure patterns in the São Paulo Metropolitan Area. J. Internet Serv. Appl. **12**(1), 1–32 (2021). https://doi.org/10.1186/s13174-021-00136-9
16. Wirth, R., Hipp, J.: CRISP-DM: towards a standard process model for data mining. In: Proceedings of the 4th International Conference on the Practical Applications of Knowledge Discovery and Data Mining (2000)

Blockchain-Powered Fish Industry: Trust Perceptions of Final Consumers on Traceable Information Availability

Ulpan Tokkozhina[1,2,3](✉) iD, Ana Lucia Martins[1,2] iD, and Joao C. Ferreira[2,3,4,5] iD

[1] Business Research Unit (BRU-IUL), Lisbon, Portugal
ulpan_tokkozhina@iscte-iul.pt
[2] Instituto Universitário de Lisboa (ISCTE-IUL), 1649-026 Lisbon, Portugal
[3] Inov Inesc Inovação/ Inesc-ID, 1000-029 Lisbon, Portugal
[4] Information Sciences and Technologies and Architecture Research Centre (ISTAR-IUL),
Lisbon, Portugal
[5] Logistics, Molde University College, NO-6410 Molde, Norway

Abstract. Blockchain is being actively discussed for business applications to digitalise supply chains. The still nascent level of blockchain adoption creates a difficulty to see the potential value that it may add to products and final consumers. Through a quantitative method, this study explores the impact of the traceability feature of products on the trust in the seller supermarket chain from the perspective of final consumers. Data from 417 questionnaires applied to buyers of fish was used to analyse such relation. Findings reveal the interest of final consumers towards traceable products and a positive relationship between the traceable information availability and the trust towards product.

Keywords: Blockchain · Fish Industry · Final Consumers

1 Introduction

Increasing competition in the market of food retail creates pressure on retailers and decreases their ability in providing more sustainable and healthy options [1]. Today consumers are paying attention not only to the availability of a product but also to its quality, where the provenance of products' origins can impact the final consumption decision [2]. To meet the expectations and needs of final consumers, supply chain (SC) stakeholders need to work together towards a mutual goal, which creates a need for close collaboration to reach their common objective. Here, another challenge of supply chain management (SCM) arises: entities are seeking a higher dedication and openness to designate mutual dependency, as the trust level between parties impacts their willingness to collaborate with each other [3].

As technological solutions are arising, one of the most promising technologies that is being actively discussed in a business context is the blockchain technology (BCT). Blockchain can be defined as a "digital, decentralized and distributed ledger in which

A. L. Martins et al. (Eds.): INTSYS 2023, LNICST 540, pp. 151–162, 2024.
https://doi.org/10.1007/978-3-031-49379-9_8

transactions are logged and added in chronological order with the goal of creating permanent and tamper-proof records" [4]. When applied in the business context, BCT can reshape current processes with its native immutable nature–all transactions and information that goes through a blockchain ledger cannot be compromised, changed, or removed later due to the nature of technology, that links the blocks together in a decentralized manner [5]. Accordingly, BCT is claimed to bring provenance of products' origins [6], ensure traceability and transparency of records [7], enable trust with final consumers, as they could easily scan and verify the product origins [8], as well as promote mutual trust between SC parties by protecting shared data [9].

Blockchain applications to SCM practices for consumer goods were studied for various categories of products, such as food and drinks [10–13], electronics [14, 15], clothing [16, 17], and others. Most of the articles in the field are conceptual model propositions and state-of-the-art, mostly focusing on the players in the SC that share information and want/need immutable information. Still poorly explored is the perspective of the final customers on the value of the traceability information and its impact on the purchase behavior of such customers, which can be potentially powered by the BCT.

Aiming at filling this gap, the purpose of this study is to explore the impact of the traceability feature of perishable products on the trust towards the product, from the perspective of final consumers. This study is based on the data collected from Portuguese consumers of fish products. Thus, the goal of this study is to reveal the potential of BCT solutions for creating value proposals by retail chains offering fish products to final consumers.

To address the purpose of this study, quantitative research was conducted and the views of final consumers on the traceability feature for fish products was investigated through an online survey. This paper contributes to the current knowledge in the area by showing that, under the scope of the analyzed sample, final consumers are interested in the traceability of products and that there is a significant and positive relationship between the availability of traceable information and the trust in the product. Such a relation may further lead to increased sales. The remaining of the paper is built as follows: a section with the review of the extant literature about BCT features and SC challenges that need to be addressed, a methodology description section, findings and data analysis, and, finally, the discussion of results and main conclusions of the study.

2   Literature Review

Supply chain players are constantly battling to understand the nature of trust and the dynamics of trust building [18]. Both the trust component of SCs and the technology component were found to have a considerable impact on collaboration between partners and operational performances of businesses. With the launching of new technologies, the trust component of SCM is also addressed. Like this, BCT is being hyped to bring to SC players "trust-free transactions" [19] by its decentralized and immutable nature.

Blockchain is a part of Distributed Ledger Technologies (DLT), that operates as an immutable ledger, keeping and recording every transaction that is instantly shared across the whole network of participants [20]. Through its decentralized nature, BCT brings transparency to the SC network, and provides reliance on products' provenance, decreasing at the same time the counterfeit possibilities, as products' origins can always be consulted in real-time [6]. BCT use was explored in many different fields, not only for consumer goods but also for industries such as medication distribution [21], chemical industry [22, 23], oil and gas industry [24], electricity trading [25, 26], and many others. This shows a universal ability of BCT to bring potential improvements to SCs in various fields.

However, various technical and regulatory issues still need to be addressed for BCT-based solutions to reach the maturity stage [27]. Some challenges, that were detected in previous studies include constraints like organizational readiness for change and a lack of technical knowledge [28], high cost of the technology and its complexity [29], comprehensive management procedures and adoption strategies for BCT-based networks when used by multi-actor SCs [30], and many others. Moreover, from the perspective of final consumers, providing them with a BCT-based tool to explore products' origin is not enough, as it needs to first create an environment of trust [31]. To move towards large-scale adoptions, final consumers need to first become active players of BCT-based networks [32], and for this technological awareness still needs to be raised among consumers [33].

3 Methodology

The data for this study was collected via an online questionnaire among fish consumers in Portugal. The questionnaire consisted of four broad sections: general information, fish consumption behavior, traceability of fish products, and trust towards traceable information. In the three last sections scales of 7 points were used. For consumer inclusion purposes, this questionnaire was made available in two languages: Portuguese (European) and English. Eligible respondents were considered as individuals with 18 years old or above, who had bought fish products in the previous year in Portugal. The questionnaire was built on Qualtrics online platform for surveys and pre-tested with 6 potential respondents of various age and education level groups. The feedback from the pre-test led to adjustments in terms of technical wording in the questionnaire.

The questionnaire was first made available online in May 2022 and the data collection took place between May 2022 and July 2022. The data collection used the snowball technique for spreading the questionnaire. The final data collected consisted of 417 filled-in questionnaires is important to note, that BCT was not mentioned anywhere in the questionnaire as a potential technology of choice, allowing a more unbiased consumer view on traceability importance for fish products, as BCT is just one of possible technologies that might bring traceability, but not an exclusive one.

Table 1. Study sample characteristics and frequencies.

Sample size = 417 responses		Frequency	Percentage (%)
Gender	Female	254	60,9%
	Male	161	38,6%
	Prefer not to say	2	0,5%
Age	18-19	108	25,9%
	30-39	105	25,2%
	40-49	84	20,1%
	50-59	70	16,8%
	60 and above	50	12%
Education	General secondary school	86	20,6%
	Technological specialization school	18	4,3%
	Bachelor's degree	144	34,5%
	Master's degree	114	27,3%
	Doctoral degree	55	13,3%
Fish consumption habits	100% fresh fish	71	17%
	About 75% fresh fish and 25% frozen fish	133	31,9%
	About 50% fresh fish and 50% frozen fish	95	22,8%
	About 25% fresh fish and 75% frozen fish	84	20,1%
	100% frozen fish	34	8,2%
Family size	1-2 persons	199	47,7%
	3-4 persons	189	45,3%
	5-6 persons	29	7%
Monthly spending on fish products	0-19.99 euros	78	18,7%
	20-39.99 euros	138	33,1%
	40-59.99 euros	108	25,9%
	60-79.99 euros	45	10,8%
	80-99.99 euros	21	5%
	100 euros and above	27	6,5%

4   Findings and Data Analysis

Table 1 shows the characterization of the respondents. The sample is quite evenly spread among age groups, resulting into 51,1% of individuals between 18 and 39 and 48,9% of individuals of 40 years and above. However, in terms of the highest education level obtained, this sample can be considered as an 'educated' one, where

75,1% of respondents have at least a Bachelor's degree. This can be explained by the snowballing technique that was applied–respondents were spreading the survey among colleagues/friends/family members with similar education background.

Regarding the fish consumption habits, the sample shows a tendency towards the consumption of more fresh fish rather than frozen. However, this can also be explained by the targeted country of the data collection–the access of Portuguese consumers to fresh fish from the ocean is an important factor that influences the habits of fish products' purchasing and consumption. Nevertheless, it is important to note, that pure frozen fish consumption, despite being low (only 8,2% of respondents), still exists, therefore fish products' consumption varies across the sample, where predominantly a mix of both fresh and frozen fish products leads.

The sample shows mostly families of up to 4 persons, which is quite natural for the current demographic situation in Portugal. Regarding the proportion of money spent per month on fish products, we can see that 77,7% spend up to 60 euros per month on fish products, which is not very high, but the overall low wages in Portugal does not allow considering this value insignificant. However, when read along with the fact that the sample is of more educated persons, i.e., persons with more income, it also signifies that, overall, the weight of expenditure in fish products in the overall income among the sample is not very high.

The interest in traceable information about fish products (Q1) and the impact of traceable information availability on purchasing decision (Q2) were evaluated using a Likert-like scale, with '1 = no interest at all/negative purchasing impact' and '7 = high interest/positive purchasing impact'. As can be seen in Table 2, on average, the respondents are moderately interested in traceability information for fish products, and it potentially brings an effect of a higher purchase intention for such traceable products. Nonetheless, the standard deviation shows that there are strong discrepancies in respondents' replies.

Table 2. Means and standard deviations of items in traceability for fish products.

Item	Mean (standard deviation)
1. Interest in having information about the origin and the processing stages of fish product(s) that are bought and the path they follow until being available at the point of sales	4.96 (1.95)
2. Impact of the availability of information about the origin and processing stages of fish product(s) on the purchasing decision	5.12 (1.73)

The Trust construct that was used for this survey consisted of three items regarding consumers' towards the correctness and authenticity of potentially traceable information (adapted from [34]) (Table 3). The items about trust were measured on a 7-point Likert-like scale, with '1 = Strongly disagree' and '7 = Strongly agree'. Prior to the questions regarding trust, respondents needed to identify the retailing chain of choice, thus keeping in mind the selected supermarket chain in the questions about trust (signified as 'supermarket X'). Figure 1 shows the histograms of the three questions: (a)

Table 3. Means, standard deviations and Cronbach's Alpha for trust construct questions.

Trust	Mean (standard deviation)	Cronbach's Alpha
I trust that if supermarket X provides information about the fish product(s), it can be traced back to the actually captured region/fish farm	4,87 (1.60)	0,90
I trust that if supermarket X provides information about the fish product(s) processing and origin, that information will be correct	4,99 (1.47)	
I trust that if supermarket X provides information about the fish product(s), it is authentic, which means it has not been falsified in any way	4,92 (1.48)	

trust that information can be traced back to the origins of the fish product; (b) trust that information provided is correct; (c) trust that information was not falsified.

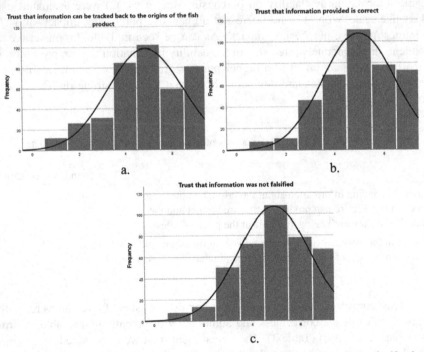

a.

b.

c.

Fig. 1. Histograms of trust construct questions: (a) trust that information can be tracked back to the origins of the fish product; (b) trust that information provided is correct; (c) trust that information was not falsified.

Table 4. Regression of trust variables with the availability of traceable information as a predictor.

Trust variables	R2	F	Significance
I trust that if the supermarket X provides information about the fish product(s), it can be tracked back to the actual captured region/fish farm	0,082	35,327	< 0, 001
I trust that if the supermarket X provides information about the fish product(s) processing and origin, that information will be correct	0,067	28,311	< 0, 001
I trust that if the supermarket X provides information about the fish product(s), it is authentic, which means it has not been falsified in any way	0,086	38,152	< 0, 001

To pursue the purpose of the study and explore the impact of the traceability feature of fish products towards trust, a regression was run. Item 2 from Table 2 was used as an independent variable and each of the three trust questions from Table 3 were used as dependent variables to check if there is any significance between the variables. The results are shown in Table 4. Keeping in mind that p-value ($p < 0.05$) was considered as a significant value, we can see that there is a positive and significant relationship between the availability of traceable information about fish products and the trust towards the information provided, therefore a higher trust towards such products. The graphical representation between the purchasing decision based on the availability of traceable information and the trust relationship can be found in Fig. 2. Here, Fig. 2 shows the following relationships: (a) the availability of traceable information and the trust that information can be traced back to the origin; (b) the availability of traceable information and trust in information correctness; (c) the availability of traceable information and trust that this information was not falsified. As can be seen in Fig. 2, the tendency of the availability of traceable information is associated with higher trust in the information that was provided, therefore, under the scope of the sample used, we can conclude that the level of trust rises with the availability of traceable information provided about the selected product.

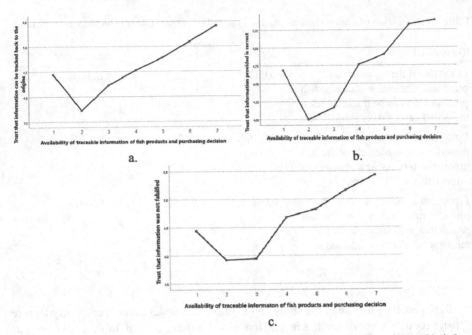

Fig. 2. Relationship between the purchasing decision based on the availability of traceable information and the trust: (a) the availability of traceable information and the trust that information can be traced back to the origin; (b) the availability of traceable information and trust into information correctness; (c) the availability of traceable information and trust that this information was not falsified

5 Discussion and Conclusions

Findings revealed real views of downstream SC players, final consumers, towards the role of traceable information about products and its potential value creation in terms of trust. At the early stages of considering the use of BCT it is crucial to see the value that this technology may bring to final consumers and understand if it is the most adequate solution.

The first important finding disclosed is the fish consumption behaviors of consumers– even in Portugal, where fresh fish is widely available, consumers still show habits of purchasing a mix of both fresh and frozen fish. This might also be explained by the type of fish that they buy, e.g. fish from the Northern seas that are not captured around Portugal might be cheaper to buy in a frozen package. [35] conducted a survey with simulations of various packages of frozen fish with BCT-based traceability option and found that only in the less familiar brand condition BCT label increases product quality perceptions to final consumers, whereas for familiar brands it does not directly influence the purchasing decision. In our study, the brand of the fish package was not mentioned, but rather respondents needed to choose one supermarket chain where they shop more often, thus here the case is more towards the trust and purchase intention for the supermarket of choice and not for a specific food brand.

Second, it is important to remember that participants of our survey were not clarified about the technology that would provide traceability information. It was done on purpose to reduce bias among those consumers that are familiar with BCT concept, for them not to be 'triggered' by the BCT application and show a higher interest in purchasing just based on the technology of choice. It was more important to understand the real value that consumers give to the traceable information–does it interest them and does it provide them added-value, if compared to those products that do not possess such option. As we saw in the previous section, the interest in traceable information for fish products in moderately high with the mean of 4,96 (SD 1.95) on the scale of 7 points maximum. This signifies that there is interest, but perhaps not all consumers realize how exactly the traceable information would be provided, thus might still be skeptical about having interest in such an option. The availability of traceable information and its consequent intention to purchase such a product shows a bit higher score with a mean of 5,12 (SD 1.73), which shows that the traceability option on a product will likely result in higher sales for supermarkets. In the case study conducted by [36], results showed that one of the main conditions for SCs to adopt BCT is related to the traceability awareness of the final consumers because the adoption is translated into higher costs for SC parties. Our study also highlights the importance to clarify how traceable information could be gained and which technologies are able to support it. We once again emphasize the fact that BCT is just a possible tool for providing traceable information, but the real importance is the value that consumers would potentially give to the traceable information provided, which was addressed in this study.

One of the key findings of this study is related to the fact that a positive and significant relationship was found between the availability of traceable information on fish products and the trust in the information provided. This means that the value that consumers give to traceability information comes out as an extra layer of trust that consumers associate with products, and consequently with the habitual supermarket chain. In Fig. 2 we can see that the high purchase intention based on the available traceable information results in higher trust towards the (1) confidence that information can be traced back; (2) correctness of provided information; and (3) reliance that the information is authentic and was not falsified. On a larger scale, [37] believes that BCT suits fisheries and the fishing industry because it motivates participating entities to demonstrate their compliance with laws and health regulations, resulting in increasing consumer demand based on trust in the product. Moreover, in our study, we assume that the trust in the information provided by the supermarket might positively affect the loyalty of consumers towards the supermarket chain, therefore brand loyalty increases. [38] believe that new technologies are reshaping not only the operational part, but also the dynamics of brand marketing, aiming at increasing brand trust and enhancing customer loyalty. Therefore, our study shows the potential that traceable information on a specific type of goods that are purchased in a habitual supermarket is adding value to final consumers and it may possibly result in increased loyalty to the supermarket chain.

This study explored the impact of the traceability feature of perishable products on the trust towards the product from the perspective of final consumers. It showed a significant and positive relationship between traceable information availability and trust towards such products. Therefore, this study provides a practical contribution for those SCs and food retailing chains that consider BCT pilots–here they can find scientifically analyzed perspectives of final consumers towards the potential availability of transparent traceable information. One of the limitations of this study is related to the sample used for the data collection–with the snowballing technique application, respondents were spreading the survey among their convenience circle, therefore in some characteristics (e.g. education) it resulted in being non-equally spread. Nonetheless, as using the information available at the points of sales is more likely to happen in younger (and therefore more educated in the Portuguese population) and the fact that more educated respondents have the tendency to have more income available to spend on these products, the sample is likely to have more adherence to the overall profile of costumers buying fish. Moreover, as the survey touched on the topic of the supermarket that consumers choose for their habitual food shopping, it would be interesting for future studies to add a brand loyalty construct and see if the traceable information actually results in increased brand loyalty. We hope that this study will serve as an impulse for future explorations of novel technology implementation for business practices and consumer experiences.

Acknowledgement. This work was supported by EEA Grants Blue Growth Programme (Call #5), Project PT-INNOVATION-0069–Fish2Fork.

References

1. Gupta, A., et al.: Factors influencing implementation, sustainability and scalability of healthy food retail interventions: a systematic review of reviews. Nutrients **14**(2), 294 (2022)
2. Hay, C., et al.: Comparing cross-cultural differences in perception of drinkable yoghurt by Chinese and New Zealand European consumers. Int. Dairy J. **113**, 104901 (2021)
3. Han, W., Huang, Y., Hughes, M., Zhang, M.: The trade-off between trust and distrust in supply chain collaboration. Ind. Mark. Manage. **98**, 93–104 (2021)
4. Treiblmaier, H.: The impact of the blockchain on the supply chain: a theory-based research framework and a call for action. Supply Chain Manag. Int. J. **23**(6), 545–559 (2018)
5. Sunny, J., Undralla, N., Pillai, V.M.: Supply chain transparency through blockchain-based traceability: an overview with demonstration. Comput. Ind. Eng. **150**, 106895 (2020)
6. Montecchi, M., Plangger, K., Etter, M.: It's real, trust me! Establishing supply chain provenance using blockchain. Bus. Horiz. **62**(3), 283–293 (2019)
7. Centobelli, P., Cerchione, R., Esposito, E., Oropallo, E.: Surfing blockchain wave, or drowning? Shaping the future of distributed ledgers and decentralized technologies. Technol. Forecast. Soc. Chang. **165**, 120463 (2021)
8. Shahid, A., Almogren, A., Javaid, N., Al-Zahrani, F.A., Zuair, M., Alam, M.: Blockchain-based agri-food supply chain: a complete solution. IEEE Access **8**, 69230–69243 (2020)
9. Al-Rakhami, M.S., Al-Mashari, M.: A Blockchain-based trust model for the internet of things supply chain management. Sensors **21**(5), 1759 (2021)
10. Feng, H., Wang, X., Duan, Y., Zhang, J., Zhang, X.: Applying blockchain technology to improve agri-food traceability: a review of development methods, benefits and challenges. J. Clean. Prod. **260**, 121031 (2020)
11. Kayikci, Y., Subramanian, N., Dora, M., Bhatia, M.S.: Food supply chain in the era of Industry 4.0: Blockchain technology implementation opportunities and impediments from the perspective of people, process, performance, and technology. Prod. Plan. Control **33**(2–3), 301–321 (2022)

12. Tan, A., Gligor, D., Ngah, A.: Applying blockchain for halal food traceability. Int J Log Res Appl 25(6), 947–964 (2022)
13. Wang, O., Scrimgeour, F.: Consumer adoption of blockchain food traceability: effects of innovation-adoption characteristics, expertise in food traceability and blockchain technology, and segmentation. Br. Food J. 125(7), 2493–2513 (2022)
14. Dasaklis, T.K., Casino, F., Patsakis, C.: A traceability and auditing framework for electronic equipment reverse logistics based on blockchain: the case of mobile phones. In: 2020 11th International Conference on Information, Intelligence, Systems and Applications, IEEE, pp. 1–7 (2020)
15. Hossain, M.M., et al.: Thwarting counterfeit electronics by blockchain. IEEE Blockchain (2022)
16. Bullón Pérez, J.J., Queiruga-Dios, A., Gayoso Martínez, V., Martín del Rey, Á.: Traceability of ready-to-wear clothing through blockchain technology. Sustainability 12(18), 7491 (2020)
17. Agrawal, T.K., Kumar, V., Pal, R., Wang, L., Chen, Y.: Blockchain-based framework for supply chain traceability: a case example of textile and clothing industry. Comput. Ind. Eng. 154, 107130 (2021)
18. Fawcett, S.E., Jones, S.L., Fawcett, A.M.: Supply chain trust: the catalyst for collaborative innovation. Bus. Horiz. 55(2), 163–178 (2012)
19. Ostern, N.: Do you trust a trust-free transaction? Toward a trust framework model for blockchain technology. In: 39th International Conference on Information Systems, San Francisco (2018)
20. Tian, F.: A supply chain traceability system for food safety based on HACCP, blockchain & internet of things. In: IEEE 2017 International Conference on Service Systems and Service Management (2017)
21. Haq, I., Esuka, O.M.: Blockchain technology in pharmaceutical industry to prevent counterfeit drugs. Int. J. Comput. Appl. 180(25), 8–12 (2018)
22. Sikorski, J.J., Haughton, J., Kraft, M.: Blockchain technology in the chemical industry: machine-to-machine electricity market. Appl. Energy 195, 234–246 (2017)
23. Zhou, X., Kraft, M.: Blockchain technology in the chemical industry. Annu. Rev. Chem. Biomol. Eng. 13, 347–371 (2022)
24. Ajao, L.A., Agajo, J., Adedokun, E.A., Karngong, L.: Crypto hash algorithm-based blockchain technology for managing decentralized ledger database in oil and gas industry. J Multidisciplinary Int. J. 2(3), 300–325 (2019)
25. Ferreira, J.C., Martins, A.L.: Building a community of users for open market energy. Energies 11(9), 2330 (2018)
26. Devine, M.T., Cuffe, P.: Blockchain electricity trading under demurrage. IEEE Trans. Smart Grid 10(2), 2323–2325 (2019)
27. Kamble, S.S., Gunasekaran, A., Sharma, R.: Modeling the blockchain enabled traceability in agriculture supply chain. Int. J. Inf. Manage. 52, 101967 (2020)
28. Zhang, J.: Deploying Blockchain Technology in the Supply Chain. Blockchain and Distributed Ledger Technology (DLT) [Working Title] (2019)
29. Zhao, G., et al.: Blockchain technology in agri-food value chain management: a synthesis of applications, challenges and future research directions. Comput. Ind. 109, 83–99 (2019)
30. Sternberg, H.S., Hofmann, E., Roeck, D.: The Struggle is real: insights from a supply chain blockchain case. J. Bus. Logist. 42(1), 71–87 (2021)
31. Sander, F., Semeijn, J., Mahr, D.: The acceptance of blockchain technology in meat traceability and transparency. Br. Food J. 120(9), 2066–2079 (2018)
32. Chiarini, A., Compagnucci, L.: Blockchain, data protection and P2P energy trading: a review on legal and economic challenges. Sustainability 14(23), 16305 (2022)
33. Cozzio, C., Viglia, G., Lemarie, L., Cerutti, S.: Toward an integration of blockchain technology in the food supply chain. J. Bus. Res. 162, 113909 (2023)

34. Dionysis, S., Chesney, T., McAuley, D.: Examining the influential factors of consumer purchase intentions for blockchain traceable coffee using the theory of planned behaviour. Br. Food J. **124**(12), 4304–4322 (2022)
35. Treiblmaier, H., Garaus, M.: Using blockchain to signal quality in the food supply chain: the impact on consumer purchase intentions and the moderating effect of brand familiarity. Int. J. Inf. Manage. **68**, 102514 (2023)
36. Fan, Z.P., Wu, X.Y., Cao, B.B.: Considering the traceability awareness of consumers: should the supply chain adopt the blockchain technology? Ann. Oper. Res. **309**, 1–24 (2022)
37. Probst, W.N.: How emerging data technologies can increase trust and transparency in fisheries. ICES J. Mar. Sci. **77**(4), 1286–1294 (2020)
38. Rejeb, A., Keogh, J.G., Treiblmaier, H.: How blockchain technology can benefit marketing: Six pending research areas. Front. Blockchain **3**, 3 (2020)

Networks

Federated Learning for Drowsiness Detection in Connected Vehicles

William Lindskog[1,2(✉)], Valentin Spannagl[2], and Christian Prehofer[1,2]

[1] DENSO Automotive Deutschland GmbH, Freisinger Str. 21, 85386 Eching,
Germany
w.lindskog@eu.denso.com
[2] Technical University of Munich, Munich, Germany

Abstract. Ensuring driver readiness poses challenges, yet driver monitoring systems can assist in determining the driver's state. By observing
visual cues, such systems recognize various behaviors and associate them
with specific conditions. For instance, yawning or eye blinking can indicate driver drowsiness. Consequently, an abundance of distributed data is
generated for driver monitoring. Employing machine learning techniques,
such as driver drowsiness detection, presents a potential solution. However, transmitting the data to a central machine for model training is
impractical due to the large data size and privacy concerns. Conversely,
training on a single vehicle would limit the available data and likely
result in inferior performance. To address these issues, we propose a
federated learning framework for drowsiness detection within a vehicular network, leveraging the YawDD dataset. Our approach achieves an
accuracy of 99.2%, demonstrating its promise and comparability to conventional deep learning techniques. Lastly, we show how our model scales
using various number of federated clients.

Keywords: Federated Learning · Driver Drowsiness · Connected
Vehicles

1 Introduction

Road accidents are predominantly caused by human errors, accounting for 90%
of incidents in the United States in 2015 [7]. While drivers and passengers benefit from the safety features of vehicles, vulnerable road users such as cyclists
and pedestrians remain at greater risk. Drowsy driving is a prevalent issue, with
a significant number of accidents attributed to this cause. The vision of fully
automated vehicles offers potential solutions to address the problem of driver
drowsiness. However, achieving fully automated driving remains a future aspira-
tion, and the current trajectory suggests the adoption of shared driver-machine
models [9]. For complex driving scenarios, the driver is required to assume control
of the vehicle, necessitating a state of readiness.

Driver readiness is contingent upon various factors and influenced by the
driver's state [18]. Automotive companies have developed different types of

© ICST Institute for Computer Sciences, Social Informatics and Telecommunications Engineering 2024
Published by Springer Nature Switzerland AG 2024. All Rights Reserved
A. L. Martins et al. (Eds.): INTSYS 2023, LNICST 540, pp. 165–178, 2024.
https://doi.org/10.1007/978-3-031-49379-9_9

Driver Monitoring Systems (DMS) to enhance road safety [11,23]. These systems analyze driver behavior and appearance to detect signs of hazardous conditions, such as distraction or drowsiness, indicating when the driver may not be prepared to assume control [5]. However, interpreting these signs can be challenging and subject to multiple interpretations. Consequently, Driver Monitoring encompasses several domains, with Driver Drowsiness Detection being one of them.

Various approaches have been employed to detect driver fatigue. Direct physiological measurements, involving the use of body sensors to track metrics like heart rate, have yielded promising results. Another approach utilizes vehicle sensors to monitor parameters like steering wheel angle, detecting anomalous patterns [21]. A third approach combines direct assessment of driver behavior with non-intrusive sensors. Optical algorithms, coupled with Deep Learning techniques, extract the driver's state from camera recordings, demonstrating improved success rates [10]. However, in-vehicle Driver Monitoring presents challenges due to the large video data size and privacy constraints.

Federated Learning (FL), a Deep Learning methodology, offers a privacy-aware solution to train Machine Learning models on distributed data. By only transmitting the model parameters through the federated network, rather than raw data, FL reduces message sizes and minimizes the potential attack surface for adversarial attacks. FL has started to see real-world implementations, mainly in medicine [20], but is being applied in other industries such as automotive [17].

In order to tackle these challenges, our study introduces an FL framework tailored for drowsiness detection in a vehicular network, employing the YawDD dataset. Remarkably, our approach attains a remarkable accuracy rate of 99.2%, showcasing its potential and comparability to conventional deep learning methods. Our main contributions are:

- Federated Learning framework for driver drowsiness detection using YawDD dataset for processing single frames and sequences.
- With our evaluation, we show how model performance scales when increasing the number of federated clients.
- We achieve great results of 99.2% when classifying normal driving, talking and yawning driver.

2   Related Work

Driver Drowsiness Detection is an actively researched area, and numerous studies have been conducted to address this critical issue. [1] developed a benchmark implementation using the YawDD dataset, focusing on in-vehicle applications. However, the accuracy of their model is limited. It is evident that there is room for improvement in achieving higher detection accuracies for driver drowsiness.

In recent works, [22] proposed a Convolutional Neural Network (CNN) architecture on the YawDD dataset, utilizing ensemble learning to achieve an impressive accuracy of approximately 99%. [19] employed a simple CNN with dropout technique, obtaining an average accuracy of 96% on YawDD by focusing on the eyes and mouth and using labels of open or closed states for these facial features. [12] introduced the PERCLOSE formulation, utilizing the eye area to determine drowsiness on the YawDD dataset. However, this approach encounters challenges when the driver's face or eyes are not detectable. [2] explored the application of Recurrent Neural Networks (RNNs) on the YawDD dataset, achieving an accuracy of 96%.

The aforementioned studies predominantly employ conventional deep learning techniques, such as ensemble learning, CNNs, and RNNs, to attain high accuracies in driver drowsiness detection. However, the integration of federated learning in the driver monitoring field remains underrepresented. [26] presented one of the few works focusing on drowsiness detection using FL. They proposed a two-stage approach, utilizing the PERCLOSE method and another drowsiness metric called FOM, to identify fatigue. The application of the federated learning strategy called Dynamic Averaging yielded promising results, and the performance evaluation was conducted on the NTHU dataset. [27] also used the NTHU dataset and the YawDD dataset. They present a privacy-preserving federated transfer learning method called PFTL-DDD for detecting driver drowsiness. The proposed method uses fine-tuning transfer learning on the FL system's initial model and a CKKS-based security protocol to encrypt exchanged parameters, protecting driver privacy. The results show that the method is more accurate and efficient compared to conventional FL methods and reduces communication costs. Nevertheless, they do not include how many clients the evaluate their models with. [16] also proposed a federated transfer learning model, but applied it to construction workers and fatigue monitoring. Lastly, [25] proposed an asynchronous federated scheme in internet of vehicles. They evaluate their model EHAFL on YawDD dataset and show how their model can reduce communication costs with 98% with a slight decrease in accuracy.

While conventional deep learning techniques have demonstrated success in driver drowsiness detection, the potential of FL in this domain remains largely untapped. Moreover, the studies that have investigated FL for DMS do not show how performance scales when number of participating clients is increased.

3   YawDD Dataset

The YawDD dataset, as documented by [1], comprises video recordings of drivers exhibiting various behaviors, with particular emphasis on yawning as a key indicator of drowsiness. To establish a baseline, normal driving videos were included to depict drivers in an alert state, free from drowsiness. Another category of videos captured drivers engaged in conversation. In a binary classification task involving yawning and normal driving, the act of mouth opening serves as an indication of yawning behavior. However, the introduction of talking data poses a challenge as this behavior can no longer be solely relied upon. The YawDD dataset consists of two subsets: one containing 322 videos and the other with 29 videos. The larger subset captures drivers from a rear mirror perspective, while the smaller subset features a camera placed in front of the driver on the dashboard, see Fig. 1. A total of 107 drivers (57 male and 50 female) were recorded, with each driver providing at least three videos for each behavior category.

Additionally, the YawDD dataset includes recordings with occlusions such as sunglasses or scarves.

Fig. 1. Samples from the YawDD dataset in two perspectives. Top: Rear mirror. Bottom: Dash [1]

3.1 Data Preprocessing

Given that the provided labels in the YawDD dataset were different, encompassing a few seconds before and after the actual yawning event in a yawning video, we performed frame-level labeling of the entire dataset to ensure precise classification for this study. Analyzing the dataset is crucial to identify its properties. The dataset is divided into two subsets based on camera perspectives: rear mirror (320 items) and dash (29 items). Despite both perspectives being realistic, the larger rear mirror set is selected for further analysis. The file names reveal a potential issue: some videos have dual labels. For instance, a sample video includes footage of talking and yawning. Upon reviewing sample videos, labeling appears more problematic as a video labeled "Yawning" contains a yawning event within normal driving. The drivers are throughout the videos driving normally, talking or yawning; thus we tackle a 3-class classification task (Fig. 2).

Fig. 2. Sample includes two categories.

Resizing is the subsequent step for data reduction while preserving crucial information. The camera used in [1] captures YawDD data at a resolution of 640×480 pixels, resulting in 307,200 pixel values per color layer. In the RGB format, this equates to 921,600 values per frame. Deep learning memory consumption scales with input data size, so minimizing input sample size is preferable. Lowering resolution causes image structures to blur. At 80×80 pixels, objects become indistinct, such as glasses merging with the eye structure. Resolutions above 160×160 pixels are recommended, with 320×320 already offering improvement compared to the original. The last step in frame pre-processing involves color representation. Since the driver drowsiness detection approach relies on behavioral measures, driver actions play a vital role. Yawning and eye blinking, identified as indicators, are not influenced by color representation. Grayscaling converts RGB to grayscale, significantly reducing data size.

4   Method for Driver Drowsiness

In this section, deep learning for spatial-temporal data and the tools applied in our study.

4.1   Deep Learning and Spatial-Temporal Data

Sequential data as input for the neural network includes the concept of spatial-temporal data. Images can be considered spatial data, where pixels correspond to locations, areas, and distances. When single frames act as input, the neural network relies on spatial information, and the task is typically image classification using CNNs. However, in YawDD, the original data is in video form, introducing temporal information. The order of frames in a video is not arbitrary, and the relation between consecutive frames is temporal. With sequences of frames, we have spatial-temporal information, and the task becomes sequence or video classification. Utilizing spatial-temporal information is desirable as it preserves an additional dimension of information. For sequential data, RNNs are a specialized variation of deep learning. [8] used an RNN extension of CNNs known as 3D CNNs, which extend CNNs to the third dimension, representing time. They achieved promising results, outperforming other methods like LSTMs. There is still nevertheless a discussion whether to use 2D or 3D CNNs for video processing [6]. Using single frames instead of sequences can help overcome hardware constraints and reduce the number of parameters to consider. Processing single frames could however result in a loss of information. Thus, we evaluate both 2D and 3D CNN on YawDD dataset.

4.2   Federated Learning Tools

Our FL architecture was implemented using the Flower framework [4] in conjunction with PyTorch. The Flower framework provides three key scripts: the *server* or *main* script, responsible for managing the federated training process; the *client* script, which handles local training and client-side evaluation; and the *utils* script, which incorporates essential functionalities such as data loading. Figure 3 depicts the Flower core framework architecture, how server and clients communicate and the possibility to simulate clients using a built-in virtual engine.

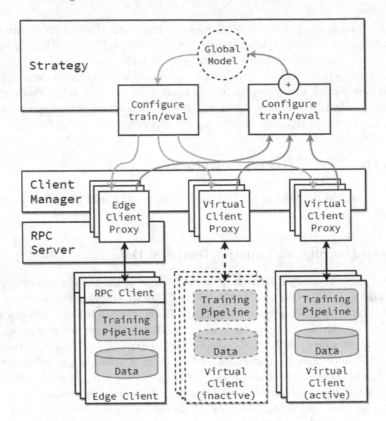

Fig. 3. Flower core framework architecture [4].

PyTorch offers a straightforward approach to load an image dataset from a folder. The *ImageFolder* function facilitates the loading and transformation of image samples along with their corresponding labels. Transformations are composed within the *transform* object, which includes operations such as grayscale conversion, conversion to Tensor format, normalization, and standardization. The label information is inferred from the folder structure, as the dataset folder comprises three subfolders for each class.

After loading the entire dataset into a variable, the next step involves splitting and assigning the subsets. We utilize the *random_split* function, which randomly permutes the dataset and splits it according to the specified length array. To ensure reproducibility, the random permutation is generated using a seeded number. Importantly, the randomization process respects the proportions of the label collections, guaranteeing that both splits maintain the same class distribution.

5   Evaluation and Results

The experiments were conducted on the Ubuntu distribution, which is built on the Linux operating system. Specifically, Ubuntu version 22.04 was utilized for this study. The hardware setup consisted of an AMD seventh-generation processor and a NVIDIA GeForce RTX 3070 graphics card.

At first, the loaded dataset size is controlled and the size 127.887 matches the number of files in the dataset folder. The 90:10 split is validated with a training set, containing 90% of the data, and a test set, which possesses 10% of the data. We also specify relevant hyperparameters before training. We search for optimal values for these and illustrate our results using the best choices found. The hyperparameter search space can be found in Table 1. Moreover, we use FedAvg [14] as a federated strategy when aggregating the client updates at the server. Adam [13] is set as an optimizer.

Table 1. Hyperparameter search space. `sequence_length` and `frame_skipping` parameters are only relevant for 3D-CNNs.

Hyperparameter	Search Space Values
`learning_rate`	$\{0.0001, 0.001, 0.002, 0.005, 0.01, 0.1\}$
`momentum`	$\{0.01, 0.02, 0.05, 0.1, 0.2, 0.5, 0.9\}$
`batch_size`	$\{2, 8, 16, 32, 64, 128\}$
`weight_decay`	$\{0.0001, 0.001, 0.002, 0.005, 0.01, 0.1\}$
`nbr_clients`	$\{2, 4, 8, 16, 20, 40\}$
`sequence_length`	$\{8, 10, 12, 14, 26, 18, 20\}$
`frame_skipping`	$\{2, 3, 4, 5, 6, 8, 10, 12\}$

5.1   3D-CNN and Video Sequence Processing

Based on [8] work, the hyperparameter values were adopted and a model was constructed as in Fig. 4. The sequence length was found to influence the results and an initial sequence length of 16 was used, but other initializations did not

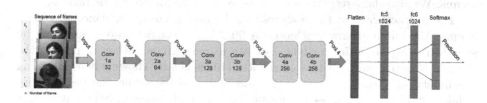

Fig. 4. 3D-CNN architecture as in [8]

improve performance. Frame skipping, introduced to enhance temporal information, showed no effect, with a commonly used frame skipping value of five. The batch size, limited by memory, was set to 2 due to the sequence length. The learning rate was the only parameter that showed some change, with smaller rates resulting in slower convergence but reduced fluctuations. The best values for frame skipping and sequence length were used after hyperparameter tuning. Highest accuracy achieved was 90.1% and processing was slow. To improve the approach and achieve better results, the process can be streamlined and simplified. Using single frames instead of sequences can help overcome hardware constraints and reduce the number of parameters to consider (Fig. 4).

5.2   2D-CNN and Image Processing

The adopted model is a 2D-Convolutional Neural Network (CNN) for image classification, in which we process the videos frame-by-frame. We draw inspiration from the work of [8] when constructing the 2D-CNN and the architecture can be found in Fig. 5.

```
Net(
   (conv1): Conv2d(1, 6, kernel_size=(5, 5), stride=(1, 1))
   (pool): MaxPool2d(kernel_size=2, stride=2, padding=0, dilation=1, ceil_mode=False)
   (conv2): Conv2d(6, 16, kernel_size=(5, 5), stride=(1, 1))
   (fc1): Linear(in_features=94864, out_features=120, bias=True)
   (fc2): Linear(in_features=120, out_features=84, bias=True)
   (fc3): Linear(in_features=84, out_features=3, bias=True)
)
...
criterion = nn.CrossEntropyLoss().to(device)
optimizer = torch.optim.SGD(net.parameters(), lr=0.01, momentum=0.9, weight_decay=1e-4)
```

Fig. 5. PyTorch code for convolutional neural network we use. The parameter values for the optimizer are initial values.

We thereafter evaluate our model using the mentioned pre-processing steps on a frame-by-frame basis. The task is a 3-class classification task in which we seek to correctly classify drivers driving normally with closed mouth, drivers talking, and drivers yawning. We illustrate our results using test accuracy and categorical cross-entropy loss. The values illustrated in Fig. 6 and 7 are averaged scores over 5 runs. We also show respective significance interval for both illustrations.

The test accuracy in Fig. 6 shows that highest accuracy is achieved using 2 clients. Maximum accuracy achieved is 99.2% and prediction outcomes can be seen in Fig. 8. We notice a slight decrease in performance when increasing the number of participating federated clients. This is clearly shown when increasing the number of clients from 16 → 20 and 20 → 40. However, the performance is fairly stable between 2 → 16 clients. The optimal choice of hyperparameters seems to be a low learning rate, weight decay, number of participating federated clients and batch size. A larger momentum gives better results.

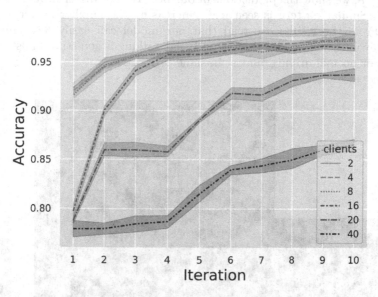

Fig. 6. Test accuracy for various number of clients. Accuracy is shown with significant intervals, averaged over 5 runs.

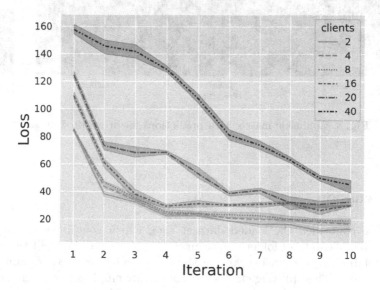

Fig. 7. Test categorical cross-entropy loss for various number of clients. Accuracy is shown with significant intervals, averaged over 5 runs.

In Fig. 8, we show the predictions of our best run for driver drowsiness using 2 clients. Similar pattern is seen when increasing the number of participating clients. From the results, we read that our model can easily distinguish the classes yawning and normal driving and that talking is sometimes mistaken for yawning or normal driving, almost in same proportion.

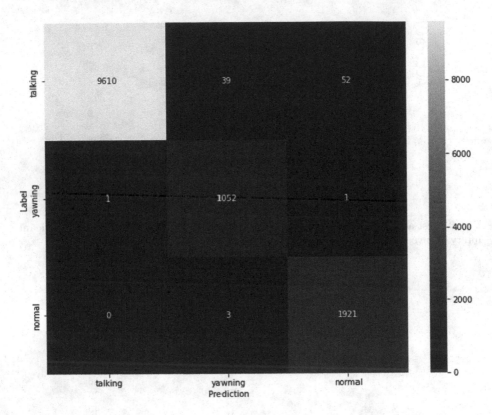

Fig. 8. Confusion matrix with predictions for driver drowsiness.

6   Discussion

Firstly, we controlled the loaded dataset size, which contained 127,887 files, ensuring that the dataset folder was accurately represented. We split the dataset into a training set, comprising 90% of the data, and a test set, containing the remaining 10%. This splitting strategy is commonly employed in machine learning to evaluate the generalization performance of models. By using this approach, we can assess how well our model performs on unseen data. To ensure optimal performance, we conducted a hyperparameter search to identify the best values for the relevant parameters.

In our experiments, we employed the FedAvg FL strategy, as proposed by [14]. This strategy enables efficient aggregation of client updates at the server while preserving data privacy. In other studies, researchers can come to evaluate other federated strategies such as FedProx [15] which could serve the area of personalized FL [24] better in case one seeks to split unique user data to individual clients. We first evaluate our 3D-CNN on YawDD data and achieve 90.1% accuracy. This is not as good as results in other studies. As mentioned, using single frames for processing can help overcome hardware limitations and reduce the number of parameters considered.

For evaluation purposes, we applied the specified pre-processing steps on a frame-by-frame basis. Our task involved a 3-class classification, where the objective was to accurately classify drivers engaged in normal driving with a closed mouth, drivers who were talking, and drivers who were yawning. To assess the performance of our model, we measured the test accuracy and the categorical cross-entropy loss. The results, shown in Fig. 6 and Fig. 7, respectively, were averaged over 5 runs to account for potential variations. Analyzing the test accuracy results presented in Fig. 6, we observe that the highest accuracy of 99.2% was achieved when using 2 clients. This finding indicates that a smaller number of participating federated clients yielded superior performance. However, we notice a slight decrease in accuracy when the number of clients increased from 16 to 20 and from 20 to 40. This decline in performance suggests that as more clients participate, the aggregation process becomes more challenging, potentially due to increased heterogeneity or more likely, size of local datasets becoming too small. With smaller local datasets, the likelihood of it including sufficient and representative data decreases and thus we may experience an increase in heterogeneity. Heterogeneous datasets or non-identical and independent (non-IID) datasets are prevalent in FL and researchers have studied this extensively [28].

Interestingly, the performance remained relatively stable when the number of clients ranged from 2 to 16. This observation implies that a moderate number of participating clients is optimal for the task at hand. To further improve the model's performance, we identified several key hyperparameters that played a crucial role. These include a low learning rate, weight decay, number of participating federated clients, and batch size. Additionally, we found that a larger momentum value yielded better results, indicating the importance of effectively leveraging momentum during the optimization process.

To gain more insights into the classification results, we analyzed the confusion matrix shown in Fig. 8. This matrix represents the predictions obtained from our best run using 2 clients. Notably, similar patterns were observed when increasing the number of participating clients. From the confusion matrix, we deduce that our model can effectively distinguish between yawning and normal driving classes. However, there is a notable confusion between the talking class and the yawning class, as well as between the talking class and the normal driving class. These misclassifications suggest that drivers who are talking exhibit certain facial movements or patterns that resemble both yawning and normal driving. Since we are operating on a frame-per-frame level, there will be certain cases where the decision boundary is "blurry", i.e., cases which look alike but belong to different classes. Further investigation into the distinguishing features between these classes could potentially lead to improvements in the model's performance. To extend this study, future research could focus on exploring additional feature engineering techniques or investigating more advanced models to further enhance the classification accuracy. Additionally, collecting more diverse and extensive datasets could provide a more comprehensive evaluation of the model's performance in real-world scenarios.

One interesting area of research is the field of Personalized FL [24]. We see that researchers can apply learnings from this field onto the problem of accurate DMS. This includes investigating different model architectures and aggregating algorithms e.g. FL with personalization layers [3].

7   Conclusion

While most of the vehicle control is handled by machines, drivers still need to be prepared to handle complex situations. Overcoming the challenges of ensuring driver readiness is crucial, and driver monitoring systems play a significant role in assessing the driver's state. These systems utilize visual cues to recognize various behaviors and associate them with specific conditions, such as drowsiness indicated by yawning or eye blinking. Consequently, an abundance of distributed data is generated for driver monitoring.

To address the task of driver drowsiness detection, machine learning techniques, such as the one employed in this study, offer a potential solution. However, transmitting the vast amount of data to a central machine for model training is impractical due to privacy concerns and the sheer size of the data. On the other hand, training the model solely on a single vehicle would limit the available data and likely result in inferior performance.

To overcome these challenges, we propose an FL framework within a vehicular network for drowsiness detection, utilizing the YawDD dataset. Our approach demonstrates impressive accuracy, achieving a rate of 99.2%. This result highlights the promise and comparability of our method to conventional deep learning techniques. Our main contributions are:

- Federated Learning framework for driver drowsiness detection using YawDD dataset for processing single frames and sequences.
- With our evaluation, we show how model performance scales when increasing the number of federated clients.
- We achieve great results of 99.2% when classifying normal driving, talking and yawning driver.

References

1. Abtahi, S., Omidyeganeh, M., Shirmohammadi, S., Hariri, B.: YawDD: a yawning detection dataset. In: Proceedings of the 5th ACM Multimedia Systems Conference, pp. 24–28 (2014)
2. Al-sudani, A.R.: Yawn based driver fatigue level prediction. In: Proceedings of 35th International Conferernce, vol. 69, pp. 372–382 (2020)
3. Arivazhagan, M.G., Aggarwal, V., Singh, A.K., Choudhary, S.: Federated learning with personalization layers. arXiv preprint arXiv:1912.00818 (2019)
4. Beutel, D.J., et al.: Flower: a friendly federated learning research framework. arXiv preprint arXiv:2007.14390 (2020)
5. Cancello Tortora, G., Casini, M., Lagna, A., Marino, M., Vecchio, A.: Detection of distracted driving: a smartphone-based approach. In: Martins, A.L., Ferreira, J.C., Kocian, A., Tokkozhina, U. (eds.) Intelligent Transport Systems, INTSYS 2022. LNICST, vol. 486, pp. 157–165. Springer, Cham (2023). https://doi.org/10.1007/978-3-031-30855-0_11
6. Chen, C.F.R., et al.: Deep analysis of CNN-based spatio-temporal representations for action recognition. In: Proceedings of the IEEE/CVF Conference on Computer Vision and Pattern Recognition, pp. 6165–6175 (2021)
7. Dingus, T.A., et al.: Driver crash risk factors and prevalence evaluation using naturalistic driving data. Proc. Natl. Acad. Sci. 113(10), 2636–2641 (2016)
8. Ed-Doughmi, Y., Idrissi, N., Hbali, Y.: Real-time system for driver fatigue detection based on a recurrent neuronal network. J. Imaging 6(3), 8 (2020)
9. Fridman, L.: Human-centered autonomous vehicle systems: principles of effective shared autonomy. arXiv preprint arXiv:1810.01835 (2018)
10. Fridman, L., Langhans, P., Lee, J., Reimer, B.: Driver gaze region estimation without use of eye movement. IEEE Intell. Syst. 31(3), 49–56 (2016)
11. Halin, A., Verly, J.G., Van Droogenbroeck, M.: Survey and synthesis of state of the art in driver monitoring. Sensors 21(16), 5558 (2021)
12. Junaedi, S., Akbar, H.: Driver drowsiness detection based on face feature and PERCLOS. J. Phys: Conf. Ser. 1090, 012037 (2018)
13. Kingma, D.P., Ba, J.: Adam: a method for stochastic optimization. arXiv preprint arXiv:1412.6980 (2014)
14. Konečný, J., McMahan, H.B., Yu, F.X., Richtárik, P., Suresh, A.T., Bacon, D.: Federated learning: strategies for improving communication efficiency. arXiv preprint arXiv:1610.05492 (2016)
15. Li, T., Sahu, A.K., Zaheer, M., Sanjabi, M., Talwalkar, A., Smith, V.: Federated optimization in heterogeneous networks. Proc. Mach. Learn. Syst. 2, 429–450 (2020)
16. Li, X., Chi, H., Lu, W., Xue, F., Zeng, J., Li, C.Z.: Federated transfer learning enabled smart work packaging for preserving personal image information of construction worker. Autom. Constr. 128, 103738 (2021)
17. Lindskog, W., Prehofer, C.: Federated learning for tabular data using TabNet: a vehicular use-case. In: 2022 IEEE 18th International Conference on Intelligent Computer Communication and Processing (ICCP), pp. 105–111. IEEE (2022)
18. Mioch, T., Kroon, L., Neerincx, M.A.: Driver readiness model for regulating the transfer from automation to human control. In: Proceedings of the 22nd International Conference on Intelligent User Interfaces, pp. 205–213 (2017)
19. Rajkar, A., Kulkarni, N., Raut, A.: Driver drowsiness detection using deep learning. In: Iyer, B., Ghosh, D., Balas, V.E. (eds.) Applied Information Processing Systems.

AISC, vol. 1354, pp. 73–82. Springer, Singapore (2022). https://doi.org/10.1007/978-981-16-2008-9_7

20. Rieke, N., et al.: The future of digital health with federated learning. npj Digit. Med. **3**(1), 119 (2020)

21. Sahayadhas, A., Sundaraj, K., Murugappan, M.: Detecting driver drowsiness based on sensors: a review. Sensors **12**(12), 16937–16953 (2012)

22. Salman, R.M., Rashid, M., Roy, R., Ahsan, M.M., Siddique, Z.: Driver drowsiness detection using ensemble convolutional neural networks on YawDD. arXiv preprint arXiv:2112.10298 (2021)

23. Sikander, G., Anwar, S.: Driver fatigue detection systems: a review. IEEE Trans. Intell. Transp. Syst. **20**(6), 2339–2352 (2018)

24. Tan, A.Z., Yu, H., Cui, L., Yang, Q.: Towards personalized federated learning. IEEE Trans. Neural Netw. Learn. Syst. 1–17 (2022)

25. Yang, Z., Zhang, X., Wu, D., Wang, R., Zhang, P., Wu, Y.: Efficient asynchronous federated learning research in the internet of vehicles. IEEE IoT J. **10**, 7737–7748 (2022)

26. Zafar, A., Prehofer, C., Cheng, C.H.: Federated learning for driver status monitoring. In: 2021 IEEE International Intelligent Transportation Systems Conference (ITSC), pp. 1463–1469. IEEE (2021)

27. Zhang, L., Saito, H., Yang, L., Wu, J.: Privacy-preserving federated transfer learning for driver drowsiness detection. IEEE Access **10**, 80565–80574 (2022)

28. Zhao, Y., Li, M., Lai, L., Suda, N., Civin, D., Chandra, V.: Federated learning with non-IID data. arXiv preprint arXiv:1806.00582 (2018)

Network Robustness Improvement Based on Alternative Paths Consideration

Jean-Claude Lebègue[1]([⊠]), Daniel Delahaye[2], and Jacco Hoekstra[3]

[1] Sopra Steria, Colomiers, France
jean-claude.lebegue@soprasteria.com
[2] Ecole Nationale de L'Aviation Civile, Toulouse, France
daniel@recherche.enac.fr
[3] TU Delft, Delft, The Netherlands
J.M.Hoekstra@tudelft.nl

Abstract. Many transportation networks have complex infrastructures (road, rail, airspace, etc.). The quality of service in air transportation depends on weather conditions. Technical failures of the aircraft, bad weather conditions, strike of the company's staff cause delays and disrupt traffic. How can the robustness of such networks be improved? Improving the robustness of air transportation would reduce the cascading delays between airports and improve the passenger journey. Many studies have been done to find critical links and nodes, but not so many analyze the paths. In this paper, we propose a new method to measure network robustness based on alternative paths. Besides improving the robustness of the French (respectively Turkish Airlines and European) low-cost flight network by 19% (respectively 16% and 6.6%), the method attempts to show the relevance of analyzing the network vulnerability from a path-based approach.

Keywords: Robust network · Topology · Passenger-centric model · Floyd-Warshall algorithm · Simulated annealing · Transport

1 Introduction

The European high-level vision aims for a 4-h door-to-door complete journey for 90% of travelers within Europe by 2050. It also forecasts that the number of commercial flights will reach 25 million. The topology of the airspace network should change to accommodate these new flights. As the number of flights on the network increases, the number of disruptions and delays will also increase if the current network structure remains unchanged. In 2022, the number of flight cancellations in the U.S. has reached 2.69% [1]. This is the highest cancellation rate in a decade, according to the Bureau of Transportation Statistics, not including 2020. These disruptions cause an economic loss every year. By making the airspace more robust, it will be possible to absorb some of the delays and reduce the recovery time. Although robustness comes at a price, taking it into account will improve the quality of service provided by airlines.

© ICST Institute for Computer Sciences, Social Informatics and Telecommunications Engineering 2024
Published by Springer Nature Switzerland AG 2024. All Rights Reserved
A. L. Martins et al. (Eds.): INTSYS 2023, LNICST 540, pp. 179–193, 2024.
https://doi.org/10.1007/978-3-031-49379-9_10

Every year, the world's population grows, and with it the size of our transportation networks (road, rail, airspace, etc.) to meet the increasing demand. At the beginning of air transportation, the Benoist Airboat Model XIV, no. 43 [2] could accommodate two people: the pilot and a passenger. Now, the Airbus A380 has a capacity of more than 500 travelers [3]. The transportation network is not only growing according to a horizontal axis but also to a vertical one. Horizontal growth is related to the increase in the size of the network associated with a transportation mode (number of vehicles and their capacities) whereas vertical growth refers to the number of transportation means. For instance, based on the European forecast air transportation is mainly concerned with horizontal growth. The bigger the network, the more complex it is.

This complexity brings a lot of new challenges to deal with. The quality of service should remain at least the same, no matter the size of the network. People expect to spend the same amount of time doing what they used to do before the network gets bigger. One of the most important challenges is the load, especially during peak hours. The network is supposed to offer an acceptable service even when capacity is reached. In a society where competition between services is a norm, it can be a reason to shift from one service to another. Finally, the network must be robust to disruptions. At a time like ours, time is a precious resource. Therefore, it is inconceivable to spend a lot of time in a traffic jam because of a disruption nor to wait for hours for the airline operators to set up a solution to make the passengers reach their final destinations.

A branch of the research in transportation theory has been devoted to the study of robustness. Researchers in this community have developed several models for analyzing networks. These models try to quantify the extent to which infrastructure elements are vulnerable to failures, congestion, attacks, etc. The methods to address this problem are numerous, but can be divided into two groups: topological vulnerability analysis and system-based vulnerability analysis. The metrics based on the former come from complex network theory and usually use graph properties without considering the dynamics of the transportation networks. The models from the latter method overcome this aspect by integrating notions from transportation theory. Vulnerability is usually quantified by the difference in cost between a nominal state and a disrupted state.

Robustness is not limited to the identification of critical elements, but also defines methods to improve the robustness of the network. The strategies to improve the robustness are numerous. The rewiring strategy gets a lot of attention lately thanks to its network properties conservation aspect, in particular, the node degree conservation. Sometimes the choice of a rewiring strategy seems to be justified by economic benefits however this kind of argument is not as evident as one may think. Firstly, it depends on the characterization of the network. On transportation networks, rewiring between non-directly connected elements involves adding a new connection. Secondly, establishing new connections at the strategic level may be a possible and interesting option. By strategic level, we mean that the flight schedule for a day is known several months in advance so the airspace topology of this day can be analyzed and improved.

The following paper presents a new topological method to improve network robustness based on alternative paths. The strategy chosen here is the addition of new links in a static state of the air network. It is well known that robustness is correlated with the number of links in a network and hence with the number of paths. However, enumerating path is a time-consuming task. Instead of using classical k shortest path algorithms, the authors propose a modified Floyd-Warshall algorithm to quantify this property and use a simulated annealing algorithm to find the set of links whose addition improves the network robustness. Knowing the future flight schedule, we search for flights to add to an air network in order to increase the number of alternative routes and make it more robust to potential disruptions or major delays. By doing so, we expect the operators to use fewer resources to deal with disruptions when they occur.

The next section presents state-of-the-art methods for improving robustness. Section 3 details the model and an algorithm for adding links that maximizes robustness. Section 4 describes the methodology. Section 5 presents the results obtained with such a method and discusses the advantages and shortcomings of our approach and the last section highlights future work.

2   Related Work

Robustness analysis is a large domain that gathers research topics such as analyzing the impact of random and targeted attacks on networks, identifying important nodes and links, defining robustness measures [4]. All these topics lead to different definitions of robustness and resilience in air traffic management (ATM). [5] define the robustness as the ability of a system to experience no stress during a time horizon. Stress refers to the deviation of a system from its reference state. For [6], robustness is the capacity of a system maintain its connectivity following random node isolation. According to [7], a system is robust if it can maintain its performance when facing a disruption.

In transportation networks and specifically in ATM, robustness is related to network connectivity and passenger delays.

In [8], it is the difference between schedule and execution efficiency over an observation period. For [9], it is difference in the global traffic travel time before and after a link disruption. [10] use graph signal processing methods to identify and quantify the abnormal distribution of delays across US airports. As [11] remark, ATM politics want to improve passenger mobility but lack passengers-oriented metrics. The paper proposes a set of passengers-centric measures to complement the already flight-centric measures to better evaluate air transportation network performance.

A lot of robustness measures in the literature model focus on network connectivity. Some models characterize robustness by the size of the largest connected component after the removal of the graph's elements (nodes or links) [12–14]. There are other robustness models based on complex network theory [15], and among them are the centrality indices [16,17]. Degree, betweenness, closeness, and eigenvector centrality are the most famous. Another attempt uses the network spectrum especially the algebraic connectivity [18,19]. This measure is a well-known qualitative index to compare OD pair's connectivity but lacks precision. The previous enumerated approaches are purely topological and therefore do not capture transportation features.

Some robustness models are based on the shortest path between OD pairs. The network efficiency [7] is a measure of the proximity of nodes in the network. Betweenness centrality [16] measures the number of shortest paths through a node. This metric can identify important nodes in a network. Both previous models consider only the shortest path. However, passengers do not necessarily choose this path for their trips. In [20], robustness is defined as the number of rerouted passengers in a disrupted network. The shortest path may not be sufficient to reroute passengers, and this alternative path may not have an acceptable travel time, which can lead to trip cancellation.

Improving network robustness is a complex task because of the size of the state of space. Different approaches were developed to address the problem, they are based on a random approach. Several papers have shown that a topological change of a network structure can significantly improve its robustness [12,14,21]. The most acknowledged strategies consist of adding and/or removing elements from a network [22–24] or rewiring existing connections to form new connections [12,25].

Floyd-Warshall's algorithm has received a lot of attention from the research community. Several studies were done to improve the computation time by different means such as GPUs and parallelism [26], cache optimization [27], matrix multiplication optimization [28]. The algorithm was also generalized to compute the k shortest paths [29]. However, it seems that nothing has been done on attempting to assess the number of paths connecting all node pairs.

The main contribution of this paper is a new passenger-centric robustness model based on alternative paths. The model differs from the literature in that it does not consider only the shortest path. From the passenger's perspective, there are several options where they can be rerouted if something unexpected happens on their original trip. These potential alternatives have a travel time that does not deviate too much from the shortest path travel time. Even if the passenger is rerouted, his total travel time (time spent in the aircraft) remains acceptable.

3   Model

Path-based models are extremely rare. Those that take this approach only focus on one path: the least-cost path. From the passenger's perspective, the cost is significant, but so are the alternatives in case of disruptions. If they are few, the re-routing solution can be stressful and tiring.

In this paper, we consider a static transportation network (Table 1) so there is no waiting time between connections. By connection, we mean a generalization of the flight leg. We focus only on passenger travel times. We are looking for a set of connections to add to this network to improve the number of alternatives, and thus, the passenger travel time in case of a disruption. We assume that the connections are not full and that there are always seats available to reassign passengers to all alternatives.

Table 1. Main variables used to describe the robustness model

Variables	Description
$\mathcal{T}$	Transportation network
$\mathcal{G}$	Strongly connected digraph
$\mathcal{N}, \mathcal{A}$	Set of nodes and links
$\mathcal{P}, \mathcal{Q}$	Set of origins, destinations
$\mathcal{L}$	Set of non existing links
$\mathcal{G}^{\mathcal{L}}$	$\mathcal{G}$ where $\mathcal{L}$ was added to $\mathcal{A}$
$\mathcal{R}_{pq}^{\mathcal{L}}$	Routes connecting node p to node q in $\mathcal{G}^{\mathcal{L}}$
$\mathbf{d} = (d_{pq})$	Fixed demand
$\mathbf{t} = (t_a)$	Link cost
$\mathbf{c} = (c_{pqr})$	Route cost

3.1   Problem Formulation

Let us consider a transportation network $\mathcal{T} = (\mathcal{G}, \mathbf{t}, \mathbf{d})$ [30,31] where:

- $\mathcal{G} = (\mathcal{N}, \mathcal{A})$ is a strongly connected digraph with $\mathcal{N}$ being the set of nodes and $\mathcal{A}$ the set of links.
- $\mathbf{t}$ is the vector of the costs of the different links of the transportation network.
- $\mathbf{d}$ represents the demand between two nodes of the network. It is the number of passengers that want to travel from an origin node p to a destination node q. Moreover, $\mathcal{P} \subseteq \mathcal{N}$ and $\mathcal{Q} \subseteq \mathcal{N}$ are respectively the sets of origin nodes and destination nodes.

In this paper, the transportation network robustness is related to the richness of alternatives. The more paths connect OD pairs, the more there are alternatives for rerouting the passengers when a disruption happens. The diversity of paths helps to maintain network connection, which is one of the most fundamental criteria when it comes to analyzing robustness because it ensures the existence of a path between all pairs of nodes.

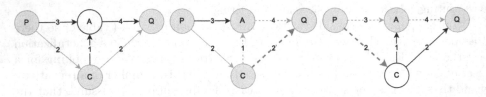

Fig. 1. Yen algorithm 3-shortest-paths (green paths) computation process between OD pair PQ based on the disconnection (red-dashed links) of each of the links forming the shortest path (green-lined path) (Color figure online)

We are interested in a robust transportation network model based on alternative paths between an OD pair. Let us consider a path $r = (p, c, a, q)$ connecting an OD pair pq and v_{pqc}, v_{pqa} being the respective robustness of the nodes c and a. These robustness values are characterized by their number of alternative paths between an internal node $i \in (c, a)$ and the destination node q. We are looking for a path model that combines these v_{pqi} values. The goal behind this definition is to capture the alternatives at each node i along the path r. A robust path always possesses an alternative to the destination in case of a disruption on the nominal path r. The model is applicable to large transportation networks, but it requires efficient computation of alternative paths for all paths connecting all OD pairs, and this operation is very time-consuming and requires a lot of memory resources.

To fully analyze the robustness of a transportation network based on the previous model, one needs a loaded network and the paths on which passengers are assigned. However, these data are not easily accessible, so instead of the model described above, we focus on a less restrictive model. In general, the shortest paths connecting two nodes are quite similar. They slightly differ from the shortest path by very few different nodes. It is based on this principle that the Yen algorithm [32] computes the k shortest paths between two nodes. As illustrated by Fig. 1, the shortest path (green-line path) between P and Q is (P, C, Q) with a cost of 4. To compute the two other paths (green-dashed paths), the algorithm is going to iteratively remove (red-dashed links) the links (C, Q) and (P, C) from the network to respectively find the paths (P, C, A, Q) and (P, A, Q). Both paths have a cost of 7. The main drawback of this algorithm is the network modification at each iteration (disconnecting and reconnecting links). Unlike the Yen algorithm, the Floyd-Warshall algorithm does not perform this operation on the network at each iteration because the paths are built progressively. Moreover, the latter algorithm is known to be efficient in computing all shortest paths between all pairs.

To make the running time acceptable, we limit the method to the computation of the paths connecting an OD pair. The main benefit of this approach is to combine the computation of the distinct paths connecting the OD pairs and the computation of the alternatives along them. The robustness of an OD pair is quantified by the paths connecting its origin to its destination.

The model proposed by the authors can be defined by the following optimization problem:

$$
\begin{cases}
\max\limits_{\mathcal{L} \in \mathcal{P}(\mathcal{N}^2 \setminus \mathcal{A})} f(\mathcal{L}) = \sum_{p \in \mathcal{P}} \sum_{q \in \mathcal{Q}} |\mathcal{R}^{\mathcal{L}}_{pq}| & (1) \\[2ex]
c_{pqr} = \sum_{a \in r} t_a & \forall r \in \mathcal{R}^{\mathcal{L}}_{pq} & (2) \\[2ex]
\mu < t_a < \eta & \forall a \in \mathcal{L} & (3) \\[1ex]
|\mathcal{L}| < \kappa & & (4) \\[1ex]
c_{pqr} < \pi & \forall r \in \mathcal{R}^{\mathcal{L}}_{pq} & (5)
\end{cases}
$$

The strategy adopted here is to add elements. The model searches for the set of links $\mathcal{L}$ that will increase the number of paths from all origin nodes to all destination nodes. $\mathcal{R}^{\mathcal{L}}_{pq}$ is the set of paths connecting nodes p and q in the graph $\mathcal{G}^{\mathcal{L}}$ where $\mathcal{L}$ has been added to the link set $\mathcal{A}$. Constraint 2 is the definition of the cost of a path r based on the cost of its links a. Constraint 3 imposes lower and upper bounds on the travel time of the newly added links. We don't want to connect airports that are too close together or too far apart. Constraint 4 fixes the maximum number of links to add to the network and finally constraint 5 fixes the maximum travel time spent by the passengers on the path r connecting p to q.

3.2 Modified Floyd-Warshall Algorithm

The heuristic chosen to solve the problem is the simulated annealing [33]. This metaheuristic is a well-known algorithm in the operations research community to deal with optimization problems. This approach can reach the quasi-global optimum solution in a reasonable computation time.

The main principle of the simulated annealing algorithm (Fig. 2) consists in generating a neighbor $\mathcal{M}$ and comparing its objective evaluation $f_{\mathcal{M}}$ with the current decision evaluation f. If $f_{\mathcal{M}}$ is better, f and $\mathcal{L}$ are updated. However, these variables have a non-null probability to be updated even if $f_{\mathcal{M}}$ is worst so that the algorithm does not stay in a local maximum. In our implementation, we used the well-known metropolis rule [33] to accept from time to time a bad solution.

The core of the simulated annealing algorithm is the neighboring operator because it is the process that is going to modify the taken decision (Fig. 3). The neighboring operator implemented is threefold: twenty-five percent of the time, the size of the decision is increased as illustrated in Fig. 3. The decision goes from one link to two. Another twenty-five percent is used to reduce the size of

Data: adjacency matrix of a strongly directed digraph
Result: set $\mathcal{L}$ of links that best improve the robustness of the network
$\mathcal{L} \leftarrow$ random set of non-existing links
$f_{\mathcal{L}} \leftarrow$ objective function evaluation for $\mathcal{L}$
$T \leftarrow$ initial temperature
repeat

    for $k <$ *number of iterations* **do**

        generate a neighbor $\mathcal{M}$ of $\mathcal{L}$

        evaluate the objective function $f_{\mathcal{M}}$ for $\mathcal{M}$

        $r \leftarrow$ random number in $[0,1]$

        if $f_{\mathcal{M}} > f_{\mathcal{L}}$ *or* $r < e^{\frac{f_{\mathcal{M}} - f_{\mathcal{L}}}{T}}$ **then**

            $f_{\mathcal{L}} \leftarrow f_{\mathcal{M}}$

            $\mathcal{L} \leftarrow \mathcal{M}$

        end

    end

    decrease the temperature T

until *temperature is sufficiently low*;

Fig. 2. Simulated annealing pseudo-code to solve the optimization problem (Eq. 1).

the decision by one element. The rest of the time is spent swapping the elements in the decision with the same number of other random elements from the absent links set.

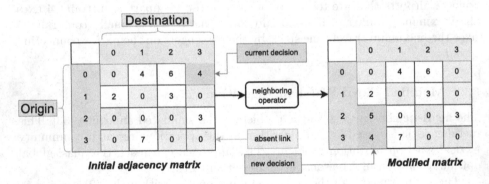

Fig. 3. Simulated annealing neighboring operator functioning. The operator modifies the current decision to a new decision according to three operations: adding, removing, and swapping.

Now that the method to solve the optimization problem has been presented, the last thing to do is to find a way to evaluate the objective function (Eq. 1). It is a tough task to do it fast, due to the number of possibilities. Here, the authors propose a modified Floyd-Warshall [34] algorithm (Fig. 4) to tackle the problem. The approach proposed here does not focus on computing the shortest paths between all pairs of nodes instead it estimates the number of alternative paths.

Data: strongly directed digraph $\mathcal{G}(\mathcal{N}, \mathcal{A})$
Result: alternative paths matrix P
$P \leftarrow$ paths set matrix
for $k \in \mathcal{N}$ **do**
    for $i \in \mathcal{N} \setminus \{k\}$ **do**
        for $j \in \mathcal{N} \setminus \{k, i\}$ **do**
            $P_{ij} \leftarrow P[i][k] \oplus P[k][j]$
            filter the paths in P_{ij}
            $P[i][j] \leftarrow P[i][j] \cup P_{ij}$
        end
    end
end

Fig. 4. Modified Floyd-Warshall algorithm to assess the number of alternative paths between all pairs of nodes without looking for the shortest paths.

Like the classical Floyd-Warshall algorithm, the version proposed in this paper builds the paths connecting OD pairs (i, j) by passing through a transit node k. The paths P_{ij} are the result of the concatenation of the paths $P[i][k]$ (connecting OD pair (i, k)) and the paths $P[k][j]$ (connecting OD pair (k, j)). Then, the set P_{ij} is filtered to remove cycles and expensive paths. Finally, the set P_{ij} of paths going through k is added to $P[i][j]$ which contains the other paths connecting (i, j).

4   Numerical Examples

The robustness improvement method presented in the previous section was tested on the French (Fig. 5a), Turkish Airlines (THY, Fig. 5b), and European (Fig. 5c) low-cost flight networks on 01/06/2018. The network data come from the Eurocontrol database. The main features and topologies of the studied networks are summarized in Fig. 5. Each node is an airport. Two nodes are connected by a link if there is at least one flight between the two airports in the data. The travel time of the leg is the difference between the departure airport's off-block time and the arrival airport's in-block time.

No information about the actual demand was available, so both sets $\mathcal{P}$ and $\mathcal{Q}$ were considered to be equal to $\mathcal{N}$ so it contains all possible pairs of the network because it is the worst-case scenario. This means that there is always at least

(a) French network: 31 nodes and 144 links

(b) THY network: 216 nodes and 610 links

(c) European network: 330 nodes and 5194 links

Fig. 5. The topology of the three strongly connected low-cost flights networks of June 1st, 2018: France, THY, Europe

one passenger who wants to go from any airport to any other airport in the air transportation network. We assume that the newly added flight was performed by an A320. We define a linear regression model to compute the new leg travel time based on the distance between the two airports of the flight. The model was fitted to the low-cost flights performed by an A320 (Fig. 6). The accuracy score of the model is 0.98. In the simulated annealing run, if the travel time between two airports was less than 20 min (roughly equivalent to a two-hour drive) or greater than 7 h and 30 min (the maximum travel time performed in the data), the travel time was set to infinity.

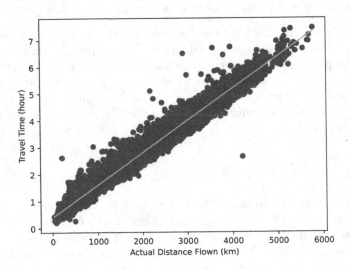

Fig. 6. A320 flight travel time model based on the distance between the two airports of the flight by doing a linear regression of the low-cost flight data done the 01/06/2018

Furthermore, the number of iterations per temperature level was set to 100 and the decreasing cooling coefficient was set to 0.97 to allow a reasonable state of space exploration. This means that from one temperature level to its lower level, the temperature is decreased by 3%. This process is repeated until the temperature reaches 0.01% of its initial value. Finally, the maximum travel time on the French (resp. THY and European) network was set to 7200 s (resp. 10800 s and 12600 s), which is about two hours, and the number of legs to 4. These upper bound were fixed based on the data. In fact, 75% of the French (resp. THY and European) flights have a travel time less than 4916 s (resp. 7380 s and 8322 s). The upper bound was determined by increasing the travel time values by 50%.

The raw data set contained internal and external flight data. In this study, we focus only on internal flights. All the external flights were removed from the data set.

5   Results

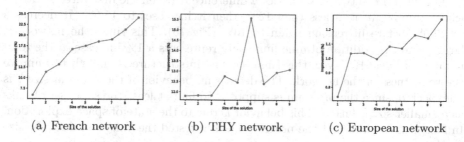

(a) French network   (b) THY network   (c) European network

Fig. 7. Improvement (percentage) of the number of alternative paths between all the node pairs for different sizes of solution (ranging from one to nine) on the French, THY, and European low-cost flight networks

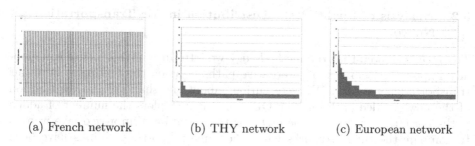

(a) French network   (b) THY network   (c) European network

Fig. 8. Distribution of the paths (sorted in decreasing order) per OD pair after adding the solution links (5% of the network links) to the low-cost flight networks

5.1   Improving the Robustness of Air Transportation Networks

Firstly, we analyze the influence of the solution size on the robustness. For the three networks, we compute the best solution for sizes ranging from one link to nine links (Fig. 7).

On the french network (Fig. 7a), the improvement is linear with the size of the solution and goes from 7.5% to 25%. This network is small (31 nodes) so adding one link represents a 0.7% improvement in the number of links whereas adding nine links represents a 6% change compared to the initial topology. The results show this structure modification has a great impact on the number of alternative paths. Unlike the two other transportation networks, the state of space is smaller therefore it is less complex to find the best solution. As we can see and expect, the larger the solution, the greater the improvement.

On the THY network, we notice a difference between the first three solutions whose improvement is less than 12%, then it increases to 15.5%. It decreases to 12.5% before increasing again to 13% (Fig. 7b). This time, the network is larger, and the addition of nine links only represents a 1% increase in the total number of links. However, this small change in structure is enough to improve the robustness of the network. The decreasing behavior of the curve at size 7 is unexpected, since the program is supposed to find at least the same set of links as a smaller-size solution. This behavior is due to the state of space exploration. In fact, it is so large that the program has not tested the links found for the size 6 solution.

Finally, we analyze the influence of the solution size on the European network. The results vary very little around 1% improvement (Fig. 7c). However, we can observe a slight increase from size one to nine.

5.2   Analysis of Flight Paths Distribution in Air Transportation Networks

The results showed that the methodology we introduce in this article can globally improve the number of alternative paths between the OD pairs in an air transportation network. We were curious about the shape of the distribution of the newly added path for each OD pair. Figure 8 plots the number of added paths per OD pair only for the OD pair that have been improved. We wanted to compare the three networks when the same proportion of links have been respectively added and analyze their new paths distribution according to their OD pairs.

In the French network, we added 7 links which are (LFML, LFMT), (LFLL, LFMP), (LFBO, LFBT), (LFBH, LFBP), (LFRB, LFBI), (LFSB, LFLL), (LFST, LFSL). These links increasing the number of alternative path by 19%. The improvement concerns 74 OD pairs over 930 (Fig. 8a). The paths are uniformly distributed among the improved OD pairs: they all received one new path.

In the THY network, we added 31 links. In Fig. 8b, we can distinguish three groups: OD pairs that receive one new path, two new paths and more than three.

This latter group is a minority. Together, 837 over 46440 OD pairs have been improved. It represents 16% new paths in the network. The OD pair (LTAC, LTFJ) obtains the maximum number of alternatives with 18 new paths. This link connects Esenboğa airport with Sabiha-Gökçen airport.

Finally, the distribution of European paths (Fig. 8c) looks similar to the THY distribution. The number of paths is increased by 6.6%. 7833 over 108570 OD pairs are improved when the solution links are integrated into the European network: 68% get one new path, 14% get two paths, and the remaining 18% get more than three paths. OD pair (EGCC, EGCN) receives the maximum number of new paths for this transportation network with 16. This link connects Manchester airport with Doncaster-Sheffield airport.

Flights on the French and European networks are operated by several different airlines. Adding the set of solutions that can increase robustness is complex for at least two reasons: firstly, how the airlines would be chosen to perform these new flights and secondly, these new routes would entail a loss of customers for other airlines. However, the process is much simpler for THY because the flights on its network are only operated by its own aircraft. Improving their network would only benefit them, with no loss of customers.

6   Conclusion

The paper has presented a new model of transportation network robustness based on alternative paths between OD pairs. We also developed a method to improve it. The method is the combination of a simulated annealing metaheuristic and a modified Floyd-Warshall algorithm. The latter is used to assess the number of paths connecting the OD pairs. The method has been tested on three static study cases: the French, THY, and European low-cost flight networks. The number of alternatives in the French (resp. THY and European) network has been improved by 19% (resp. 16% and 6.6%), and these alternatives concern 8% (resp. 2% and 3%) of the OD pairs. The difference in results between these studies is due to the size and the topology of the networks. By slightly changing the network topology (5% new links have been added in each network), the studies have shown it is possible to greatly improve the number of alternatives among the passenger OD pairs. In this study, the passenger can move from any airport to any other airport. Having several alternatives is interesting during a disruption because it reduces the costs generated and the resources to mobilize to reassign the passengers. The most interesting benefit is that if a disruption happens on an improved OD pair, there is at least one solution for the passengers to reach their destination with little delays. For a company, robustness is a guarantee of the quality of service and insurance to reroute the passengers if a disturbance happens on its network.

Although we consider the OD pairs, we did not simulate disruptions nor manage the potential stranded passengers. Our interest here was to globally improve the robustness of a transportation network from a passenger perspective. The next step to validate this work is to ensure that there are always enough seats on the alternative paths for all the passengers and to reassign the stranded passengers to them.

The current version of the model only maximizes the global number of alternative paths in the network. However, it is not relevant to find more alternatives than the number needed to reassign all passengers. By considering this constraint, we can maximize the number of improved OD pairs.

The model is also static. We did not take into account the waiting time and focused only on the travel time of the passengers. However, the latter variable should be considered so that all aspects of the disruption are captured in the simulation. By extending the model to a dynamic version, we will take into account all these important features and make the model more realistic. Considering schedules, load factors, and operational constraints on aircraft can help analyze the quality of the solution. On the other hand, it can reduce the state of the decision space and the number of alternatives to be computed.

References

1. Bureau of Transportation Statistics: Airline On-Time Statistics and Delay Causes. U.S. Department of Transportation (2023). https://www.transtats.bts.gov/ot_delay/OT_DelayCause1.asp?20=E
2. Michaels, W.: The story of the world's first airline (2012). https://www.iata.org/en/about/history/flying-100-years/firstairline-story/
3. Airbus. A380. https://www.airbus.com/en/products-services/commercial-aircraft/passenger-aircraft/a380
4. Sun, X., Wandelt, S.: Robustness of air transportation as complex networks: systematic review of 15 years of research and outlook into the future. Sustainability **13**, 6446 (2021)
5. Gluchshenko, O., Foerster, P.: Performance based approach to investigate resilience and robustness of an ATM system. In: Tenth USA/Europe Air Traffic Management Research and Development Seminar, Chicago (2013)
6. Lordan, O., Sallan, J.M., Simo, P., Gonzalez-Prieto, D.: Robustness of the air transport network. Transp. Res. Part E Logist. Transp. Rev. **68**, 155–163 (2014)
7. Zhou, Y., Wang, J., Huang, G.Q.: Efficiency and robustness of weighted air transport networks. Transp. Res. Part E Logist. Transp. Rev. **122**, 14–26 (2019)
8. Zhou, Y., Wang, Y.: Measuring the resilience of airlines operation networks (2021)
9. Cai, Q., Ma, C., Alam, S., Duong, V.N., Sridhar, B.: Airway network flow management using Braess's paradox. In: 13th USA/Europe Air Traffic Management Research and Development Seminar, Vienna, Austria (2019)
10. Li, M.Z., Gopalakrishnan, K., Balakrishnan, H., Pantoja, K.: A spectral approach towards analyzing air traffic network disruptions. In: 13th USA/Europe Air Traffic Management Research and Development Seminar (2019)
11. Cook, A., Tanner, G., Cristobal, S., Zanin, M.: Delay propagation-new metrics, new insights. In: Eleventh USA/Europe Air Traffic Management Research and Development Seminar. EUROCONTROL/FAA (2015)
12. Schneider, A.A.M.C.M., Andrade, S.H.J.S., Herrmann, H.J.: Mitigation of malicious attacks on networks. Proc. Natl. Acad. Sci. **108**, 3838–3841 (2011)
13. Cai, M.P.Q., Alam, S.: Interdependency and vulnerability of multipartite networks under target node attacks. Complexity **2019**, 1–16 (2019)

14. Zeng, A., Liu, W.: Enhancing network robustness for malicious attacks. Phys. Rev. E Stat. Nonlinear Soft Matter Phys. **85**(6), 066130 (2012)
15. Sydney, M.Y.A., Scoglio, C.M., Schumm, P.: Characterizing the robustness of complex networks. arXiv Networking and Internet Architecture (2008)
16. Bröhl, T., Lehnertz, K.: Centrality-based identification of important edges in complex networks. Chaos **29**(3), 033115 (2019)
17. Yu, D.C.E., Zhao, J.: Identifying critical edges in complex networks. Sci. Rep. **8**, 14469 (2018)
18. Sydney, C.M.S.A., Gruenbacher, D.M.: Optimizing algebraic connectivity by edge rewiring. Appl. Math. Comput. **219**, 5465–5479 (2013)
19. Fiedler, M.: Algebraic connectivity of graphs. Czechoslov. Math. J. **23**, 298–305 (1973)
20. Wandelt, S., Sun, X., Cao, X.: Computationally efficient attack design for robustness analysis of air transportation networks. Transportmetrica A Transp. Sci. **11**(10), 939–966 (2015)
21. Wang, J.W.: Robustness of complex networks with the local protection strategy against cascading failures. Saf. Sci. **53**, 219–225 (2013)
22. Beygelzimer, R.L.A., Grinstein, G., Rish, I.: Improving network robustness by edge modification. Phys. A Stat. Mech. Appl. **357**, 593–612 (2005)
23. Abbas, W., Shabbir, M., Jaleel, H., Koutsoukos, X.: Improving network robustness through edge augmentation while preserving strong structural controllability. In: 2020 American Control Conference (ACC), pp. 2544–2549. IEEE (2020)
24. Van Mieghem, P., et al.: Decreasing the spectral radius of a graph by link removals. Phys. Rev. E **84**(1), 016101 (2011)
25. Chan, H., Akoglu, L.: Optimizing network robustness by edge rewiring: a general framework. Data Min. Knowl. Disc. **30**, 1395–1425 (2015)
26. Djidjev, H.N., Thulasidasan, S., Chapuis, G., Andonov, R., Lavenier, D.: Efficient multi-GPU computation of all-pairs shortest paths. In: 2014 IEEE 28th International Parallel and Distributed Processing Symposium, pp. 360–369 (2014)
27. Park, J.S., Penner, M., Prasanna, V.K.: Optimizing graph algorithms for improved cache performance. IEEE Trans. Parallel Distrib. Syst. **15**, 769–782 (2004)
28. Han, S.C., Franchetti, F., Püschel, M.: Program generation for the all-pairs shortest path problem. In: 2006 International Conference on Parallel Architectures and Compilation Techniques (PACT), pp. 222–232 (2006)
29. Minieka, E.: On computing sets of shortest paths in a graph. Commun. ACM **17**, 351–353 (1974)
30. Delahaye, D.: Optimisation de la sectorisation de l'espace aérien par algorithmes génétiques, Ph.D. dissertation, ENAC, Toulouse, France (1995)
31. Patriksson, M.: The Traffic Assignment Problem: Models and Methods. Dover Books on Mathematics. Dover Publications (2015)
32. Yen, J.Y.: Finding the k shortest loopless paths in a network. Manage. Sci. **17**(11), 712–716 (1971). https://doi.org/10.1287/mnsc.17.11.712
33. Delahaye, S.C.D., Mongeau, M.: Simulated annealing: from basics to applications. In: Handbook of Metaheuristics (2018)
34. Floyd, R.W.: Algorithm 97: shortest path. Commun. ACM **5**, 345 (1962)

Machine Learning Methods to Forecast Public Transport Demand Based on Smart Card Validations

Brunella Caroleo[1]([envelope]) [iD], Silvia Chiusano[2] [iD], Elena Daraio[2] [iD], Andrea Avignone[2] [iD],
Eleonora Gastaldi[2], Mauro Paoletti[3], and Maurizio Arnone[1] [iD]

[1] LINKS Foundation, Via P.C. Boggio 61, 10135 Turin, Italy
`{brunella.caroleo,maurizio.arnone}@linksfoundation.com`
[2] Politecnico di Torino, c.so Duca degli Abruzzi 24, 10129 Turin, Italy
`{silvia.chiusano,elena.daraio,andrea.avignone}@polito.it`,
`eleonora.gastaldi@studenti.polito.it`
[3] Granda Bus, Via Circonvallazione 19, 12037 Saluzzo, Italy
`mauro.paoletti@grandabus.it`

Abstract. This paper explores the forecasting of public transport demand using mobility data obtained from electronic tickets and smart cards. The research aims to estimate the demand for a selected route at a specific bus stop on a given day and time slot. The study utilizes a large dataset of historical demand data, including approximately 10 million validations collected in 2019 by the Piedmont transport operator Granda Bus, and combines it with additional information such as weather conditions, anonymized user data, and temporal segmentation of the yearly calendar. To identify the peculiarities in demand forecasting for each bus route and stop, a clustering analysis is performed, resulting in the identification of six cohesive and homogeneous clusters. Various machine learning models are tested and compared to determine the most suitable model for forecasting public transport demand at each stop within one-hour time slots. The results demonstrate that machine learning algorithms consistently outperform average-based techniques: the machine learning algorithms exhibit a significant improvement (up to 50% compared to the baseline) when demand uncertainty is greater. The proposed methodology framework is replicable and transferable to other areas, providing a valuable tool for optimizing resource allocation and network planning, while enhancing user satisfaction by accurately forecasting passenger demand at each stop and desired time slot.

Keywords: public transport demand · machine learning · clustering · forecasting

1 Introduction

Estimating the public transport demand has become a great concern for the public transport agencies: it would allow to improve the service offered to the customer and to optimize the physical resources and the operating costs to the service provider.

A. L. Martins et al. (Eds.): INTSYS 2023, LNICST 540, pp. 194–209, 2024.
https://doi.org/10.1007/978-3-031-49379-9_11

This objective has many challenges to overcome: the number of passengers which need to travel at specific place and time may depend on several factors, thus subject to a great variability. The potential directions are toward a reliable forecasting method, able to consider the specific features of the territory, of the service and of the demand, or towards the design of an on-demand transport service.

To estimate the demand for a certain trip, travel documents analysis can provide useful information to create suitable models [1]. Among the ticketing typologies, smart cards generate large amounts of data revealing more insights in passengers' travel behavior [2], allowing the analysis of the current public transport usage and the prediction of the future one.

This paper addresses the problem of forecasting public transport demand at a certain bus stop for each route (denoted as *bus stop-route couple*) of a geographical zone at each hour of the day of the following week.

Data examined in this paper come from the public transport operator Granda Bus of the Piedmont Region (Italy). Smart cards of this operator allow to charge both subscriptions and transport credit documents. The first case (subscriptions) refers to a fare which gives the right to travel within a certain area and for a certain time of validity, which can start with the purchase or with the first validation. In the latter case (transport credit), a certain amount of money is charged on the card and, at each travel, the corresponding cost is subtracted according to the departure and the arrival location. Smart cards are usually validated only when on-boarding (tap-in/check-in), especially in the case of subscriptions. If check-out is not validated, the final destination of the journey can be inferred as stated in the reference literature [3, 4]. If properly exploited, information coming from the smart cards can be extremely precious.

To forecast public transport demand at a certain *bus stop-route couple* of a geographical zone at a given 1h-timeslot, this paper proposes a novel approach that combines already known techniques but in an innovative and customized way according to the context of analysis. The proposed approach is based on the main concept of the bus stop-route couple, meaning that each bus stop of the public transport infrastructure is analyzed separately for each route that passes by it (details in Sect. 3). Starting from this concept and to pursue the forecasting goal, the proposed approach is structured as a two-level methodology designed in the following way. The first level is based on a clustering analysis, whose objective is to identify similarities among the bus stop-route couples. The second level is based on a regression analysis contextualized with respect to each cluster, previously identified through the first level of the methodology, whose objective is to evaluate the best suitable model and its configuration to forecast the demand. Within the proposed methodology, the data about service demand and supply are enriched with additional information about the meteorological conditions and other temporal information (details in Subsect. 3.1).

This paper is organized as follows: after a review of the literature in Sect. 2, Sect. 3 contains a description of the proposed approach, while Sect. 4 reports the main obtained results and their analysis. Finally, conclusions and recommendations for future research are provided in Sect. 5.

2 Related Works

The literature presents different issues that can be dealt using smart card data: segmenting customers according to their personal data or to their mobility patterns [1, 2], forecasting the most likely destination given the boarding stop [4–6], forecasting individual mobility and trip chain [7, 8], estimating the time at which a vehicle will arrive a certain stop [9, 10], predicting travel and dwell time [11, 12], predicting bunching and preventing it [13], reorganizing the routes of the public transport basing on travel/dwell times and on demand at each stop [14]. Similarly, clustering techniques are employed to reveal insights about popular stations and group of passengers [15], as well as for the mining of travels [16] and for characterizing the structure of cities [17].

The focus of this paper is the problem of forecasting mobility demand of public transport at a certain stop to predict how many people will need a particular mobility service, at a certain place, within a specific time slot. There are different approaches in the literature, mainly differing in terms of type of model used for the prediction, input variables, and time horizon of the prediction. Some previous studies focused on predicting bus passenger demand with deep learning and machine learning techniques. For example, [18] proposes the use of a SAE-DNN model (a hybrid deep network of unsupervised SAE and supervised DNN) to predict the hourly passenger flow using a three-stage deep learning architecture. [19] used Gradient Boosting Decision Trees to forecast the number of alighting passengers up to 15–30 min, using also the demand data of the adjacent bus stops. The authors of [20] used a LSTM (Long short-term memory) recurrent neural network (RNN) architecture to forecast the demand using also weather features, with a 10-min time horizon. LSTM technique has also been used in [21] in comparison with SVR (Support Vector Regression). Other approaches are presented in [22] (ARIMA/SARIMA) and [23] (Random Forest).

However, none of these works has analyzed the entire supply network of a public transport operator, crossing with the historical demand data, and detecting the peculiarities in terms of prediction of each route/stop with respect to the other ones.

After a preliminary exploration conducted in [24, 25], this paper proposes a novel data analysis approach to cover this gap. Specifically, it aims at identifying the most proper model to predict public transport demand at each stop of the entire transit network covered by a transport operator for each 1-h timeslot. The features characterizing each bus stop are: time series of the demand at that bus stop, working/school holiday days, weather conditions, type of users (students/retirees/others), segmentation of the yearly calendar depending on the transport supply, the cluster to which the bus stop belongs.

3 Methodology

The proposed methodology is based on data coming from a public transport operator, that consists in the public transport supply and demand of the whole year 2019. The dataset is provided by Granda Bus, a consortium of 16 transport agencies founded in 2004, mostly operating in the area of Cuneo, in North-Western Italy. Data provided by Granda Bus consortium are totally anonymous and comply with the specifications of the privacy authority and the GDPR.

From the supply side, the involved public transport operator collects and stores data in the General Transit Feed Specification (GTFS) format. This is a standard representation of the scheduled public transport services, including also geographical information. In the selected year, the service includes 237 routes, 6,069 trips and 7,371 stops.

From the demand side, for the whole 2019, Granda Bus provided data of users' validations, the typology of the tickets and the category of users. In more detail, from each validation there are: (i) *temporal information*, i.e. date and time at which the validation occurs, (ii) *spatial information*, i.e. the stop at which the validation occurs and the corresponding bus route, (iii) *ticketing information*, i.e. its typology (e.g., single ticket, carnet, weekly, annual subscriptions) and its type (if the validation refers to a check-in or a check-out), and (iv) *anonymized personal information*, as age, sex, birthplace and category (students/retirees/others) in case of smart cards (i.e. subscriptions).

Data retrieved from the public transport operator have been enriched in this study with external data sources, as detailed in Subsect. 3.1. The proposed framework is made of three main building blocks represented in Fig. 1, namely the *Data acquisition, collection and enrichment*, the *Clustering analysis*, the *Forecasting model: analysis and assessment*. Each block will be detailed in the next subsections.

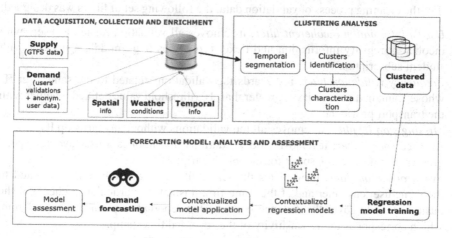

Fig. 1. The proposed framework.

The current methodology is based on the core concept that each bus stop can be better modelled if considered with respect to the route that goes by it. As an example, the route that connects the two municipalities of Saluzzo and Cuneo is identified by route_id = B91 (route_long_name = SALUZZO-CUNEO). This bus route has a stop at Saluzzo railway station (stop_id = 1). The same bus stop also serves other bus routes in addition to B91 (e.g., B95TO, B104, B105). Since each bus stop is characterised by different validation trends according to the considered route, each possible bus stop-route couple has been considered separately. For this reason, from now on we will refer to this concept as the bus stop-route couple, e.g., the couple (1, B91) refers to the *stop_id* = 1 (Saluzzo railway station) of the route_id = B91 (SALUZZO-CUNEO).

3.1 Data Acquisition, Collection and Enrichment

The first block of the framework refers to the acquisition and collection of public transport data, in terms of both supply and demand and including the personal users' data when available (in case of subscriptions). The following additional information has been added to enrich the information retrieved from the public transport operator:

- *Weather conditions*: meteorological information is retrieved from 3bMeteo [26] with daily or hourly temporal granularity (one station for each municipality). Temperature (minimum and maximum) and quantity of rain precipitation are hourly information, while the categorical description of the weather condition (i.e., sunny, partly cloudy, cloudy, variable, rainy, snowy, rainy-snowy, stormy, foggy) is daily;
- *Temporal information*: temporal information is computed from the validation timestamp to further characterise the data in terms of *weekday* (Monday - Sunday), *day type* (working day, holiday day or pre-holiday day) and *school holiday* (boolean equal to 1 for the days in which the schools are closed);
- *Spatial information*: type of zone in which the bus stop of the validation is located (residential, working, or mix).

For the cleaning process of validation data, the following set of filters was designed:

- *User's information incoherent filter*: it removes all validation related to users with incoherent registry information and ticket typologies (e.g., middle-aged user with student subscription);
- *Frequency validation filter*: it discards the validations related to the same user ID whose count in the same day is greater than 10 (threshold value defined together with the transport provider);
- *Missing stop ID filter*: it removes all the validations without any bus stop ID;
- *Average speed filter*: it removes the validations that implies a user average speed greater than the average speed for the relative trip;
- *Synchronisation filter*: it evaluates the feasibility of two validations associated to the same user/customer and at the same time instant. In particular, it checks if the customer could cover the distance between the reported stops in less than 1 min, which corresponds to the sensitivity of the recorded timestamp.

Due to the presence of categorical variables (i.e., the day of the week, the day type and the meteorological conditions), the one-hot-encoding has been selected to exploit the translation into numerical variables.

3.2 Clustering Analysis

The second building block of the proposed methodology exploits cluster analysis to partition the bus stop-route couples and find the optimal forecasting model for each stop. The model which best fits the data related to the most representative bus stop-route couple of the cluster (i.e., the centroid) is used for forecasting the demand at the other stops of the same cluster. It entails two main steps of the analysis: (i) the *temporal segmentation of analysed data*, to properly analyse the mobility data by a temporal point of view, and (ii) the first level of the proposed two-level methodology, which consists of the *clustering method selection*, together with its tuning and the evaluation of the obtained clusters. Both these steps are here after described more in details.

Temporal Segmentation: according to the characteristics of the public transport service supply, it is possible to identify different time periods that follow external conditions variations, such as the school holiday period which highly affects the daily routines. Three temporal segments have been identified:

- *Working segment*: it refers to the period during which schools are open and days are referred to as working days (from the second week of January to the first week of June and from the second week of September until the third week of December);
- *Holiday segment*: it refers to the period during which schools are closed and days are referred to as holiday days (from the second week of June to the first week of September, plus the Christmas holidays);
- *Hybrid segment*: it refers to the weeks composed by both working and holiday days (e.g. Carnival's week, Easter's week and the 25th April's week).

Clusters Identification: the cluster identification step aims to select the most suitable clustering algorithm to identify clusters of similar bus stop-route couples.

To model the bus stop-route object, the current methodology is based on the following concepts: given a time bin *tb*, each bus stop-route couple is modelled in terms of demand *d* at *tb* (i.e. d_{tb}). For each bus stop-route couple, the corresponding demand d_{tb} is computed based on two features: (i) the *sum of the validations occurred in each time bin* d_{tb}^{sum}, and (ii) the *variance of demand at each time bin* across the days in the dataset d_{tb}^{var}. According to this model, each bus stop-route is characterized by *time_bins* $\cdot$ 2 features. To evaluate the right cluster set and if it is possible to keep it as fixed across different time periods, the clusters' identification needs to be performed on temporal segments while comparing the obtained results.

The proposed methodology explored the suitability of the algorithms available in literature by evaluating different kinds of approaches: the k-means algorithm, the hierarchical agglomerative algorithm and the DBSCAN density-based algorithm. Each of them requires the fine-tuning of parameters configuration through a grid search.

To evaluate the quality of the identified cluster set, the following indices are chosen:

- the *Sum of Squared Errors* (SSE): it is defined as the sum of the squared distances between the centroid and each member of the cluster. It evaluates the cluster compactness and the best number of clusters for k-means using the Elbow method;
- the *Davies-Bouldin index* (DB index): it is defined for each cluster as the maximal ratio between the sum of the spatial dimensions among itself and another cluster and the distance between the two clusters. Then, the values are averaged. It is a measure of compactness and separation from other clusters.
- the *Silhouette Score* (SS): it is defined as the ratio between *b-a* and *max(a, b)*, where *a* is the mean distance from the other elements of the same cluster, while *b* is the mean distance from the elements of the nearest cluster. It ranges between -1 (worst case) and 1 (best case). It is also a measure of compactness and separation from other clusters.

3.3 Forecasting Model: Analysis and Assessment

The third building block entails the second level of the proposed two-level methodology, which consists of the regression model selection and fine tuning. Within this research activity, the authors selected some of the most known algorithms, such as Random Forest (RF) and its version with most important features only (RF-MF), Gradient Boosted Decision Tree (GBDT), Support Vector Regressor (SVR) and Seasonal Auto Regressive Integrated Moving Average (SARIMA).

The performances of the abovementioned algorithms have been compared with two wise-baselines: the *Average Response (AR)*, which computes the average validation among the corresponding hours of the same type of day (working/holiday), and the *Median Response (MR)*, which is the same as the AR but it computes the median value. These wise-baselines are simple and they do not require parameters setting, so they are useful to evaluate the benefits of the adoption of machine learning techniques.

For each predictive model, a grid search has been conducted to determine the optimal configuration setting, both in terms of hyperparameters and in terms of training set length. In particular, the proposed methodology evaluates the model goodness when trained on multiples of a week, which means 7 days, 14 days, and so on.

Forecasting and temporal segmentation: the forecasting has been performed by taking into consideration the temporal segmentation previously described in Subsect. 3.2. To forecast the demand of the working segment, the model has been trained only on weeks of the working segment and analogously for the holiday segment. The approach for the hybrid segment is slightly different: these weeks have been evaluated combining the usage of working and holiday models, according with the type of each day of the week under analysis, as represented in Fig. 2.

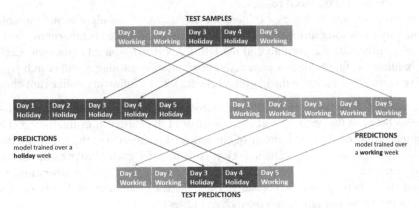

Fig. 2. Forecasting approach in the hybrid segment.

Model assessment: the last part of the proposed methodology provides evidences of the performance in the demand forecasting, obtained through the regression models introduced above. In particular, the quality of forecasting is quantified through a set of common quantitative metrics. Thus, as a result of this block, some useful guidelines to support the service provider in the decision-making process could be provided.

The contextualised models are evaluated in terms of: (i) *Mean Absolute Error (MAE)*, measuring the difference between the predicted value and the real one; (ii) *Mean Absolute Scaled Error (MASE)*, a scale-free error metric that never deals with undefined or infinite values, representing a good choice for intermittent-demand series, which can occur in our analysis context due to the service interruption during some timeslots (like during night); (iii) the coefficient of determination *R squared* (R^2), evaluating the ratio between the variance of the error and the variance of the measured data.

To evaluate the performance on each temporal segment, the authors propose to train as many models as possible that can be then tested on the week right after the training period, averaging the performance metrics computed for each model.

4 Results

The computing environment for the experimental evaluation was mainly based on Python, using the most popular libraries (e.g., pandas, numpy, sklearn, geopy).

4.1 Data Acquisition, Collection and Enrichment

The dataset refers to all the bus tickets validations of the Granda Bus consortium for the whole year 2019. The map in Fig. 3 shows an example of geographical distribution of the bus stops in one month of the year under examination (October 2019, retrieved from the GTFS provided by the transport operator), where the colour of the stop points ranges from white to blue depending on the number of incoming validations (at least onc), while stops with no validations in October are in pink.

Data retrieved from each validation is: timestamp (date and time), stop_id (the bus stop where the validation occurred), trip_id and route_id (the trip and the route corresponding to the validation), ticket typology (single ticket/carnet/subscription/students' subscriptions/over65 subscriptions), and if it is a check-in or a check-out. In case of smart card, information of each user has been included. The recorded information includes about 1,000 travel documents and 100,000 users. The dataset has been enriched with weather, temporal and spatial information introduced in Subsect. 3.1.

Since the objective of the study is to forecast the demand at each hour of the day for the following week, data were resampled in hourly time slot. The study takes as unit of measure one week (24*7 = 168 records): this means that the size of the training dataset is a multiple of one week, and the size of the test dataset is fixed to one week, so that each week can be separately forecasted.

As a result of the data cleaning described in Sect. 3.1, 89% of raw data for the whole year have been considered for further analysis: this percentage can be interpreted as a good quality of the dataset provided by the transport operator.

4.2 Clustering Analysis

A clustering of all the bus stop-route couples has been performed according to the methodology described in Sect. 3.2, using validation data of one representative month (October) in 6,714 stop-route couples.

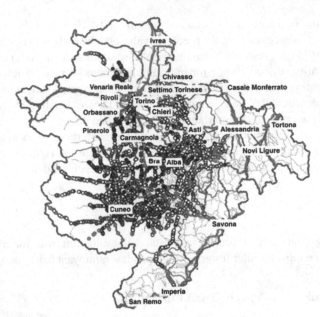

Fig. 3. Geographical distribution of stop points: example on the validations of October 2019. (Color figure online)

Three clustering techniques have been compared: density-based DBSCAN, Ward hierarchical agglomerative, and k-means. Density-based clustering provided the worst results, while k-means resulted to be preferable with respect to Ward agglomerative clustering, due to a slightly higher silhouette and lower DB index with the same number of clusters. As regards the choice of the number of clusters, a slowdown in the decreasing of SSE can be observed at 6 and 7 clusters. Since the second value showed a local maximum of DB index and a local minimum of silhouette, the first option has been preferred. Thus, the algorithm chosen for the creation of the clusters is the k-means, with $k = 6$. The algorithm receives as input the data collected in October 2019 and provides in output six clusters of bus stop-route couples. Such partitioning has been obtained by the assessment of the number of validations and the relevance of each stop-route couple in terms of supply (number of trips, terminal stop, number of interchanges within the route and frequency provided) and the volume of the demand.

The distribution of the most significant variables characterizing each cluster is shown in Fig. 4 and in Fig. 5, separately for each partition (from #1 to #6) and related to working days. In Fig. 4, variables are related to the supply (*dens_pop* represents the density of population in the census zone of each stop_id, *num_trips* is the total number of trips passing by each stop, *terminal* is a binary variable denoting if the stop is the first or the last one of the trip, averaged over days), while Fig. 5 refers to the demand (*stud* is referred to validations coming from students' subscriptions, *ret* refers to validations coming from over65 subscriptions, while *other* to other ticket typologies).

Cluster #1 is the one with higher cardinality (6,303 samples), characterized by bus stop-route couples located in isolated places, with very few validations from all ticket

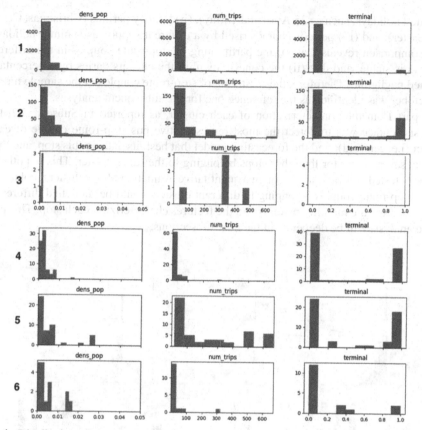

Fig. 4. Distribution of the most significant variables related to the supply across the clusters, numbered from 1 to 6.

typologies, a very low number of trips' interchanges; in addition, these stops are rarely terminals. The opposite holds for Cluster #3 (5 samples): it contains few stop-route couples, but corresponding to a very high demand, especially from students and others, which are the most likely to commute at train stations. The train stations of Saluzzo, Alba and another in the centre of Cuneo belong to this cluster. Also in Cluster #5, formed by 50 elements, there are stop points very relevant from the supply side (in terms of *num_trips* and *terminal*), but with a lower demand if compared with cluster #3. Stop-route couples belonging to Cluster #4 are located in high-density census zones, i.e., mainly in Cuneo and Turin. Cluster #2 (including 264 elements) is also characterized by high relevance in terms of supply and less in terms of demand, but stops belonging to this cluster are located in sprawled areas. Finally, the demand and the supply relevance of the stops are reduced for Cluster #6 (17 elements) and even more for Cluster #4 (75 elements, mainly in rural areas).

Clustering was assessed in an example month (October) characterised by the absence of special holidays and a pattern that is the prevailing one during the calendar year (working days). The analysis was then replicated in months characterised by: (i) public holidays (isolated holidays, such as 25 April and 1 May), (ii) holiday periods (Christmas, Carnival, Easter), and (iii) periods characterised by a different supply, as summer holidays. The comparison reveals that: (i) the partitioning of stop-route couples in the different clusters is stable, and that (ii) the cohesion within the clusters varies by a percentage deemed negligible. Therefore, the clustering of stop-route couples in the sample month of October was identified as the reference one for the subsequent analyses.

Apart from the characterization of each cluster, as reported in Subsect. 3.2, the analysts' choice was to detect the most representative bus stop-route couple of each cluster (i.e. centroid), find the forecasting model that best fits data on this stop, and then use the same model for the other stops belonging to the same cluster. This hypothesis has been tested and validated through a quantitative evaluation of the clusters' cohesion. Thus, stop-route couples belonging to different clusters could be modelled differently to best capture the mobility patterns and the features characterizing each stop. This part of the analysis will be deepened in the next subsections.

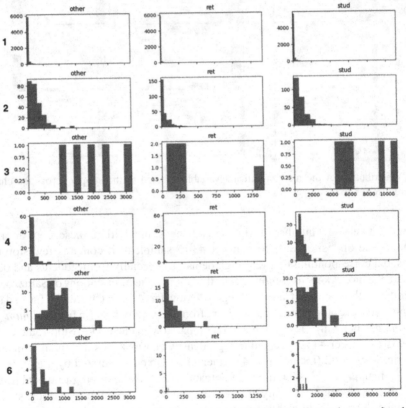

Fig. 5. Distribution of the most significant variables related to the demand across the clusters, numbered from 1 to 6.

4.3 Forecasting Model: Analysis and Assessment

Regression analysis was performed for each centroid of the clusters identified in the previous section. Table 1 reports the centroid information for each cluster, since it is the representative bus stop-route couple element of the specific cluster. The centroid is described by its stop-route name.

Table 1. Centroids of each cluster.

Cluster #	Centroid - Stop name (City)	Centroid - Route name
1	Corso Unione Sovietica (Torino)	Torino (TO) – Saluzzo (CN)
2	Bus station (Saluzzo)	Cuneo (CN) – Saluzzo (CN)
3	Piazza Caio Mario (Torino)	Torino (TO) – Saluzzo (CN)
4	Corso Giolitti (Cuneo)	Cuneo (CN) – Saluzzo (CN)
5	Bus station (Alba)	Bivio Cast. (CN) – Alba (CN)
6	Railway station (Mondovì)	Mondovì (CN) – Cuneo (CN)

As introduced in Subsect. 3.3, several Machine Learning (ML) techniques have been tested for each centroid, comparing the performance with two wise-baselines: the Average Response (AR baseline) and the Median Response (MR baseline).

By comparing the two wise-baselines, it has been observed that the AR baseline performs better with respect to the MR one in the working and in the hybrid temporal segments, while it is slightly worse in the holiday segment. The difference in this last temporal segment is negligible, so the authors selected the AR baseline as reference to evaluate the performance of the machine learning algorithms. With no need of parameters setting, the baseline is useful to evaluate the benefits of the adoption of ML with respect to simple average-based techniques that the Public Transport Operator can already perform without any deep knowledge of ML. For each abovementioned predictive model, a grid search has been conducted to determine the optimal size of the training dataset window (N, number of training days) and the hyperparameters.

The demand forecasting has been performed taking into consideration the temporal segmentation previously introduced (Fig. 2): working, holiday and hybrid segment. For each ML technique investigated, Table 2 shows the best size of the training window (N) obtained from the grid search in each temporal segmentation. The proper N size has been obtained after a deep joint analysis of MAE, MASE and R^2 (see Subsect. 3.3) for each possible value of N (multiples of 7 days, to obtain a number of training weeks required for forecasting).

Finally, each model -fitted for the centroid of each detected cluster (Subsect. 4.2)- has been applied to the given dataset. Table 3 reports, for each cluster and for each temporal segment: (i) the best predictive model identified; (ii) the corresponding size of training window (N); (iii) the corresponding MASE; (iv) the *gain*, i.e., the MASE error gain of using the best identified forecasting model over using the AR baseline.

Thus, the gain provides a quantitative and comparable advantage of using forecasting models with respect to average-based techniques.

Table 2. Grid search results: size of the training window for each ML technique investigated.

ML technique	Temporal segmentation	N	Hyperparameters tuned
RF	Working	21	Number of estimators (from 10 to 200, step 10)
	Holiday	21	Depth of Trees ([3, 5, 7, None])
	Hybrid	14	
RF-MF	Working	21	Number of estimators (from 10 to 200, step 10)
	Holiday	21	Depth of Trees ([3, 5, 7, None])
	Hybrid	14	
GBDT	Working	28	Number of estimators ([10, 20, 50, 100, 200, 500])
	Holiday	14	Maximum depth ([2, 3, 4, 5, 6, 7])
	Hybrid	28	Learning rate ([0.0001, 0.001, 0.1, 1.0])
SVR	Working	21	Kernel ([linear, polynomial, radial basis function])
	Holiday	21	C ([1, 10, 100, 1000, 10000])
	Hybrid	21	gamma ([0.001, 0.01, 0.2, 0.5, 0.6, 0.9])
SARIMA	Working	7	Autoregressive order, p (*auto_arima* function)
	Holiday	7	Moving average order, q (*auto_arima* function)
	Hybrid	7	Differencing order, d (*auto_arima* function)

By comparing the wise-baseline with the ML algorithms results, the ML algorithms always outperform the results obtained through the AR baseline. As a matter of fact, the gain is always positive, and varies in the range [+2%, + 50%] according to the temporal segment. The best ML algorithm in most cases is the Support Vector Regression: across all temporal segments, the gain of SVR approach over the baseline improves performance by 14% (on average).

If the model that best fits each cluster is chosen within the working segment, the average gain of the MASE error is 10%, within the holiday segment it is 12% and within the hybrid it raises up to 26%. The gain from using ML algorithms is especially positive in the holiday and hybrid segments, where the centroid model is more effective than the AR baseline. This is due to the fact that these are segments with little data (because they are shorter periods during the year with respect to the working segment): in this case, therefore, the use of ML techniques is particularly effective.

Table 3. Best predictive techniques for each cluster in the three different temporal segments: gain of each model with respect to the AR baseline.

Cluster#	Centroid	Temporal segment	Best forecasting model	N	MASE	Gain wrt baseline
1	Corso Unione Sovietica (Torino)	Working	SVR	21	0.57	**+38%**
		Holiday	SARIMA	7	0.97	+28%
		Hybrid	SVR	21	0.85	+7%
2	Bus station (Saluzzo)	Working	SVR	21	0.23	+8%
		Holiday	RF	21	0.77	+2%
		Hybrid	SARIMA	7	0.37	**+50%**
3	Piazza Caio Mario (Torino)	Working	RF	28	0.56	+3%
		Holiday	SVR	35	0.96	**+30%**
		Hybrid	SARIMA	7	0.76	+23%
4	Corso Giolitti (Cuneo)	Working	RF	28	0.47	+2%
		Holiday	SVR	35	0.95	+2%
		Hybrid	RF	28	0.68	+7%
5	Bus station (Alba)	Working	SVR	28	0.71	+7%
		Holiday	SVR	21	0.95	+6%
		Hybrid	RF	28	0.73	**+31%**
6	Railway station (Mondovì)	Working	RF	14	0.43	+4%
		Holiday	SVR	28	0.97	+5%
		Hybrid	SVR	28	0.67	**+38%**

5 Discussion and Conclusions

This study is aimed at predicting public transport demand at each bus stop of the entire transit network covered by a transport operator. This objective has been achieved by the cross analysis of the supply network and the historical demand data (about 10 million validations collected in 2019), and by the enrichment of such data with other sources: weather conditions, users' type, temporal segmentation of the yearly calendar depending on the transport supply. In order to detect the peculiarities in terms of prediction of each route/stop with respect to the other ones, a clustering of all the bus stop-route couples of the transport network has been performed: six clusters were identified, being cohesive and homogeneous in terms of demand prediction. Different machine learning models have been tested and compared to identify the most proper model to forecast public transport demand for each 1-h timeslot at each stop of the transport network.

The first result of this study is the importance of the segmentation of stops resulting from the clustering: it allows to group together bus stop-route couples with similar features in terms of supply and demand so that all the elements of each cluster can be analysed using the same model within the same temporal segment, thus improving the performance of the subsequent forecasting.

As regards the forecasting, the results of the analysis show not only that machine learning algorithms lead always to better results with respect to average-based techniques, but also a quantitative assessment of such gain is provided. In more detail, the advantage in using ML models is more evident within the hybrid temporal segment (up to + 50% of gain with respect to the Average Response baseline), when the trend of validations is more variable over the weeks. Also, regarding holiday periods, ML algorithms lead to significant improvement in terms of forecasting performance (up to + 30% of gain) with respect to the baseline. So, the gain highly depends on the characteristics of the temporal segment: the contribution of ML algorithms is higher when the demand is more irregular (hybrid segment) and the wise-baseline is not able to catch its behaviour, while estimating the demand is still valuable for transport operators. When the demand is more regular (working period), a simpler model (e.g., average-based) is an acceptable alternative to more complex ML models. This is reasonable, since -in the working temporal segment- students and commuters are used to follow their own daily routine, thus the demand variability is lower. However, these cases represent times with more crowding, so even a slight increase in accuracy can lead to benefits in terms of operational efficiency and more comfortable travel experience.

The proposed methodology, that is replicable and transferable in other zones, allows to forecast the passengers' demand at each stop in each desired timeslot. This is fundamental to optimize the allocation of resources (personnel and vehicles), the network planning, and therefore to reduce operating costs and increase users' satisfaction.

References

1. Costa, V., Fontes, T., Costa, P.M., Dias, T.G.: Prediction of journey destination in urban public transport. In: Pereira, F., Machado, P., Costa, E., Cardoso, A. (eds.) EPIA 2015. LNCS (LNAI), vol. 9273, pp. 169–180. Springer, Cham (2015). https://doi.org/10.1007/978-3-319-23485-4_18
2. Briand, A.S., Côme, E., Trépanier, M., Oukhellou, L.: Analyzing year-to-year changes in public transport passenger behaviour using smart card data. Transp. Res. Part C: Emerg. Technol. **79**, 274–289 (2017)
3. Arnone, M., Delmastro, T., Giacosa, G., Paoletti, M., Villata, P.: The Potential of e-ticketing for public transport planning: the piedmont region case study. Transp. Res. Procedia **10**, 3–10 (2016)
4. Arnone, M., Delmastro, T., Negrino., Arneodo, F., Botta, C., Friuli, G.: Estimation of public transport user behaviour and trip chains through the piedmont region e-ticketing system. In: Proceedings of 14th ITS European Congress, Lisbon, Portugal, ITS-SP 2273 (2020)
5. Trépanier, M., Tranchant, N., Chapleau, R.: Individual trip destination estimation in a transit smart card automated fare collection system. J. Intell. Transp. Syst.: Technol. Plan. Oper. **11**, 1–14 (2007)
6. He, L., Trépanier, M.: Estimating the destination of unlinked trips in transit smart card fare data. Transp. Res. Rec.: J. Transp. Res. Board **2535**, 97–104 (2015)
7. Toqué, F., Côme, E., El Mahrsi M.K., Oukhellou, L.: Forecasting dynamic public transport origin-destination matrices with long-short term memory recurrent neural networks. In: IEEE 19th International Conference on Intelligent Transportation Systems (ITSC), Rio de Janeiro, Brazil, pp. 1071–1076 (2016)
8. Zhao, Z., Koutsopoulos, H., Zhao, J.: Individual mobility prediction using transit smart card data. Transp. Res. Part C Emerg. Technol. **10**, 19–34 (2018)

9. Yu, H., Wu, Z., Chen, D., Ma, X.: Probabilistic prediction of bus headway using relevance vector machine regression. IEEE Trans. Intell. Transp. Syst. **18**, 1–10 (2016)
10. Sun, F., Pan, Y., White, J., Dubey, A.: Real-time and predictive analytics for smart public transportation decision support system (2016)
11. Othman, M.S., Tan, G.: Predictive simulation of public transportation using deep learning. In: Proceedings of 18th Asia Simulation Conference, Kyoto, Japan, 27–29 October, pp. 96–106 (2018)
12. Cristóbal, T., Padrón, G., Quesada-Arencibia, A., Hernández, F., de Blasio, G., García, C.: Using data mining to analyze dwell time and nonstop running time in road-based mass transit systems. Proceedings **2**(19), 1217 (2018)
13. Yu, H., Chen, D., Wu, Z., Ma, X., Wang, Y.: Headway-based bus bunching prediction using transit smart card data. Transp. Res. Part C: Emerg. Technol. **72**, 45–59 (2016)
14. Asmael, N., Waheed, M.: Demand estimation of bus as a public transport based on gravity model. MATEC Web Conf. **162**, 01038 (2018)
15. El Mahrsi, M.K., Côme, E., Oukhellou, L., Verleysen, M.: Clustering smart card data for urban mobility analysis. IEEE Trans. Intell. Transp. Syst. **18**(3), 712–728 (2017)
16. Kieu, L.M., Bhaskar, A., Chung, E.: Passenger segmentation using smart card data. IEEE Trans. Intell. Transp. Syst. **16**(3), 1537–1548 (2015)
17. Kim, K.: Identifying the structure of cities by clustering using a new similarity measure based on smart card data. IEEE Trans. Intell. Transp. Syst. **21**(5), 2002–2011 (2020)
18. Liu, L., Chen, R.C.: A novel passenger flow prediction model using deep learning methods. Transp. Res. Part C: Emerg. Technol. **84**, 74–91 (2017)
19. Ding, C., Wang, D., Ma, X., Li, H.: Predicting short-term subway ridership and prioritizing its influential factors using gradient boosting decision trees. Sustainability **8**, 1100 (2016)
20. Liu, Y., Liu, Z., Jia, R.: DeepPF: A deep learning based architecture for metro passenger flow prediction. Transp. Res. Part C Emerg. Technol. **101**, 18–34 (2019)
21. Guo, J., Xie, Z., Qin, Y., Jia, L., Wang, Y.: Short-term abnormal passenger flow prediction based on the fusion of SVR and LSTM. IEEE Access **7**, 42946–42955 (2019)
22. Milenkovic, M., Svadlenka, L., Melichar, V., Bojovic, N., Avramovic, Z.: SARIMA modelling approach for railway passenger flow forecasting. Transport, 1–8 (2015)
23. Toqué, F., Khouadjia, M., Côme, E., Trépanier, M., Oukhellou, L.: Short and long term forecasting of multimodal transport passenger flows with machine learning methods, pp. 560–566 (2017)
24. Gastaldi, E.: Forecasting public transport demand using smart cards data. https://webthesis.biblio.polito.it/20414/. Accessed 24 July 2023
25. Attili, A.: The demand for public transport: analysis of mobility patterns and bus stops. https://webthesis.biblio.polito.it/17338/. Accessed 24 July 2023
26. 3bmeteo. https://www.3bmeteo.com/. Accessed 30 May 2023

Taxonomy for Integrated Passenger—Freight Transportation Models as an Alternative for Urban Logistics

Jorge Chicaiza-Vaca[1,2](✉) (iD), Benjamín Barán[3] (iD), Fernando Sandoya[4,5] (iD), and Michel Barán[6] (iD)

[1] Center for International Migration (GIZ/CIM), Dag-Hammarskjöld-Weg 1-5, Eschborn, Germany
[2] Ecuadorian Chamber of Freight Transport and Logistics Companies, Av. El Inca Oe1-70, Quito, Ecuador
investigacion@ctpp.org.ec
[3] Comunera University, Dr. Juan Eulogio Estigarribia, Asunción, Paraguay
bbaran@cba.com.py
[4] ESPOL Polytechnic University, Vía Perimetral km 30.5, Guayaquil, Ecuador
fsandoya@espol.edu.ec
[5] Universidad de Guayaquil, Av. Delta s/n y Av. Kennedy, Guayaquil, Ecuador
fernando.sandoyas@ug.edu.ec
[6] Catholic University of Asunción, Cordillera de Amambay casi, Asunción, Paraguay
mbaran@cba.com.py

Abstract. The integration of passenger and freight transport through urban areas could be an effective way to reduce traffic in cities, and its negative externalities, making transport activities more efficient and respectful of the environment. This could be done by sharing infrastructure, such as roads and railways, or by sharing vehicles. This paper proposes a novel taxonomy based on seven classification criteria: Type of Study, Type of Analysis, Objective Focus, Solution Method, Geographic Location, Type of Transportation, and Type of Integration, to better understand the performance of integrated passenger and freight initiatives and identify trends in their development. The proposed taxonomy identifies important research gaps. They include the need for intelligent transportation system applications that enable data exchange between passenger and freight systems, theoretical and practical studies, incorporating stakeholder desires through a multi-objective approach, and the use of alternative fuel vehicles for the first and last mile of goods transportation in combination with passenger transportation. If we close these gaps, we can optimize the merger of passenger and cargo transport, leading to a more sustainable and efficient urban transportation system. In addition, the integration will promote a high efficiency of the passenger transport network and improve living conditions in metropolitan areas.

This work was partially supported by the GIZ/CIM Grants - Return Expert program.

A. L. Martins et al. (Eds.): INTSYS 2023, LNICST 540, pp. 210–227, 2024.
https://doi.org/10.1007/978-3-031-49379-9_12

Keywords: Taxonomy · Freight Transportation · Integrated Urban Logistics

1   Introduction

The rise of e-commerce and same-day delivery has led to a decline in the number of people commuting to crowded city centers and shopping malls. This is because people can now buy almost anything they need online and have it delivered to their door, often within hours. This trend has had a number of implications for cities, including reduced traffic congestion, lower air pollution, and increased energy efficiency. Meanwhile, cargo boxes have been taking up the seats that travelers and attendees of conferences in far-off destinations once occupied on passenger airplanes. Alternatively, the COVID-19 pandemic activated significant disruptions in the global supply chain, revealing inherent weaknesses within the system. As a result, delays and unstocked shelves became commonplace. Hospitals faced supply shortages of critical equipment and supplies, while grocery stores encountered unprecedented scarcity of food and other essential items [1, 2].

COVID-19 pandemic led to a significant decrease in demand for freight transportation in the post-crisis economic landscape, giving place to a considerable shift in the old balance between passenger and freight transportation. This situation presents an opportunity to transform the traditional mobility sector by creating a comprehensive transportation system that addresses both passenger and freight needs and tackle the ongoing climate crisis. It is critical to prioritize integrating passenger and freight transportation, thus increasing the resilience and sustainability of the whole mobility system. While various terms describe passenger and freight transportation, such as freight in transit, cargo hitching, and passenger-and-package sharing, exploring additional options can further enhance our transportation capabilities [3–6].

According to the WEF [7], the demand for last-mile deliveries in cities is projected to increase by 78% by 2030, leading to a 35.9% growth in delivery vehicles in the world's top 100 cities. City planners must, therefore, prioritize the planning of delivery and storage of goods to avoid potential damage to the transportation system, with congestion, secondary parking, and the use of sidewalks as makeshift distribution centers. While certain cities have already established specific plans for urban freight, more comprehensive planning is essential to ensure efficient and sustainable last-mile deliveries [2].

Many large as well as small businesses rely on a daily collection and transportation of goods in today economy. Consequently, several researchers have already studied different ways of taking advantage of existing public systems, such as inner-city subways or trams, for goods transportation in crowded urban areas.

Some authors, such as Jansen et al. [8], Ghilas et al. [9], and Li et al. [10] show how the freight transportation sector, including public transportation agencies, manufacturers, shippers, carriers, and receivers, can derive economic benefits from moving goods using their spare transportation capacity. Additionally, public agencies can financially benefit from increased sustainability of transit operations, resulting in less burdensome transit operations; thus, paving the way for delivery and passenger services. These services are better located in shrinking areas and improve their attractiveness to current and future populations, providing sustainable transportation to and from crucial transit hubs or corridors.

Given the steady evolution of urban logistics systems worldwide, examining the similarities and differences in the elements that characterize the integration is interesting. However, to our knowledge, no integrated passenger and cargo transportation classification in the literature provides a systematic and complete understanding of this topic. As a result, it is difficult to identify important characterizing factors, filter out and understand success factors, and analyze trends worldwide.

This paper aims to introduce a novel taxonomy of passenger and freight transportation through an analysis of a wide range of works from around the world. This taxonomy is divided into seven classification criteria: Type of Study, Type of Analysis, Objective Focus, Solution Method, Geographic Location, Type of Transportation, and Type of Integration. We will discuss these criteria in detail in the following sections.

2   Related Work

Urban logistics (UL) is a critical aspect of urban mobility, as it encompasses the delivery and collection of goods in urban areas. The customary under- takings of transferring, manipulating, and preserving commodities, supervising stock, waste, and remissions, along with home delivery conveniences, typically fall under logistics. The proliferation of literature on this topic reflects a growing preoccupation with this issue [11–14].

This paper uses two approaches: a theoretical view and an emphasis on practical implementations.

2.1   Theoretical Approach

Theoretically, the issue can be approached by extending existing transportation and allocation models, such as the well-known pickup and delivery problem with time windows and scheduled lines, as explained in Ghilas et al. [9]. Their work addresses the challenge of scheduling vehicles to comply with requests, considering the multimodality of modes of transportation that are designed for the movement of passengers, such as taxis, buses, trains, or trams. They present an arc-based mixed-integer programming formulation incorporating passenger and parcel pickup and delivery orders.

Several other researchers have made noteworthy contributions to this field. For instance, Massion et al. [20] and Li et al. [10] developed optimization algorithms and techniques to help decision-makers optimize urban logistics (UL) systems that involve both passengers and goods. While Strale et al. [21] explored the potential use of light rail for freight transportation, using Brussels as an example. They propose an effective transportation system that combines passenger and freight rapid transit to improve the sustainability of urban logistics.

Li et al. [10] integrate passenger and parcel flows using taxis to support taxi routing. The authors propose MIP formulations for both static and dynamic planning situations. They conclude that computationally intensive algorithms are necessary for solving realistic scenarios. Subsequently, Li et al. [15] later developed a modified version of the algorithm described earlier. This version accounts for uncertainty related to transportation times and delivery locations. They present a two-stage mixed-integer stochastic programming model and an adaptive algorithm for exploring large neighborhoods.

In a case study in the La Rochelle-France, Masson et al. [20] proposed a solution to optimize the daily distribution of urban goods in a business to business context. They proposed integrating passenger and freight flows using a homogeneous fleet of buses and a homogeneous fleet of Environmentally friendly urban freight vehicles that can carry one mobile container to the final destination.

Fatnassi et al. [22] consider that although passenger and freight transportation have different destinations and constraints, mixing their trips on the same network aligns with the trend. They explores how passenger and freight rapid transit can share a network and use the available transportation capacity within a city more efficiently by linking them. Based on the common characteristics of these two modes of transportation, this paper proposes a new and efficient transportation solution to improve the sustainability of urban logistics.

Arvidsson and Browne [23] summarized the main issues related to the first and last mile in freight and passenger transport. They explored passenger and freight transportation synergies to enable resource sharing regarding time, space, and vehicles. They presented several examples of resource sharing in passenger and freight transportation. They found that combining passenger and freight traffic in cities could be an effective way to address the last-mile challenge.

Zhao et al. [24] proposed a method for constructing an integrated logistics system for the metro by locating distribution hubs. They first segmented the urban metro network into subnetworks. Then, they used complex network theory to select indicators or measures to rate the relevance of each metro station. The weight of each evaluation index was calculated using the analytical hierarchy process method. The relevance of each metro station was then assessed using the TOPSISO model, which is an acronym for Technique for Order Preference by Similarity to an Ideal Solution. This identified the metro distribution nodes eligible for the location model. Finally, a locational decision model was formulated to decide the final distribution hubs from the candidates. The Shanghai metro system was used as a case study. The mathematical formulation of the location model for metro distribution nodes is defined by the following objective function: Minimize the total distance between demand points and metro distribution nodes for all deliveries. The relative relevance of each metro station was assessed using the TOPSISO model, and the metro hubs nodes under consideration were determined using the P-median model.

Behiri et al. [25] studied urban freight transportation using the rail passenger network. First, they identify the relevant problems at strategic, tactical, and operational levels. Then, they looked at the Freight-Rail-Transport-Scheduling Problem, proposing many heuristics to solve it. They have also developed a framework for discrete-event simulation. The problem was first formulated as a MIP problem. The authors then prove that the problem is NP-hard and equivalent to the generalized assignment problem and proposed two heuristics to solve the problem: a dispatch rule-based heuristic and a simple train-based decomposition metaheuristic algorithm. The effectiveness of these heuristics is assessed using a discrete-event simulation approach. This provides a general way for decision-makers to simulate and analyze the performance of various solutions for a given system in multiple situations.

Cieplinska et al. [26] developed a workable model for a company organizing the movement of people and goods in urban areas. The proposed model could be an effective tool for local authorities to improve passenger and freight transportation in urban areas. The study analyzed practical solutions in the field in European metropolitan areas. The paper presents a framework for organizing urban agglomerations with conceptual modeling. The theoretical part of the paper is based on the existing materials from public sources and the authors' research experience.

Cargo hitching was studies by Romano-Alho et al. [27] to consider the use of spare capacity in passenger transportation. This contribution to the cargo hitching studies the following dimensions: a) Application of an agent-based simulation framework to understand the impact of cargo hitching from different perspectives: transportation companies, travel customers and regulators. The simulation framework is used for modeling of mobility-on demand services on the supply as well as the demand side, explicitly capturing the interactions between supply and demand; b) Comprehensive simulations to understand different freight demand allocation strategies using a 2030 model of Singapore to gain insights into the potential impacts of cargo hitching. The platform SimMobility was used to get a high-resolution agent-and activity-based simulation for flows of passenger and freight.

Barán et al. [28] examined a collaborative passenger and freight transportation system in a multi-objective context, as a sustainable option for urban logistics (UL). They proposed a model for parcel delivery services, considering the metro of Quito-Ecuador as a typical case study with metro stations used for parcel pickup and delivery. This study suggested a mixed-integer linear multi-objective programming model to represent this problem of joint transportation of passengers and parcels, including some criteria and constraints that represent real operational and business rules. Finally, a well-known evolutionary multi-objective algorithm called NSGA-II (Non-dominated Sorting Genetic Algorithm, version 2) was implemented to solve the proposed model.

2.2 Practical Approach

Real-world examples of successful integration between passenger and freight transportation are needed to demonstrate the potential of this approach. This is particularly important given the close link between UL, the urban mobility system, and the main actors of urban management and economies including public administrations, commercial actors, manufacturers, carriers, and residents. In their study, Ghilas et al. [9] analyzed the UL system in detail, considering door-to-door passenger transport, parcel transport, and fixed public services. They developed different scenarios with different levels of integration. Establishing profitable cooperation is necessary for the success of an integration process, but it requires time and great political effort. For example, Fatnassi et al. [22] showed that sharing goods and passengers across a network could lead to significant sustainability gains, such as improved service times and reduced energy waste.

Traditionally, urban transportation planning has treated the movement of people and goods as separate entities, even though they utilize the same road infrastructure and exert mutual influence. By integrating both types of traffic flow, we can optimize the utilization of available capacity, reduce the number of vehicles and drivers required to meet transportation needs, and create new business opportunities [32]. In their work, Boudoin et al. [33] discuss the advantages of such integration. However, recent studies in urban logistics emphasize the importance of integrated management of freight movements in urban areas, which combines various actors and services and encourages the emergence of new business models that promote agile distribution using smaller, less-polluting vehicles, such as bicycles [34].

The concept of integrating passenger and freight transportation has been explored not only theoretically, but also through initial pilot studies. These studies have focused on shared-use approaches and have yielded some valuable insights, which we briefly present below.

- *India*: In India, the Dabbawala organization is a lunchbox delivery and return system that achieves high service performance with low cost and a simple operating system based on color-coded and numbered lunchboxes [35]. Every morning, a dabbawala collects lunchboxes from homes and offices in their area on foot or by bicycle, goes to the local train station, and sorts the lunchboxes by destination. The lunchboxes are then placed on the trains and delivered to the appropriate dabbawalas at their destination. The dabbawalas then deliver the lunchboxes to the owners by bicycle. The empty lunchboxes are then collected by the dabbawalas and returned to the homes and offices.
- *Sweden*: In Sweden, Bussgods is a nationwide transportation system that provides transportation for both businesses and individuals using existing bus routes. This makes Bussgods one of the most environmentally friendly and punctual transportation options as they carry both passengers and packages at the same time [36]. Bussgods has a few agencies and service points in the main cities in Sweden. Customers can find the nearest agents and track their packages through the website.

- *Nederlands*: In 2007, CityCargo Amsterdam launched the CargoTram project to reduce the number of trucks circulating in the urban core by 50 (%) and decrease pollution by 20 (%). A successful trial run was conducted during which two empty CargoTrams were tested on the network for a month. However, CityCargo Amsterdam filed for bankruptcy in 2009 [23].
- *Germany*: Meanwhile, DVB Dresden's CarGoTram transported car parts to Volkswagen's "Transparent Factory" in downtown Dresden between 2001 and 2020. Up to eight daily trips resulted in 25 avoided truck journeys [37]. Additionally, Hermes and the Frankfurt University of Applied Sciences carried out a pilot "LastMileTram" project in Frankfurt in 2019. Specialized transport containers were conveyed by tram from a depot outside the city to the urban core. Subsequently, they were transported to their ultimate delivery destination by special e-bikes. Although the pilot study demonstrated the feasibility of transporting goods by tram, the costs were somewhat higher than those for delivery by road [38,39].
- *Switzerland*: The Cargo Tram has facilitated the disposal of electronic waste and bulky items in Zurich since 2003. Eleven designated stops are made according to a fixed schedule, where citizens can drop off their e-waste or bulky waste free of charge. This approach has resulted in several hundred tons of unmanageable waste being disposed of annually, corresponding to reduced road traffic [40].

3   Taxonomy Dimensions

This section introduces our novel taxonomy and explains the main features we considered in its construction. It is based on a comprehensive review of 36 papers published between 2014 and 2023, representing very different approaches and addressing various issues related to passenger and freight transportation integration. The seven classification criteria ensure coherence and parsimony without compromising comprehensiveness. Each classification criterion has a specific component, as follows.

1. *Type of Study:* The literature on integrated passenger and freight transport models can be broadly divided into three focal points: theoretical investigations, practical applications, and survey-based studies.
   Theoretical studies develop new models and methodologies to facilitate integration and explore underlying principles and mechanisms. Practical applications demonstrate the feasibility of implementing these models in urban logistics systems. Finally, survey-based studies provide a comprehensive overview of the current state of research and practice in the field, identifying key trends, challenges, and opportunities. These three focal points offer a comprehensive framework for understanding the diverse range of studies related to integrated transport, providing valuable insights for researchers, practitioners, and policymakers alike.

2. *Type of Analysis:* When examining the literature on integrated passenger and freight transportation models, the type of analysis employed can be broadly categorized into two main approaches: qualitative and quantitative perspectives.

   Qualitative analyses typically rely on non-numerical data, such as observations, interviews, and case studies, to develop insights into the complex social, economic, and environmental factors that influence the integration of passenger and freight transport. These studies often emphasize the importance of context and seek to understand the subjective experiences and perceptions of individuals and communities affected by transport systems. In contrast, quantitative analyses focus on numerical data and employ statistical and mathematical models to measure integrated transport systems' effectiveness, efficiency, and sustainability. In addition, these studies often prioritize objective measures and seek to quantify the impact of transport policies and interventions on key outcomes such as travel time, cost, and emissions.

3. *Objective Focus:* The literature on integrated passenger and freight transport models can also be analyzed based on the number of objectives considered, broadly categorized into two perspectives: single and multi-objective.

   Single-objective perspectives focus on optimizing a single objective, such as reducing travel time or minimizing emissions, while holding other factors constant. These research often employ mathematical optimization techniques to identify the best solution for a given objective. In contrast, multi-objective perspectives consider multiple goals simultaneously, recognizing that optimizing one purpose may come at the cost of another. These studies often employ decision-making frameworks that allow for trade-offs between objectives, such as multi-criteria decision analysis or Pareto optimization.

4. *Solution Method:* We identified five primary perspectives: exact methods, heuristics and metaheuristics, hybrid methods, simulation, and scenario analysis.

   Exact methods utilize mathematical optimization techniques to find the optimal solution to a given problem, often focusing on minimizing travel time, cost or emissions. Heuristics and metaheuristics offer alternative approaches to optimization that are often faster and more efficient than exact methods but may not guarantee the optimal solution. Hybrid methods combine elements of both exact and heuristic methods to balance efficiency and accuracy. Simulation methods use computer models to simulate the behavior of integrated transport systems and predict their performance under different scenarios. Finally, scenario analysis involves developing and analyzing various scenarios representing potential futures for integrated transport systems, allowing for exploring different policy interventions and their possible outcomes.

5. *Geographic Location:* According to the geography classification criteria, integrated passenger and freight transport models can also be analyzed based on

geographic location, which can provide insights into the regional differences and similarities in research and practice. The literature can be broadly classified into six continents: Europe, North America, Asia, Latin America, Oceania and Africa. Studies from Europe and North America are relatively more numerous and established, given these regions' more comprehensive research and development history. In contrast, studies from Asia, Latin America, and Africa tend to focus on specific local contexts and often address the unique challenges and opportunities of developing economies. Oceania is relatively underrepresented in the literature, but a few notable studies are from Australia and New Zealand.

6. *Type of Transportation:* Another way to categorize the literature on integrated passenger and freight transport models is based on the kind of transportation systems considered. The combination of passenger and freight transport can be realized in various types of transport, including buses, metros and trains, trams, and private vehicles (such as small cars).
   Integrating passenger and freight transport in bus systems is relatively common, as buses are versatile and can accommodate passenger and freight needs. Metro and train systems also offer opportunities for integration but are often constrained by the need for specialized infrastructure and the potential for safety concerns. Tram systems provide a more localized form of transport that can be tailored to specific urban contexts and effectively reduce congestion and improve air quality. Finally, integrating passenger and freight transport in private vehicles, such as small cars, is an emerging area of research, with potential applications in last-mile delivery and other localized transport needs.

7. *Type of Integration:* In general, there are three types of integration: shared track, shared vehicle, and shared wagon.
   - *Shared track:* The shared track model involves transporting freight in a separate vehicle that only shares infrastructure with public transport vehicles. This approach is often used in metro and train systems, where dedicated freight cars can be attached to passenger trains or transported separately on the same tracks.
   - *Shared vehicle:* The shared vehicle model involves transporting freight in a separate carriage on light railways or a trailer affixed to vehicles, such as buses. This approach is often used in bus rapid transit systems, where freight can be transported in dedicated trailers attached to passenger buses.
   - *Shared wagon:* in the shared wagon model, freight is transported with passengers in a shared wagon or compartment. This approach is often used in trams and light rail systems, where cargo can be transported in dedicated compartments integrated with passenger cars.

Table 1 presents a complete summary of the proposed taxonomy, where the taxonomy and its content are sketched.

Table 1. Summary of the classifications.

1. Type of Study	
1.1 Theory	[6, 9, 10, 15, 18–20, 42–44]
1.2 Practical	[2, 4, 8, 22, 24, 25, 27–30], [31, 45, 46], [47–51]
1.3 Survey, review	[3, 5, 17, 23, 35, 52]
2. Type of Analysis	
2.1 Qualitative	[2, 3, 5, 17, 23, 28, 35, 44]
2.2 Quantitative	[4, 6, 8–10, 15], [18–20, 22], [24, 25, 27, 29–31, 42, 43, 45], [46, 47, 51]
3. Objective Focus	
3.1 Single Objective	[4, 6, 9, 10, 15, 18, 20, 22, 24, 25], [29, 42, 43, 50]
3.2 Multi-Objective	[28, 31, 48],
4. Solution Method	
4.1. Exact methods	[6, 9, 15, 20, 22, 24, 25, 42, 43]
4.2. Heuristics and Metaheuristics	[15, 20, 25, 28, 29, 31, 48, 50]
4.3. Hybrid methods	[27, 31, 49, 50]
4.4. Simulation	[8, 18, 19, 22, 25, 27, 30, 47, 49, 51]
4.5. Scenarios Analysis	[9, 18, 19, 30, 44–46, 49]
5. Geographic Location	
5.1. Europa	[2, 3, 5, 8, 17, 20, 22, 23, 25, 30, 42], [43–47, 51, 52]
5.2. Asia	[4, 18, 19, 24, 27, 29, 31, 35, 48, 49], [50]
5.3. Latin American	[28]
5.4. North America	[3, 17]
5.5. Africa	Not found
5.6. Oceania	Not found
6. Type of Transportation	
6.1. Bus	[3–6, 8, 9, 17, 20, 22, 42, 52]
6.2. Metro and Train	[3, 5, 9, 17–19, 24, 25, 27, 28], [29–31, 35, 43, 45–49], [50–52]
6.3. Tram	[2, 3, 5, 17, 22, 23, 44, 46, 52]
6.4. Particular	[4, 8–10, 15, 27]
7. Type of Integration	
7.1. Shared track	[2, 17, 22, 23, 45, 46, 52]
7.2. Shared vehicle	[4–6, 10, 15, 17, 20, 24, 27, 29], [30, 31, 42, 43, 47–50, 52]
7.3. Shared Wagon	[3, 5, 18, 19, 25, 28, 35, 44, 51, 52]

3.1   Type of Study

There are a variety of approaches taken in the literature regarding integrated passenger and freight transportation models, with differing levels of theoretical and practical emphasis (Fig. 1). The literature surveyed includes ten theoretical contributions that provide a conceptual framework for understanding integrated transport, and 18 applied contributions that demonstrate the implementation of these concepts in practical scenarios. In addition, six contributions that explore the topic based on a survey and a literature review, without proposing a clear taxonomy.

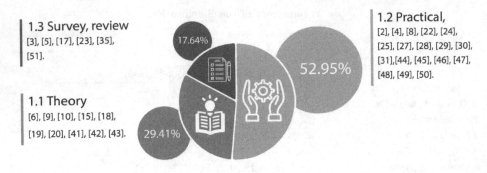

1.3 Survey, review
[3], [5], [17], [23], [35], [51].

1.1 Theory
[6], [9], [10], [15], [18], [19], [20], [41], [42], [43].

1.2 Practical,
[2], [4], [8], [22], [24], [25], [27], [28], [29], [30], [31],[44], [45], [46], [47], [48], [49], [50].

Fig. 1. Type of Study

3.2 Type of Analysis

We found eight papers with a qualitative analysis of passanger and freight integration. At the same time, we found 22 articles with quantitative analysis (Fig. 2).

2.1 Qualitative
[2], [3], [5], [17], [23], [28], [35], [43].

2.2 Quantitative
[4], [6], [8], [9], [10], [15], [18], [19], [20], [22], [24], [25], [27], [29], [30], [31], [41], [42], [44], [45], [46], [50].

Fig. 2. Type of analysis

3.3 Objective Focus

In 14 papers, only a single objective function is considered, generally minimizing total cost or distance. Only three papers consider a multi-objective perspective, such as transportation cost, level of service, used capacity, travel time, and reduction of carbon emissions (Fig. 3).

3.4 Solution Method

First, nine papers, mainly with a single objective function, exact methods or comparisons with heuristics were used as solution methods. Second, heuristics and metaheuristics were presented in eight papers, mainly Greedy randomized

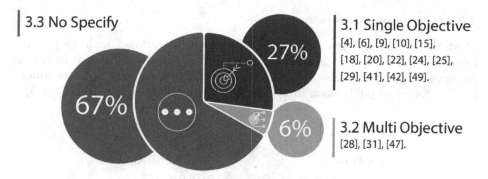

Fig. 3. Objective focus

adaptive search procedure (GRASP), population-based algorithms such as genetics methods, Tabu Search, ant colony, and particle swarm algorithms. Third, for multi-objective models, most of the time, the non-dominated classification genetic algorithm version 2 (NSGA-II) was used. Third, a hybrid scheme combining different solution methods or optimization with simulation approaches was used in four papers. Fourth, ten papers used simulation as an analysis method to evaluate different models for combining passenger and freight transportation. Finally, the scenario analysis was used in eight papers to address the issue from a statistical point of view (Fig. 4).

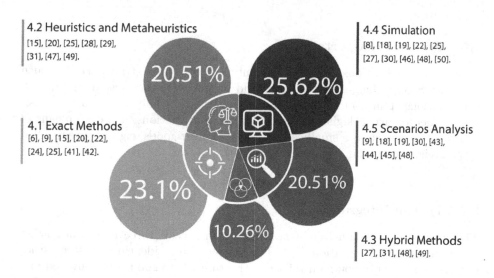

Fig. 4. Solution method

3.5   Geographic Location

Most theoretical and practical applications were in Europe, with 18 papers, followed by Asia with 11 articles. Only two of the applications were in North America. There is only one publication studying implementation in Latin America. We found no publication from Africa or Oceania implementations (Fig. 5).

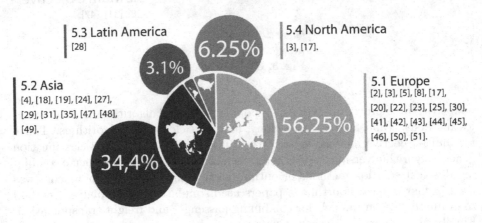

Fig. 5. Geographic location

3.6   Type of Transportation

First, in 11 applications, freight was combined with public transportation such as buses. Second, long-distance trains and metros were the most used, with 22 contributions. Third, nine contributions used trams or light rail as a new business model for urban logistics. Finally, in six contributions, a special means of transportation such as a small car, is used to deliver goods, e.g., a system called Uber Freight or similar schemes [41] (Fig. 6).

3.7   Type of Integration

The literature on urban freight transportation reveals three main approaches concerning to the integration type. The first approach, identified in seven studies, involves using of common rail infrastructure where goods are conveyed in a distinct/separate vehicle that shares the tracks with public transport vehicles. The second approach, found in 19 papers, pertains to shared vehicles in which freight is carried in a separate wagon attached to light rail or buses. Finally, ten contributions focus on shared wagons, where passengers and cargo are transported together in the same compartment or wagon, sharing not only the travel

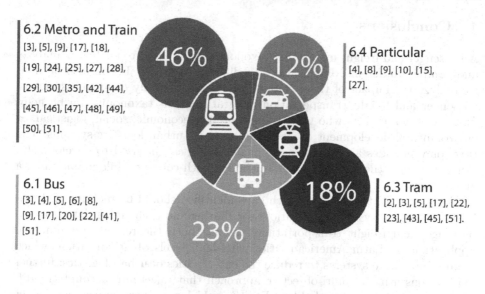

Fig. 6. Type of transportation

route, time, and distance but also the physical space (Fig. 7). It is essential to carefully evaluate the advantages and disadvantages of each approach in the context of the specific urban environment and transportation system to ensure efficient, safe, and sustainable urban freight transportation.

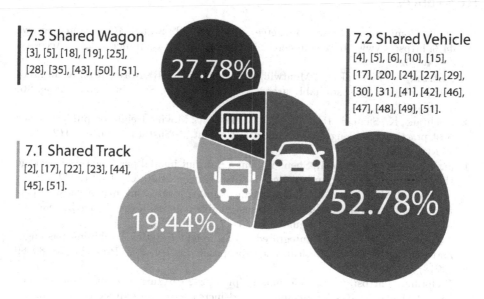

Fig. 7. Type of integration

4   Conclusions

A passenger and freight integration taxonomy can be used to evaluate, analyze, and compare different configurations in different contexts. It can also be used to analyze the impact of these configurations and to study common aspects of passenger and freight transportation integration. This taxonomy can be helpful for decision-makers who want to promote the economic, social, logistical, or environmental development of cities through new urban logistics systems. The taxonomy provides a comprehensive analysis and can be used to develop solutions that meet the logistical requirements of each context while maintaining a global view.

At this point, the main research gaps identified should be mentioned: Intelligent Transport Systems applications for sharing and exchanging data between passenger and freight transportation systems; both theoretical and practical applications in Latin American cities with high levels of urbanization, which require innovative systems to reduce the externalities of urban logistics; further applications using a multi-objective approach that takes into account the different perspectives of stakeholders. Electric vehicles can also be used for freight transportation, especially for the first and last mile, which can be combined with the passenger transportation system. However, further research is needed to identify potential gaps and opportunities in this area.

For all of these reasons, there is a general opportunity for studies in a variety of practical and academic areas when it comes to integrating passenger and freight transportation models.

References

1. DigitalCommerce, Digital-commerce 360. United States e-commerce grows 44%. https://www.digitalcommerce360.com/article/us-ecommerce-sales. Accessed 4 May 2022
2. Pietrzak, K., Pietrzak, O., Montwiłł, A.: Light Freight Railway (LFR) as an innovative solution for sustainable urban freight transport. Sustain. Urban Areas **66**, 102663 (2021)
3. Cochrane, K., Saxe, S., Roorda, M.J., Shalaby, A.: Moving freight on public transit: best practices, challenges, and opportunities. Int. J. Sustain. Transp. **11**(2), 120–132 (2017)
4. Ji, Y., Zheng, Y., Zhao, J., Shen, Y., Du, Y.: A multimodal passenger-and-package sharing network for urban logistics. J. Adv. Transp. **2020**, 6039032 (2020)
5. Mazzarino, M., Rubini, L.: Smart urban planning: evaluating urban logistics performance of innovative solutions and sustainable policies in the Venice Lagoon-the results of a case study. Sustainability **11**(17), 4580 (2019)
6. Pimentel, C., Alvelos, F.: Integrated urban freight logistics combining passenger and freight flows-mathematical model proposal. Transp. Res. Procedia **30**, 80–89 (2018)
7. Weforum. https://www.weforum.org/press/2020/01/urban-deliveries-expected-to-add-11-minutes-to-daily-commute-and-increase-carbon-emissions-by-30-until-2030-without-effective-intervention-e3141b32fa/. Accessed 24 June 2022

8. Jansen, T.A.M.: Development of a design model for integrated passenger and freight transportation systems. Ph.D. thesis. Master's thesis, Eindhoven University of Technology, The Netherlands (2014)

9. Ghilas, V., Demir, E., Van Woensel, T.: The pickup and delivery problem with time windows and scheduled lines. INFOR: Inf. Syst. Oper. Res. **54**(2), 147–167 (2016)

10. Li, B., Krushinsky, D., Reijers, H.A., Van Woensel, T.: The share-a-ride problem: people and parcels sharing taxis. Eur. J. Oper. Res. **238**(1), 31–40 (2014)

11. Gonzalez-Feliu, J.: Sustainable Urban Logistics: Planning and Evaluation. Wiley, London (2018)

12. Gonzalez-Feliu, J., Chong, M., Vargas Florez, J., Padilla Solis, J.: Handbook of Research on Urban and Humanitarian Logistics. IGI Global, Hershey (2019)

13. Gonzalez-Feliu, J., Semet, F., Routhier, J.L.: Sustainable Urban Logistics: Concepts, Methods and Information Systems. Springer, Heidelberg (2014). https://doi.org/10.1007/978-3-642-31788-0

14. Taniguchi, E., Fwa, T.F., Thompson, R.G.: Urban Transportation and Logistics: Health, Safety, and Security Concerns. CRC Press, Boca Raton (2013)

15. Li, B., Krushinsky, D., Van Woensel, T., Reijers, H.A.: The share-a-ride problem with stochastic travel times and stochastic delivery locations. Transp. Res. Part C Emerg. Technol. **67**, 95–108 (2016)

16. Ranieri, L., Digiesi, S., Silvestri, B., Roccotelli, M.: A review of last mile logistics innovations in an externalities cost reduction vision. Sustainability **10**(3), 782 (2018)

17. Cleophas, C., Cottrill, C., Ehmke, J.F., Tierney, K.: Collaborative urban transportation: recent advances in theory and practice. Eur. J. Oper. Res. **273**(3), 801–816 (2019)

18. Dong, J., Hu, W., Yan, S., Ren, R., Zhao, X.: Network planning method for capacitated metro-based underground logistics system. Adv. Civil Eng. **2018**, 6958086 (2018)

19. Dong, J., Xu, Y., Hwang, B.G., Ren, R., Chen, Z.: The impact of underground logistics system on urban sustainable development: a system dynamics approach. Sustainability **11**(5), 1223 (2019)

20. Masson, R., Trentini, A., Lehu'ed'e, F., Malh'en'e, N., P'eton, O., Tlahig, H.: Optimization of a city logistics transportation system with mixed passengers and goods. EURO J. Transp. Logistics **6**(1), 81–109 (2017)

21. Strale, M.: The cargo tram: current status and perspectives, the example of Brussels. Sustain. Logistics **6**, 245–263 (2014)

22. Fatnassi, E., Chaouachi, J., Klibi, W.: Planning and operating a shared goods and passengers on-demand rapid transit system for sustainable city-logistics. Transp. Res. Part B Methodol. **81**, 440–460 (2015)

23. Arvidsson, N., Browne, M.: A review of the success and failure of tram systems to carry urban freight: the implications for a low emission intermodal solution using electric vehicles on trams. Eur. Transp./Trasporti Europei **54**, 6 (2013)

24. Zhao, L., et al.: Location selection of intra-city distribution hubs in the metro-integrated logistics system. Tunn. Undergr. Space Technol. **80**, 246–256 (2018)

25. Behiri, W., Belmokhtar-Berraf, S., Chu, C.: Urban freight transport using passenger rail network: scientific issues and quantitative analysis. Transp. Res. Part E Logistics Transp. Rev. **115**, 227–245 (2018)

26. Cieplin'ska, J.R.: The role of transport organisers in the integration of passengers and goods flows within urban areas. Transp. Res. Procedia **39**, 453–461 (2019)

27. Romano-Alho, A., et al.: Simulation-based evaluation of a Cargo-Hitching service for E-commerce using mobility-on-demand vehicles. Future Transp. **1**(3), 639–656 (2021)

28. Barán, M., Sandoya, F., Chicaiza-Vaca, J., Barán, B.: Integrated passenger-freight transportation model: Metro of Quito (Ecuador) as a case study. In: Martins, A.L., Ferreira, J.C., Kocian, A., Tokkozhina, U. (eds.) Intelligent Transport Systems, INTSYS 2022. LNCS, Social Informatics and Telecommunications Engineering, vol. 486, pp. 215–230. Springer, Cham (2023). https://doi.org/10.1007/978-3-031-30855-0_15

29. Zheng, C., Gu, Y., Shen, J., Du, M.: Urban logistics delivery route planning based on a single metro line. IEEE Access **9**, 50819–50830 (2021)

30. Villa, R., Monz'on, A.: A metro-based system as sustainable alternative for urban logistics in the era of e-commerce. Sustainability **13**(8), 4479 (2021)

31. Sun, X., Hu, W., Xue, X., Dong, J.: Multi-objective optimization model for planning metro-based underground logistics system network: Nanjing case study. J. Ind. Manage. Optim. (2021). https://doi.org/10.3934/jimo.2021179

32. Bektas, T., Crainic, T. G., Van Woensel, T.: From Managing Urban Freight to Smart City Logistics Networks. Research Papers, CIRRELT-2015-17 (2015)

33. Boudoin, D., Morel, C., Gardat, M.: Supply chains and urban logistics platforms. In: Gonzalez-Feliu, J., Semet, F., Routhier, J.L. (eds.) Sustainable Urban Logistics: Concepts, Methods and Information Systems. EcoProduction, pp. 1–2. Springer, Heidelberg (2014). https://doi.org/10.1007/978-3-642-31788-0_1

34. Schliwa, G., Armitage, R., Aziz, S., Evans, J., Rhoades, J.: Sustainable city logistics—making cargo cycles viable for urban freight transport. Res. Transp. Bus. Manag. **15**, 50–57 (2015)

35. Baindur, D., Mac'ario, R.M.: Mumbai lunch box delivery system: a transferable benchmark in urban logistics? Res. Transp. Econ. **38**(1), 110–121 (2013)

36. Bussgods (2021). Bussgods http://www.bussgods.se/om-oss. Accessed 24 June 2022

37. Dresdner Verkehrsbetriebe, A.: Die dresdner güterstraßenbahn-ein system für alle fälle? (2020). http://www.dvb.de/-/media/files/die-dvb/dvb-vortragcargotram.pdf. Accessed 24 June 2022

38. Riemann, H.: Logistiktram (2021). http://www.logistiktram.de/ancorpartner/. Accessed 24 June 2022

39. Schocke, K.O., Schäfer, P., Höhl, S., Gilbert, A.: Bericht zum forschungsvorhaben "lastmiletram empirische forschung zum einsatz einer güterstraßenbahn am beispiel frankfurt am main" (2020). https://www.frankfurt-university.de/fileadmin/standard/Hochschule/. Accessed 24 June 2022

40. Stadt Zürich, Z.: Cargo-tram und e-tram (2021). https://www.stadt-zuerich.ch/. Accessed 24 June 2022

41. Byrne, R.O.: The uberisation of logistics. MHD Supply Chain Solutions **46**(5), 36–38 (2016)

42. Donne, D., Alfandari, L., Archetti, C., Ljubic, I.: Freight-on-Transit for urban last-mile deliveries: a strategic planning approach (2021). Available at SSRN

43. Filippi, C., Plebani, F.: Metro stations as crowd-shipping catalysts: an empirical and computational study. arXiv preprint arXiv:2109.08069 (2021)

44. Kelly, J., Marinov, M.: Innovative interior designs for urban freight distribution using light rail systems. Urban Rail Transit **3**(4), 238–254 (2017)

45. Bruzzone, F., Cavallaro, F., Nocera, S.: The integration of passenger and freight transport for first-last mile operations. Transp. Policy **100**, 31–48 (2021)

46. De Langhe, K., Meersman, H., Sys, C., Van de Voorde, E., Vanelslander, T.: How to make urban freight transport by tram successful? J. Shipping Trade **4**(1), 1–23 (2019)
47. Galbiati, F.: An Innovative Last Mile Logistics based on Hybrid Subway Deliveries in Urban Areas. https://federicogalbiati.com/pdf/. Accessed 24 June 2022
48. Guo, J., Xiao, X., Ye, Y., Yan, L.: An urban metro network-based method to evaluate carbon emission and distribution cost of express delivery. J. Intell. Fuzzy Syst. **41**(4), 5021–5034 (2021)
49. Hu, W., Dong, J., Hwang, B.G., Ren, R., Chen, Z.: Hybrid optimization procedures applying for two-echelon urban underground logistics network planning: a case study of Beijing. Comput. Ind. Eng. **144**(4), 106452 (2020)
50. Hu, W., Dong, J., Hwang, B.G., Ren, R., Chen, Z.: A preliminary prototyping approach for emerging metro-based underground logistics systems: operation mechanism and facility layout. Int. J. Prod. Res. **59**(24), 7516–7536 (2021)
51. Potti, P., Marinov, M., Sweeney, E.: A simulation study on the potential of moving urban freight by a cross-city railway line. Sustainability **11**(21), 6088 (2019)
52. Elbert, R., Rentschler, J.: Freight on urban public transportation: a systematic literature review. Res. Transp. Bus. Manage. **45**, 100679 (2021)

Modeling Other Road Users' Acceptance to an Automated Shuttle Service

Rim Rejeb[1]([✉]) [iD], Natacha Métayer[1] [iD], Arnaud Koustanaï[2], Stéphanie Bordel[3] [iD], and Juliette Massoulié[2]

[1] VEDECOM, Versailles, France
rim.rejeb@vedecom.fr
[2] Renault Group, Boulogne-Billancourt, France
[3] Cerema, Rhone-Alpes, France

Abstract. To guarantee a smooth implementation of automated vehicles on the common road, it is essential to have the public acceptance of this technology. Looking to the literature, less is known about the acceptance of the other road users (i.e., conventional drivers, cyclists, or pedestrians). Based on social psychology models of acceptance, we study the determinants of the other road users' acceptance for the implementation of an automated shuttle between Nantes and Carquefou (France). With a sample of 229 participants and using Structural Equation Modeling, we identify the main determinants of the behavioral intention to interact with the automated vehicle. Relying on the findings of the tested model, we propose recommendations for industrials and policymakers to increase public acceptance.

Keywords: automated vehicle · acceptance · SEM · other road users · shuttle service

1 Introduction

With the numerous developments that the automotive industry is seeing, the emergence of semi-automated to fully automated vehicles pledge travelers a new safer, accessible, and more ecologically sustainable transportation alternative. Despite its attractiveness, the public still have concerns about this technology and its adoption is limited [1, 2]. This context justifies the increasing interest of industrials, policymakers, and researchers in better understanding the determinants of the individual acceptance of automated vehicles. Acceptance is defined as the "the attitude towards, or the willingness for use (or non-use), that an individual has of an advanced system" [3].

The growing literature focuses on evaluating the end-user acceptance expressed through their stated intentions to adopt an automated vehicle [4–7]. The recent meta-analyses presenting the defining factors of these intentions, either for using private or shared automated vehicles [3, 8, 9], recognize the significant effects of the socio-demographic characteristics of the respondent (e.g., income, age) or the vehicle attributes

A. L. Martins et al. (Eds.): INTSYS 2023, LNICST 540, pp. 228–246, 2024.
https://doi.org/10.1007/978-3-031-49379-9_13

(e.g., trip duration, cost). Most importantly, these studies emphasize the significant effects of psychological factors (e.g., individual attitudes or perceptions). There is a consensus that these latter should be further considered in the study of automated vehicles' acceptance.

The study of these psychological factors is generally based on theoretical frameworks such as the Technology Acceptance Model (TAM2) [10], the Unified Theory of Acceptance and Use of Technology (UTAUT) [11] or the Theory of Planned Behavior (TPB) [12]. With the increasing interest in the study of automated vehicles we also find the Self-Driving Car Acceptance Scale (SCAS) [13] which is an extension of the factors included in the previously mentioned acceptance models but adapted to the case of studying the technology of automated vehicles (e.g., compatibility, reliability, trust). All these models agree on the idea that the potential user acceptance of the automated vehicle could be expressed in terms of his stated intentions to adopt this mode of transport. Thus, the stronger the stated intentions are, the more accepting the individual is.

We notice that the existing literature focuses mostly on modeling the acceptance of the end-users of automated vehicles giving less interest to studying the acceptance process of another category of individuals who may be impacted by the implementation of an automated vehicle. We refer to the other road users (e.g., conventional drivers, cyclists, or pedestrians) who are external to the automated vehicle but could interact with it. We believe in the importance of considering this category of road users before the introduction of the automated vehicle on the road since they need to accept to cohabitate with it and share a common space. Indeed, the acceptance of this interaction by other road users should facilitate the introduction of these increasingly automated vehicles and therefore reduce the risk of incivility against them [14].

To the best of our knowledge, there are only three previous studies that focus on the other road users sharing the road with an automated vehicle. First, Koustanaï and co-authors [15] studied the influence of perceived safety of conventional drivers on their acceptance of a Level 3 SAE automated vehicle on highways. Based on the SCAS, they showed that perceived safety predicted perceived reliability, which influenced trust, the direct determinant of intention to interact with the automated vehicle. Second, the work of Deb and co-authors [16] focuses on modeling the pedestrian acceptance to cross the road in the presence of an automated vehicle, a concept they call receptivity. Results showed that both safety and interaction scores were the main two determinants of pedestrian acceptance. Third, Pammer and co-authors [17] studied the motorcyclists and cyclists' perceptions of the automated vehicle. Using correlation and regression analyses on Australian data, they found that motorcyclists and cyclists have low trust in both human drivers and automated vehicles. However, the participants think that automated vehicles are safer than human drivers, especially in respecting a safe distance.

These papers offer interesting insights for industrials and policymakers but only consider the acceptance of a private (or individual) automated vehicle. We contribute to this literature by answering the question: *What are the psychological factors that define the acceptance of the other road users toward a shared automated vehicle?*

Answering this question, we identify two main originalities. First, we focus on a shared automated shuttle which presents different challenges and opportunities than a private automated vehicle. For instance, a shared automated vehicle is usually presented as a solution for congestion, a mode that reduces air pollution through the general use of electric energy, and offering new use cases (e.g., first and last kilometer). These elements could influence the perceptions and attitudes of the other road users which need to be investigated. Second, there is no previous psychological model that studies the acceptance of other road users including at the same time conventional drivers, cyclists, and pedestrians. Using original data, collected on the experimental automated shuttle service located between Nantes and Carquefou in France, we test a theoretical model including factors from the TPB and the SCAS. We also take into consideration technophilia and perceived safety as additional factors that were previously demonstrated to be important in the study of new technologies' acceptance [6, 18]. Using Structural Equation Modeling (SEM), we were able to identify the most influencing factors of the other road users' intentions to interact with the automated vehicle.

The remaining of this article is organized as follows: Sect. 2 presents the theoretical model and the tested hypotheses, Sect. 3 introduces the collected data and the used analysis method, Sect. 4 displays the results and their discussion, and Sect. 5 is the conclusion.

2 Theoretical Model and Hypotheses

Based on the literature review of automated driving and acceptance research, we contribute to the understanding of the determining factors of the acceptance of the other road users by testing the theoretical model illustrated in Fig. 1. The present model is an extended version of the TPB assuming that stated intentions are the direct precedent of the real behavior, expressed here as the acceptance of other users of the road to interact with an automated vehicle. We extend this model by introducing influential factors from the SCAS in addition to a couple of factors that have been demonstrated to be determining of the acceptance of new technology such as technophilia and perceived safety. The tested relations in this model are summarized in Table 4.

We suppose that the intentions (i.e., acceptance) are mainly predicted by the level of technophilia (H1d), the individual attitudes toward the automated vehicle (H7b) and the level of perceived behavioral control (H8). These factors are assumed to be positively related to the intentions and these assumptions are grounded in the existing literature. First, previous research has emphasized that a higher degree of technophilia (also called, personal innovativeness) influences positively the acceptance of end-users of the technology expressed as intentions of use, specifically automated vehicles [4, 5, 18]. In this respect, we expect a similar positive relation between technophilia and intentions to interact with the automated vehicle for other road users. Second, positive attitudes have been demonstrated to be a significant determinant of positive intentions of using automated vehicles [4, 5]. Thus, we expect other road users who have positive attitudes to be more willing to accept the circulation of automated vehicles. Third, perceived behavioral control, usually related to concept of self-efficacy [19], has been previously identified as an influential factor of the intentions to adopt new technologies [19–21]. Accordingly, we think that other road users who believe that they have the required resources and opportunities to manage an interaction with the automated vehicle would express higher acceptance of it circulating on the same road.

We also suppose that the intentions to interact with the automated vehicle are determined indirectly by the combination of a number of factors that interact within each other. We specifically test the relationship between subjective norms, reliability, compatibility, trust, and perceived safety assuming that all the factors are positively related between each other and in their prediction of intentions (see Table 4 for details). These assumptions join the results of previous studies on user or non-user of the acceptance of the automated vehicles [4–6, 15].

Lastly, we note that we control for the effects of age and gender[1]. We assume that all the psychological factors included in the model could be influenced by these individual characteristics [21].

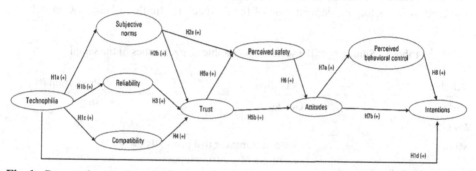

Fig. 1. Proposed research model for investigating the acceptance of automated vehicles by other road users.

3   Data and Methods

3.1   Participants and Procedure

We use original data collected through a twenty-minutes online survey conducted between May and June 2022 as part of the SAM project (Safety and Acceptability of Automated Driving and Mobility). The survey aimed to evaluate the acceptance of inhabitants and users of the Nantes-Carquefou area (France) regarding the introduction of automated vehicles (a shuttle service[2]) using part of the former Nantes-Carquefou railway line (see the red line in the map in Fig. 3). The presented automated vehicle would allow accommodating 6 to 50 people to make 20 min connecting ride from Carquefou to Nantes with an average speed of 20 km/h. The participants had no previous experience with the automated vehicle service deployed at the Nantes-Carquefou site. This allowed us to study their preconceived opinions, attitudes and perceptions influencing their acceptance of the automated shuttle.

---

[1] We consider the participants regardless of their specific usual mobility practices (being a driver, cyclist or pedestrian) since including this variable did not bring any improvement in the predictive power of intentions to interact with the vehicle. Thus, we opt for the most parsimonious model.

[2] Experimented by SNCF and the Stellantis Group (formerly PSA Peugeot-Citroën).

Each participant received by e-mail an individualized participation link to answer the questionnaire that is composed of three main parts: 1) a presentation of the automated vehicle, 2) the acceptance questionnaire and 3) the socio-demographic questionnaire. The final sample was composed of 445 participants divided into 216 potential users of the automated vehicle and 229 potential other road users who could interact with it. As previously mentioned, in the present paper, we only focus on studying the acceptance of the potential other road users. These participants are equally distributed between males and females. The whole sample's mean age is 51 years old with the majority (60.26%) stating being usual car users. Additionally, the sample is composed of a large share of individuals who declare frequently traveling in the tested area of circulation of the automated vehicle. Thus, these are individuals who are most likely going to be directly impacted by the actual implementation of the connecting shuttle of Nantes-Carquefou.

Table 1. Summary of the socio-demographic characteristics of the sample

Variable	Definition	Proportion (%)
Male	Gender	50.22
Female		49.78
Mode	Mode of transport that is usually used regardless of the trip purpose	
Car (as a driver)		60.26
Public transport		14.85
Bicycle		9.61
Walk (or wheelchair)		3.93
Train		1.31
Motorcycle (or scooter)		0.87
Other		9.17
Potential interaction	Travel frequency in the circulation area of the automated vehicle	
Every day or almost every day		40.17
3 or 4 times a week		16.59
1 or 2 times a week		16.16
2 or 3 times a month		9.61
About once a month		6.55
Less often		7.86
Never		3.06
		Mean (*SD*)
Age	In years	50.58 (0.99)

Notes: SD: Standard Deviation, Sample = 229 participants

3.2 Measures

The studied psychological factors are defined and measured using modified versions of existing instruments and items summarized in Table 2. The measuring items are affirmations that the participant is asked to evaluate and declare on a 6-points Likert scale whether they 1 "totally disagree" to 6 "totally agree".

Table 2. Measuring items of the psychological factors included in the model

Psychological factor	Theory	Definition	Measuring items	Mean (*SD*)
Intentions	TPB	The individual readiness to interact with the automated vehicle and accept its circulation in the same area	When I travel... Whenever possible, I intend to avoid running into automated vehicles I will not avoid places where automated vehicles circulate As far as possible, I will stay away from the automated vehicle	4.10 (1.48)
Attitudes	TPB	Personal favorable or unfavorable evaluation of the automated vehicle	Sharing public space with automated vehicles would be a good idea I think that integrating automated vehicles into public space will improve the quality of life for the residents I will not want to share the street with the automated vehicle I think that the presence of automated vehicles will improve traffic flow I support the presence of the automated vehicle in public space Sharing the public space with the automated vehicle will be pleasant	4.39 (1.24)

(*continued*)

Table 2. (*continued*)

Psychological factor	Theory	Definition	Measuring items	Mean (*SD*)
Perceived behavioral control	TPB	The individual's perception of his capacity (ease or difficulty) to manage the situation when interacting with the automated vehicle	I will travel with ease in places where the automated vehicle is present I will not be afraid to be around the automated vehicle I will not be sure what to do if I run into the automated vehicle	4.46 (1.26)
Subjective norms	TPB	The individual's beliefs about his entourage's attitudes about the automated vehicle	I don't think my relatives would mind being in the same area as the automated vehicle I think the people I care about would advise me to avoid automated vehicles My relatives would not hesitate to go to a place where the automated vehicle is present	4.38 (1.22)
Compatibility	SCAS	The individual's opinion about the readiness of the automated vehicle to circulate without supervision in public spaces	It is essential that a supervisor be on board to retake control of the automated vehicle I think that automated vehicles are not yet advanced enough to drive on public roads I don't think the automated vehicle will be able to handle all driving situations	3.70 (1.31)

(*continued*)

Table 2. (*continued*)

Psychological factor	Theory	Definition	Measuring items	Mean (*SD*)
Reliability	SCAS	The individual's opinion about the risks of failures of the automated vehicle	I don't think automated vehicles will have any failures I think automated vehicles will have failures I think the automated vehicle will be reliable	3.33 (1.16)
Trust	SCAS	The individual's confidence in the maturity of the technology to be able to function correctly	I will have confidence that the automated vehicle correctly detects people and objects around it I will have confidence in the automated vehicle to handle complex traffic situations I will trust the automated vehicle to look out for me	4.26 (1.38)
Perceived safety	Extension	The individual's opinion about the risk of having/not having an accident with the automated vehicle that could harm his personal safety	I think the automated vehicle will be able to avoid me in all circumstances I will not feel safe in a place with the automated vehicle I don't think I will have an accident with the automated vehicle	4.14 (1.26)
Technophilia	Extension	The individual's attraction to testing new technologies	If I hear about a new technology, I try to experiment with it quickly I like to discover new technologies	4.23 (1.34)

Notes: The measuring items are translated from French; The scales of the negatively formulated measuring items were reversed before calculating the means; *SD* = Standard Deviation

3.3 Data Analyses

Confirmatory Factor Analysis (CFA)

The proposed model is based on the previously mentioned literature including psychological factors previously included in the TPB or SCAS. However, we verify the structure of the questionnaire and the robustness of our model by running a CFA. It is a necessary step before running a structural model to assess the relevance of the factors in the tested model compared to the theory (known as the measurement model). This is done by conducting several statistical tests, namely computing the model fit indices, to determine the adequacy of model fit to the data such as the chi-square test, the Root Mean Square Error of Approximation (RMSEA), the Comparative Fit Index (CFI), the Tucke-Lewis index (TLI), the Standardized Root Mean Square Residual (SRMR), etc.

Structural Equation Modeling (SEM)

When studying relationships between psychological factors that are measured using several declarative questions, the most appropriate and widely used method is SEM. The objective of a SEM is to test hypotheses of relationships between several variables of a theoretical model. Actually, it is a combination of a measurement model and several regression models used to understand the paths between the psychological factors. In the present paper we test the way the previously mentioned psychological factors interact in predicting the individual intentions to interact with the automated vehicle as an expression of the acceptance of this mode by the other road users (see the tested model in Fig. 1).

All these analyses have been done on R-4.2.1 using the lavaan package [22].

4 Results and Discussions

4.1 Confirmatory Factor Analysis – Measurement Model

Carrying out the CFA to test the internal consistency of the theoretical model, we use the diagonally Weighted Least Squares method with a Mean and Variance correction (WLSMV) instead of the widely used Maximum Likelihood (ML) estimation method. Our scale is ordinal and our data does not follow a normal distribution based on the results of the Shapiro-Wilk test of normality of data [23]. Actually, WLSMV method has been demonstrated to perform better with ordinal data than the ML method [24] which justifies our choice of estimation method.

The results of the CFA suggest that the model has acceptable adjustment to the data since the model fit indices respect the required thresholds: RMSEA = 0.070 (between 0.05 and 0.08 [25, 26]); SRMR = 0.048 (< 0.08 [27]); CFI = 0.970 and TLI = 0.964 (both > 0.95). The factor loading results are all above 0.6 except for two items of the measure of reliability having factor loadings just above 0.5 (See Table 3). Based on the results of the factor analyses, the underlying psychological constructs demonstrate, both, satisfactory validity and reliability (Cronbach's Alpha (CA) coefficients above 0.7 threshold and calculated Average Variance Extracted (AVE) all very close or above the 0.5 threshold). Thus, these factors can be used to calculate a structural equation model.

Table 3. Evaluation of the psychological factors

Psychological factor	Number of used items	Factor loadings range	CA	AVE
Intentions	3	0.653–0.880	0.692	0.543
Attitudes	6	0.643–0.927	0.888	0.658
Perceived behavioral control	3	0.681–0.909	0.804	0.676
Subjective norms	3	0.749–0.840	0.771	0.637
Compatibility	3	0.613–0.769	0.710	0.476
Reliability	3	0.509–0.935	0.748	0.484
Trust	3	0.867–0.919	0.894	0.800
Perceived safety	3	0.688–0.888	0.740	0.593
Technophilia	2	0.861–0.899	0.829	0.774

Notes: CA = Cronbach's Alpha, AVE = Average Variance Extracted

4.2 Structural Equation Model

Figure 2 presents the results of the estimated structural model with solid lines representing the significant relationships and the dotted lines representing the non-significant ones. Table 4 summarizes the supported or rejected tested hypotheses. A total of 68.1% of the variance in the intentions of the other road users to interact with the automated vehicle was accounted for in the model. Besides, the model fit indices are acceptable: RMSEA = 0.065; CFI = 0.970; TLI = 0.969 and SRMR = 0.048.

With a standardized coefficient equal to 1.536 ($p < 0.001$), the perceived behavioral control seems to be the most important direct predictor of the intentions. The analyses reveal a significant positive relationship between attitudes and perceived behavioral control (0.949, $p < 0.001$), trust as a positive predictor of the individual perception of safety of the automated vehicle (0.947, $p < 0.001$) and, in turn, this trust is positively related to the reliability (0.519, $p < 0.01$) and compatibility (0.484, $p < 0.01$). Lastly, positive subjective norms and thinking the automated vehicle is reliable and compatible is more likely for a technophile participant (respectively, 0.932; 1.067; 1.074, $p < 0.001$).

The decomposition of the effects testing the significance of the indirect and total effects (see Table 5) of the psychological factors on intentions (and between each other) identifies the significant indirect effect of the attitudes on intentions which is mediated by the perceived behavioral control (1.458, $p < 0.001$). The results also show that trust (1.403, $p < 0.001$) and technophilia (2.426, $p < 0.001$) indirectly predict the intentions to interact with the automated vehicle.

Controlling for the effects of age and gender (see estimation results in Table 6), the intentions of the participants (i.e., their acceptance) did not significantly vary in function of these individual characteristics. However, we identify several significant effects on other psychological factors in relation to these intentions. Regarding the age factor, we find that younger participants are more likely to be technophile (-0.275, $p < 0.05$)

and to perceive that they have the necessary capacities to handle a situation where the automated vehicle is present (-0.088, $p < 0.05$). On the contrary, older participants are more likely to perceive the automated vehicle as reliable (0.427, $p < 0.001$) and compatible (0.293, $p < 0.05$) as well as being influenced by the attitudes of those around them (0.282, $p < 0.05$). Age did not have significant effects on perceived safety, trust nor on attitudes. Concerning the gender effect, we find that men are more likely to be technophile (0.414, $p < 0.001$), to be more trusting of the automated vehicle (0.100, $p < 0.05$), and to perceive that they have the capabilities to handle a situation where the automated vehicle is present in their traveling area (0.124, $p < 0.01$). Parallely, women are more likely to perceive the automated vehicle as reliable (-0.516, $p < 0.001$) and compatible (-0.405, $p < 0.01$) as well as being influenced by the attitudes of those around them (-0.444, $p < 0.001$). We identifiy no significant gender effects on the perceived safety nor on the attitudes.

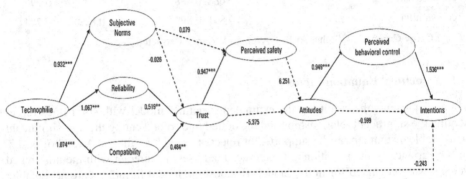

Fig. 2. Standardized regression weights of the model of acceptance of other road users

4.3 Discussion

We contribute to the understanding of the acceptance of automated vehicles by the other road users expressed as stated intentions to interact with it. Relying on the TPB and SCAS, we identify through a SEM that perceived behavioral control is the main predictor of these intentions. Meaning that an individual would be more accepting of the automated vehicle if they believe in their capacity (having the necessary personal or external factors) to handle a situation where they are confronted with this technology. This finding is in line with previous research where perceived behavioral control was found to be a significant predictor of intentions to adopt automated vehicles [7, 29].

The results of the model also showed that the attitudes were not a significant predictor of the intentions which goes against expectations and the previous findings of various acceptance studies of the automated vehicle [4, 5, 7]. This divergence could be explained by the lack of consideration of the role of perceived behavioral control in these previous studies. In our case, this factor has a strong relation with intentions, and it plays the role of a full mediator in the attitudes-intentions relationship.

Table 4. Results of the tested hypotheses

Tested hypothesis		Standardized Estimate	p-value	Conclusion
H1a	Technophilia → Subjective norms	0.932	0.000	Supported
H1b	Technophilia → Reliability	1.067	0.000	Supported
H1c	Technophilia → Compatibility	1.074	0.000	Supported
H1d	Technophilia → Intentions	−0.243	0.301	Rejected
H2a	Subjective norms → Perceived safety	0.079	0.179	Rejected
H2b	Subjective norms → Trust	−0.026	0.726	Rejected
H3	Reliability → Trust	0.519	0.004	Supported
H4	Compatibility → Trust	0.484	0.005	Supported
H5a	Trust → Perceived safety	0.947	0.000	Supported
H5b	Trust → Attitudes	−5.375	0.250	Rejected
H6	Perceived safety → Attitudes	6.251	0.177	Rejected
H7a	Attitudes → Perceived behavioral control	0.949	0.000	Supported
H7b	Attitudes → Intentions	−0.599	0.191	Rejected
H8	Perceived behavioral control → Intentions	1.536	0.000	Supported

We additionally found that trust indirectly predicted intentions. This relation is mainly mediated by perceived behavioral control. This means that the trust that an individual has in this technology is internalized in his stated perceived behavioral control which, then, would influence the individual acceptance. A number of previous studies [4–6, 15] confirm the importance of considering the trust-acceptance relationship in the context of the use of automated vehicle. Trust was found to be a direct positive predictor of the use intentions or having an indirect effect on intentions when considering the perceived safety as a mediator of this relation [30].

All these results raise for the industrials and the policymakers the importance of finding ways to reinforce the perceived behavioral control if they want to guarantee a better acceptance of other road users. Based on our model, this could be done either by acting directly on the concerned psychological factor or by programming measures on other influential factors (namely, trust and attitudes) related to the factor of interest.

In the present paper, we defined the perceived behavioral control as the perceived ease of interaction with the automated vehicle. But, since this technology is not available to the public yet, numerous question marks still surround it. To bring answers to the public, and based on the results of the model, industrials and policymakers could increase the individuals' knowledge about automated vehicles through advertising and media campaigns. This would establish a better awareness of the vehicle's features. In turn, it would improve the perceived ease of interaction with the vehicle on the road. Discovering

Table 5. Decomposition of the effects

Dependent variable	Explanatory variable	Direct effects	Indirect effects	Total effects
Subjective norms	Technophilia	0.932***	N/A	N/A
Reliability	Technophilia	1.067***	N/A	N/A
Compatibility	Technophilia	1.074***	N/A	N/A
Trust	Subjective norms	−0.026	N/A	N/A
	Reliability	0.519**	N/A	N/A
	Compatibility	0.484**	N/A	N/A
	Technophilia	N/A	1.048***	1.048***
Perceived safety	Subjective norms	0.079	-0.025	0.054
	Trust	0.947***	N/A	N/A
Attitudes	Trust	−5.375	5.918	0.543***
	Perceived safety	6.251	N/A	N/A
Perceived behavioral control	Attitudes	0.949***	N/A	N/A
	Perceived safety	N/A	5.935	5.935
Intentions	Attitudes	−0.599	1.458***	0.860***
	Perceived behavioral control	1.536***	N/A	N/A
	Trust	N/A	1.403***	1.403***
	Technophilia	−0.243	2.426***	2.504***

Notes: N/A = Not Applicable, * $p < 0.05$; ** $p < 0.01$; *** $p < 0.001$, Significance of the indirect and total effects tested using the Sobel test [28]

these facilitating features could also be done through controlled trials where the potential concerned individuals would be put in a realistic setting to interact with the vehicle before its actual introduction on the road and have a better sense of their capacities to manage a situation with its presence. Additionally, individuals need to be reassured about the existence of adequate infrastructures (e.g., a specific color of traffic light to signal the presence of the automated vehicle) to easily accommodate the circulation of the automated vehicle in the presence of the other modes of transport.

Concerning the possible measures to have positive individual attitudes, we recommend industrials and policymakers to emphasize the benefits of introducing an automated vehicle for other road users. This could take the form of communication campaigns highlighting the improved road safety, the better access to mobility (e.g., disabled individuals or elderlies), optimization of traffic flow (e.g., an automated shuttle would allow reaching the destination faster and opting less for the private vehicle) and reducing the greenhouse gas and other pollutant emissions thanks to reduced road traffic.

Lastly, policymakers and industrials should consider programming measures to gain the trust of the other road users by demonstrating the reliability and compatibility of the automated vehicle. The other road users need to be convinced by the maturity of the technology and its readiness to circulate safely in interaction with the random external factors. We advise manufacturers to be transparent about the capabilities of the vehicle, for example by communicating key statistics (e.g., impact of the introduction of the vehicle to accidentology) or the quality control process (e.g., number of vehicle overhauls for a defined period). Besides, policymakers should share the future improvement projects of the infrastructure which would allow to increase the compatibility of the automated vehicle with the existing traffic network.

It would therefore be relevant, for future work, to implement all or part of these proposals in order to confirm their impact on acceptance.

5 Conclusion

We proposed and empirically tested an automated vehicle acceptance model for other road users including psychological factors from the TPB, factors from the SCAS, perceived security and technophilia. Our findings confirmed the important relationship between the individual perceived behavioral control to easily handle a situation in the presence of the vehicle and the intentions to interact with it. Thus, the present paper contributed to clarifying the relationships between the determinants of acceptance and giving new levers that industrials and policymakers should consider before introducing automated vehicles on the common roads.

However, some limitations of this work should be mentioned. First, the used data lacks age representativity of the populations of Nantes and Carquefou[3]. We have a sample with a mean age of 51 years old. Still, most of the participants are directly concerned with the implementation of the automated vehicle since they are frequent users of the studied traffic area. About 57% of the sample declare going in this area at least three times a week. Thus, the sample gives a good representation of the future people that may interact with the automated vehicle.

Second, the proposed model highly depends on the way the psychological factors have been defined and measured. Even though we based our choice of measures on literature and tested their robustness, using other scales could give different results than the ones found here. For instance, when considering the perceived safety, we mainly relate the definition of this factor to the avoidance of collisions. But the safety related to an automated vehicle could also include, for example, aspects of cyber security [33] that were not defined here and should be considered in future studies.

---

[3] Compared to the age distribution of the population of Nantes and Carquefou in 2019 [31, 32].

Lastly, the proposed model is the first to consider the acceptance of other road users with different mobility practices. Nonetheless, comparative studies should be conducted using data from other experimental automated vehicles (private and shared) to further validate this model. We also believe that this model should be extended by including other potentially influential factors of acceptance. The automated vehicle is expected to have social, environmental and health benefits. Accordingly, factors as the individual environmental awareness [34], level of altruism [35] or health motivations [36] could be included in the acceptance models of other road users.

Acknowledgement. This work was supported by the SAM project (Safety and Acceptability of Automated Driving and Mobility), SNCF and the Stellantis Group.

Officially launched on June 20, 2019, the SAM project is the result of the EVRA (Expérimentation de véhicules routiers automatisés – Experiment of automated vehicles on open roads) call for projects as part of the Investments for the Future Program (PIA) which is at the heart of the national strategy for the development of automated vehicles presented by the Government in May 2018. The project was co-funded by the French Agency for Ecological Transition (Ademe).

We thank Marlène Bel, Aurore Lemonnier and Florence Rosey for their contributions to the questionnaire used for data collection.

Appendices

A. Map of the Nantes-Carquefou Automated Vehicle Implementation

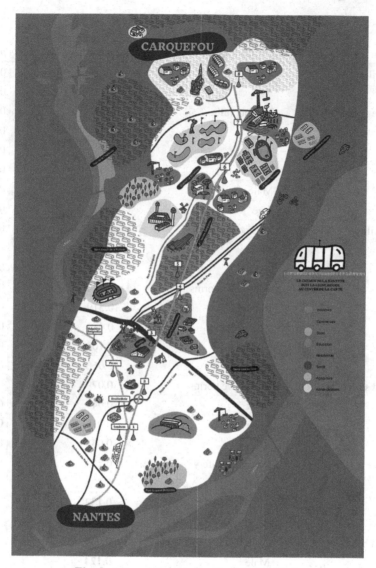

Fig. 3. Map of the automated vehicle's circuit

B. Model Estimation Results

Table 6. Model estimation results

Dependent variable	Explanatory variable	Standardized Estimate	p-value
Technophilia	Male	0.414	0.000
	Age	−0.275	0.022
Subjective norms	Technophilia	0.932	0.000
	Male	−0.444	0.000
	Age	0.282	0.014
Reliability	Technophilia	1.067	0.000
	Male	−0.516	0.000
	Age	0.427	0.001
Compatibility	Technophilia	1.074	0.000
	Male	−0.405	0.003
	Age	0.293	0.024
Trust	Subjective norms	−0.026	0.726
	Reliability	0.519	0.004
	Compatibility	0.484	0.005
	Male	0.100	0.052
	Age	0.066	0.176
Perceived safety	Subjective norms	0.079	0.179
	Trust	0.947	0.000
	Male	0.019	0.689
	Age	−0.054	0.220
Attitudes	Perceived safety	6.251	0.177
	Trust	−5.375	0.250
	Male	−0.132	0.668
	Age	0.294	0.479
Perceived behavioral control	Attitudes	0.949	0.000
	Male	0.124	0.004
	Age	−0.088	0.014
Intentions	Technophilia	−0.243	0.301
	Perceived behavioral control	1.536	0.000
	Attitudes	−0.599	0.191
	Male	0.010	0.943
	Age	−0.133	0.295

Notes: The estimated covariances are not included in this table for reasons of parsimony

References

1. Lee, D., Hess, D.J.: Public concerns and connected and automated vehicles: safety, privacy, and data security. Hum. Soc. Sci. Commun. **9**(1), 1–13 (2022)
2. Kaur, K., Rampersad, G.: Trust in driverless cars: Investigating key factors influencing the adoption of driverless cars. J. Eng. Technol. Manage. **48**, 87–96 (2018)
3. Kaye, S.A., Somoray, K., Rodwell, D., Lewis, I.: Users' acceptance of private automated vehicles: a systematic review and meta-analysis. J. Saf. Res. **79**, 352–367 (2021)
4. Nastjuk, I., Herrenkind, B., Marrone, M., Brendel, A.B., Kolbe, L.M.: What drives the acceptance of autonomous driving? An investigation of acceptance factors from an end-user's perspective. Technol. Forecast. Soc. Change **161**, 120319 (2020)
5. Herrenkind, B., Brendel, A.B., Nastjuk, I., Greve, M., Kolbe, L.M.: Investigating end-user acceptance of autonomous electric buses to accelerate diffusion. Transp. Res. Part D: Transp. Environ. **74**, 255–276 (2019)
6. Zhang, T., et al.: Automated vehicle acceptance in China: social influence and initial trust are key determinants. Transp. Res. Part C: Emerg. Technol. **112**, 220–233 (2020)
7. Jing, P., Huang, H., Ran, B., Zhan, F., Shi, Y.: Exploring the factors affecting mode choice intention of autonomous vehicle based on an extended theory of planned behavior—A case study in China. Sustainability **11**(4), 1155 (2019)
8. Lécureux, B., Bonnet, A., Manout, O., Berrada, J., & Bouzouina, L.: Acceptance of shared autonomous vehicles: a literature review of stated choice experiments (2022)
9. Lemonnier, A., Adelé, S., Dionisio, C.: The determinants of acceptability and behavioural intention of automated vehicles–a review. Le travail humain **4**, 297–342 (2020)
10. Venkatesh, V., Davis, F.D.: A theoretical extension of the technology acceptance model: Four longitudinal field studies. Manage. Sci. **46**(2), 186–204 (2000)
11. Venkatesh, V., Morris, M.G., Davis, G.B., Davis, F.D.: User acceptance of information technology: Toward a unified view. MIS Q., 425-478 (2003)
12. Ajzen, I.: The theory of planned behavior. Organ. Behav. Hum. Decis. Process.Behav. Hum. Decis. Process. **50**(2), 179–211 (1991)
13. Nees, M.A.: Acceptance of self-driving cars: an examination of idealized versus realistic portrayals with a self-driving car acceptance scale. In: Proceedings of the Human Factors and Ergonomics Society Annual Meeting, pp. 1449–1453. SAGE Publications Sage CA, Los Angeles (2016)
14. Haué, J.-B., Merlhiot, G., Koustanaï, A., Barré, J., Moneger, F.: Hey Robot, let me the way Automated vehicle and incivility
15. Koustanaï, A., Bel, M., Bordel, S., Metayer, N., Massoulié, J.: Modeling perceived safety and acceptance of AV in traffic. In: ITS European Congress Toulouse, 2022 (2022)
16. Deb, S., Strawderman, L., Carruth, D.W., DuBien, J., Smith, B., Garrison, T.M.: Development and validation of a questionnaire to assess pedestrian receptivity toward fully autonomous vehicles. Transp. Res. Part C: Emerg. Technol. **84**, 178–195 (2017)
17. Pammer, K., Gauld, C., McKerral, A., Reeves, C.: "They have to be better than human drivers!" Motorcyclists' and cyclists' perceptions of autonomous vehicles. Transp. Res. Part F: Traffic Psychol. Behav. **78**, 246–258 (2021)
18. Dastjerdi, A.M., Kaplan, S., e Silva, J.D.A., Nielsen, O.A., Pereira, F.C.: Use intention of mobility-management travel apps: the role of users goals, technophile attitude and community trust. Transp. Res. Part A: Policy Pract. **126**, 114–135 (2019)
19. Luarn, P., Lin, H.H.: Toward an understanding of the behavioral intention to use mobile banking. Comput. Hum. Behav.. Hum. Behav. **21**(6), 873–891 (2005)
20. Ajjan, H., Hartshorne, R.: Investigating faculty decisions to adopt web 2.0 technologies: theory and empirical tests. Internet High. Educ. **11**(2), 71–80 (2008)

21. Venkatesh, V., Morris, M.G., Ackerman, P.L.: A longitudinal field investigation of gender differences in individual technology adoption decision-making processes. Organ. Behav. Hum. Decis. Process.Behav. Hum. Decis. Process. **83**(1), 33–60 (2000)
22. Rosseel, Y.: Lavaan: an R package for structural equation modeling. J. Stat. Softw.Softw. **48**, 1–36 (2012)
23. Shapiro, S.S., Wilk, M.B.: An analysis of variance test for normality (complete samples). Biometrika **52**(3/4), 591–611 (1965)
24. Li, C.-H.: The performance of MLR, USLMV, and WLSMV estimation in structural regression models with ordinal variables. Michigan State University (2014)
25. Kaplan, D.: Structural Equation Modeling: Foundations and Extensions, vol. 10. SAGE publications, New York (2008)
26. Hu, L.T., Bentler, P.M.: Cutoff criteria for fit indexes in covariance structure analysis: Conventional criteria versus new alternatives. Struct. Equ. Model.: Multidisc. J. **6**(1), 1–55 (1999)
27. Schreiber, J.B., Nora, A., Stage, F.K., Barlow, E.A., King, J.: Reporting structural equation modeling and confirmatory factor analysis results: a review. J. Educ. Res. **99**(6), 323–338 (2006)
28. Sobel, M.E.: Asymptotic confidence intervals for indirect effects in structural equation models. Sociol. Methodol.. Methodol. **13**, 290–312 (1982)
29. Buckley, L., Kaye, S.A., Pradhan, A.K.: Psychosocial factors associated with intended use of automated vehicles: a simulated driving study. Acc. Anal. Prevent. **115**, 202–208 (2018)
30. Liu, P., Yang, R., Xu, Z.: Public acceptance of fully automated driving: effects of social trust and risk/benefit perceptions. Risk Anal. **39**(2), 326–341 (2019). https://doi.org/10.1111/risa.13143
31. Dossier complet − Commune de Nantes (44109) | Insee. https://www.insee.fr/fr/statistiques/2011101?geo=COM-44109. Consulté 30 Mars 2023
32. Dossier complet − Commune de Carquefou (44026) | Insee. https://www.insee.fr/fr/statistiques/2011101?geo=COM-44026. Consulté 21 Avril 2023
33. Garidis, K., Ulbricht, L., Rossmann, A., Schmäh, M.: Toward a user acceptance model of autonomous driving. In: Proceedings of the 53rd Hawaii International Conference on System Sciences, 7–10 January 2020, pp. 1381–1390. Wailea-Makena, Hawaii, University of Hawai'i at Manoa (2020)
34. Wu, J., Liao, H., Wang, J.W., Chen, T.: The role of environmental concern in the public acceptance of autonomous electric vehicles: a survey from China. Transp. Res. Part F: Traffic Psychol. Behav. **60**, 37–46 (2019)
35. Arısal, İ, Atalar, T.: The exploring relationships between environmental concern, collectivism and ecological purchase intention. Procedia-Soc. Behav. Sci. **235**, 514–521 (2016)
36. Rojas Rueda, D., Nieuwenhuijsen, M.J., Khreis, H., Frumkin, H.: Autonomous vehicles and public health. Ann. Rev. Publ. Health **41**(1), 329–345 (2020)

Smart-Routing Web App: A Road Traffic Eco-Routing Tool Proposal for Smart Cities

José R. Lozano-Pinilla⏺, Iván Sánchez-Cordero⏺,
and Cristina Vicente-Chicote⁽✉⁾⏺

Quercus SEG, University of Extremadura, Cáceres, Spain
{joserralp,cristinav}@unex.es

Abstract. The use of routing services has witnessed a notable surge in recent years. While most of them provide users with the shortest and the fastest routes, only a few of them provide information about the most eco-friendly route or gather information about the vehicle or the user preferences. Eco-routing has demonstrated its potential to significantly reduce both fuel consumption and Greenhouse Gas Emissions (GGE). However, most of the routing applications supporting this feature do not consider the specific car features, the road slope or the traffic conditions, providing only a rough estimation of the fuel consumption (mainly based on travel distance and type of fuel). Integrating such additional information would result in more flexible and powerful routing applications, allowing end-users to prioritize different features (travel time, distance, fuel consumption, etc.) according to their needs or preferences. In this context, we propose an easy-to-configure smart-routing web framework, providing end-users with alternative routes for their trips, including the most common ones (minimum distance and minimum expected travel time) together with an eco-friendly route, computed in a more precise way than current routing services.

Keywords: Eco-Routing · Route Optimization · Smart Cities

1 Introduction

A few decades ago, the only way to plan travel routes was by using physical road maps. Currently, navigation apps (installed in our mobile phones or even integrated in our cars) help us plan and carry out our trips in a more user-friendly and sustainable way, as maps are automatically updated (there is no need to regularly buy new versions of printed maps) and include plenty of additional useful information.

Currently, navigation apps increasingly integrate features related with smart mobility, including eco-route planning, real-time traffic status, or information about accidents or road works, among others. These features not only help individual drivers to plan and carry out their trips, but also aim at contributing to

© ICST Institute for Computer Sciences, Social Informatics and Telecommunications Engineering 2024
Published by Springer Nature Switzerland AG 2024. All Rights Reserved
A. L. Martins et al. (Eds.): INTSYS 2023, LNICST 540, pp. 247–258, 2024.
https://doi.org/10.1007/978-3-031-49379-9_14

global traffic management, one of the key aspects in *Smart Cities*. Some of these smart features (e.g., traffic status) build on information automatically gathered from users' mobile devices. This is the case of Google Maps [1]: one of the leading navigation apps today, and a precursor to many others. Google Maps provides users with many valuable features: it is free, easy to configure and use, and is available both as a web and a mobile application. However, some users report limited offline functionality, excessive battery consumption, and many privacy issues related with personal data collection, storage and exploitation. In this sense, the use of Internet of Things (IoT) technologies could help implementing more privacy-respectful navigation systems, as traffic information could be collected in an aggregated and anonymous way from different sensors placed in the cities' infrastructure (rather than from the users' devices). The use of this information for intelligent decision-making related to traffic management would contribute to achieve real Smart Cities. However, the integration of IoT devices in cities is not being as fast or uniform as promised, resulting in unreliable performance and lack of information for many places.

One of the most recent features included in Google Maps is eco-routing. This concept, coined by Ericsson et al. [2] in 2006, aims at computing the route that minimizes the energy required to complete a trip, taking into account several factors such as the current status of the traffic, the road topology (e.g., slope, road type, diversions, etc.) and the specific features of the vehicle (e.g., weight, fuel type, etc.), among others. Reducing vehicles' energy consumption implies not only reducing the cost of the trip, but also the Greenhouse Gas Emissions (GGE). Besides, specifically to Electric Vehicle (EV) drivers, eco-routing also reduces "range anxiety", i.e., drivers' anxiety for not being able to complete their trip before the vehicle runs out of battery. Despite these advantages, eco-routes tend to be longer in terms of travel time since, e.g., they may consider roads with less slope that may require traveling longer distances. In fact, the study carried out in Japan by Kono et al. [3] concluded that eco-routes, compared to shortest routes, reduce fuel consumption in about 9%, while they increase travel time also in 9%. Despite the longer travel times, Zeng et al. highlight in [4,5] the benefits of choosing eco-routes compared to shortest or fastest routes.

Eco-route calculation is a computation-intensive process involving big amounts of input data. Although Google Maps supports this feature, it offers just a rough estimation of eco-routes, namely based on fuel type and travel distance. In this context, the Smart-Routing Web App presented in this paper aims at computing eco-routes in a more accurate way, while keeping the process efficient and preserving users' privacy. Apart from eco-routes, the application will also provide drivers with the fastest and shortest routes, allowing them to choose among the three of them according to their needs or preferences.

The rest of the paper is organized as follows. Firstly, Sect. 2 reviews related research focused on eco-routing. Secondly, Sect. 3, outlines the architecture of the proposed web application, describing its main components. Then, Sect. 4 describes how road topology information is obtained, processed and used to compute the eco-routes according to the workflow then detailed in Sect. 5. Finally, Sect. 6 draws some conclusions and outlines future works.

2 Related Works

Eco-routing is a hot research topic today due to its relevance in smart mobility: one of the pillars of Smart Cities. Smart mobility aims at reducing travel times and congestion, improving network and traffic management, increase safety by preventing accidents, and ensure environmental and economic sustainability.

Many research works focused on eco-routing can be found in the literature. Zeng et al. [6] develop an eco-routing algorithm for navigation systems that finds the route with the minimum fuel consumption satisfying on-time arrival requirements. Aguiar et al. [7] define MobiWise, an eco-routing decision support system that leverages Internet of Things (IoT) technologies, real traffic data and a calibrated digital twin, being limited to a middle-sized European city as Porto (Portugal). Some works focus on reducing emissions and air pollution. For instance, Vamshi et al. [8] propose a dynamic route planning algorithm that distributes traffic density in real-time to low-density traffic areas, trying to minimize the number of congested junctions by uniformly distributing traffic in order to reduce air pollution, available only with traffic information on the Surat area in Gujarat (India). Similarly, Ghaffari et al. [9] introduce a novel algorithm to find the shortest route based on traffic congestion and air quality, not considering road topology or vehicle features.

Internet of Vehicles (IoV), an evolution of the Vehicular Ad-hoc Networks (VANETs), is another active research field in which it is possible to find some works focused on eco-routing. For instance, Xiaofeng [10] introduces a hybrid genetic algorithm and social spider optimization algorithm for an energy-aware routing schema to optimize traffic congestion. Also in this line, Alfaseeh et al. [11] propose a multi-objective eco-routing system for Connected and Autonomous Vehicles (CAVs). Both IoV and CAVs assume that vehicles are equipped with sensors, software, and other technologies to collect and exchange information over the Internet with other vehicles or smart devices. However, these technologies are not expected to be available in most private vehicles until 2040 [12,13].

Finally, among the navigation systems currently supporting eco-route calculation it is worth highlighting Google Maps [14] and EmiLa App [15]. The former was first introduced by Google in the United States in October 2021. Nowadays, it is available in many other countries, more than 40 in Europe [16], including Spain, France, Germany and the UK. Google Maps allows drivers to configure the type of engine of their vehicles: diesel, gasoline, electric or hybrid and, according to that, it displays the eco-route and a rough estimation of the fuel savings. However, as previously mentioned, the eco-route proposed by Google Maps seems not to consider, e.g., relevant changes in the route slope, which may drastically affect energy consumption. On the other hand, EmiLa App integrates life-cycle assessments of various means of transportation into classic route planning algorithms by considering different sustainability factors in addition to typical metrics such as distance, travel times or cost. This application motivates users to choose eco-routes through gamification. However, the criteria for eco-route selection and emission calculation are not clearly defined and it seems to be still a theoretical artifact rather than an actual product.

Despite the advances achieved in the eco-routing field, most of the reviewed works have important limitations either in the geographical areas of application, in the technologies required for their implementation or in the incomplete information being used for the calculations. In response to these limitations, our proposal aims to address worldwide eco-route calculation using currently available technologies and accurate topology information.

3   Proposed Architecture

The software architecture of the Smart-Routing Web Application proposed in this paper gathers several components. These components are deployed and connected in a loosely coupled way, making it easier to replace any of them with other services offering similar functionalities. The architecture of the proposed framework is shown in Fig. 1, along with its components and their relationships. Each of these components is described below, along with their core functionality and the technologies involved.

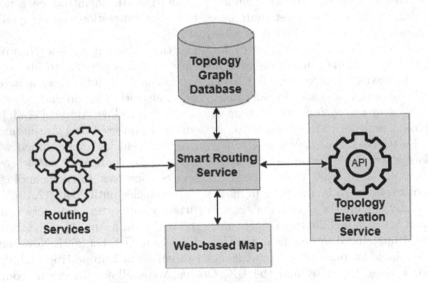

Fig. 1. Smart Routing Web Application architecture.

– **Routing Services (RS).** This component currently gathers three third-party routing services, although it could be easy extended to support new (either third-party or self-made) ones. The three services currently supported build on OpenStreetMap, as a baseline for route calculation: (1) OpenRoute-Service [17] (ORS), which provides global spatial services such as route calculation or time-distance matrices calculated using only public open-source data; (2) Open Source Routing Machine [18, 19] (OSRM), a high-performance routing engine for calculating shortest and fastest routes in road networks, among other functionalities; and (3) GraphHopper [20, 21], an open-source fast and memory-efficient routing engine, which allows users to calculate the distance, time, turn-by-turn instructions, and road features for any route between two or more points. All these services calculate routes based on different metrics, allowing users to easily retrieve them using different programming languages. Although all these services are third-party, some of them have been deployed locally using Docker containers.

– **Topology Elevation Service (TES)**. Since one of the main contributions of this framework is to accurately calculate eco-routes, knowledge of the road network topology is essential due to its direct impact on fuel consumption. There are several services that allow us to determine the elevation (altitude) of any GPS coordinate on Earth such as (1) Open-Elevation API [22], a free and open-source API that allows retrieving elevation information for geographical coordinates; (2) Google Elevation API [23], a pay-per-request API that returns elevation data for a given location or path; and (3) OpenTopo-Data [24], a free REST API for elevation data that can be deployed both locally or remotely. We chose the later as it allows users to easily select different data sources and load them in the API. The process for loading and processing geospatial and topology data is later described in Sect. 4.

– **Web-Based Map (WBM)**. This component serves as an interface between the SRS component and the end-users, allowing them to select the source and destination of their trip and view the different routes calculated between them. The application is based on an interactive map, meaning that users can select locations directly clicking on it and interact with the output routes to retrieve additional information, such as the distance or the estimated travel time or fuel consumption. Additionally, this application provides turn-by-turn directions for the selected routes, offering specific road information at each route segment. Figure 2 shows a mock-up of the web application with all its detailed features. This component has been developed using the Flask micro-framework, along with Python and Jinja to handle user interactions, and the interactive and easy to customize maps provided by OpenStreetMap.

– **Topology Graph Database (TGD)**. In order to store the different routes and efficiently perform operations on them, we decided to use a graph-oriented database. Among the different options considered (e.g., ArangoDB or Redis-Graph), finally Neo4J was chosen because it supports both directed and undirected graphs, and offers several libraries and predefined route optimization algorithms such as A*, shortest path, and Yen's k-shortest paths, among others.

– **Smart Routing Service (SRS)**. This component is the core of the framework as it interconnects all other services. The SRS is responsible for retrieving the different routes provided by the RS, processing and storing them in the

TGD and plotting them graphically in the WBM. Route processing involves several steps: (1) retrieving the full routes; (2) splitting them into different route segments and nodes; and (3) retrieving and calculating the topology information for these segments, including their slope, number of lanes or maximum speed, among other features. For the last step, the Overpass API [25], an OpenStreetMap read-only service that allows users to retrieve OSM-map-related information, is used. The SRS component has been developed using Python and Flask, along with several additional libraries and packages.

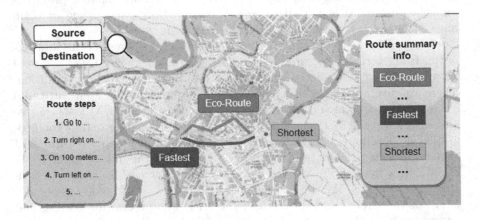

Fig. 2. Smart Routing Web App mock-up

Some of the external services used in the framework can also be deployed locally, which facilitates the development and testing processes. These local services are deployed using Docker containers and the Docker-Compose orchestration tool, as shown in Fig. 3, where the architecture of the local components, their properties and relations are described using the *Containers Modeling Tool (CML)* [26]: a Docker-Compose modeling tool developed by the authors. Components used remotely are not represented in the model, while all local containers have a related volume, where their functionality information is stored.

Despite its benefits, local deployment has also some limitations. For instance, some of the routing services do not provide all the features supported by their online versions, e.g., the route step descriptions or the topology database may be limited to the information stored on the local device, even when using a worldwide dataset. These limitations have been considered and addressed in the framework by obtaining any missing information from other external sources.

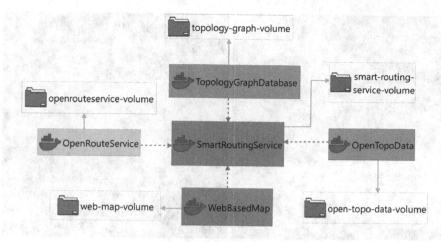

Fig. 3. Docker-Compose schema of the Smart Routing Web App.

4   Topology Information

The topology information obtained by the TES component is very valuable as it allows calculating optimal eco-routes in a more precise way. In the proposed Smart-Routing Web Application, one the sources providing topology information is the OpenTopoData API, which is deployed locally and allows loading almost any kind of geospatial dataset (ASTER, ETOPO1, SRTM both 30m and 90m, Mapzen, etc.). The framework loads and uses several datasets, including the one provided by the NASA's Shuttle Radar Topography Mission (SRTM) [27]. This dataset covers almost all of the earth's surface (from -60 to $60°C$ latitude) with a precision of 1 arc-second (30 m at the equator). As this dataset covers a huge extension, it is divided into several chunks of information, each one covering different areas, as shown in Fig. 4, which displays two adjacent SRTM30m files.

The full dataset is publicly available worldwide for testing purposes, consisting of 14,297 files with an estimated total size of 345 GB. As the full dataset could not be stored and managed efficiently on a local device, we restricted the data downloaded (using the 30-meter SRTM Tile Downloader tool [28]) to Spain (88 files, totaling around 2 GB). This information is loaded into the OpenTopoData API service and used to test the framework, however, it is easy to modify.

Several tests were performed to determine the accuracy of the information provided by this dataset, resulting in a very low error of around a few meters. These tests involved comparing the altitude obtained from different datasets and APIs, as well as conducting empirical experiments in which the authors physically visited several locations to verify the accuracy of the data.

The geospatial information retrieved by the system was subsequently used to calculate metrics related to the different routes and their segments, such as distances and slopes. In order to calculate the slope of a given segment, information about the distance between its two coordinates and their respective altitudes is

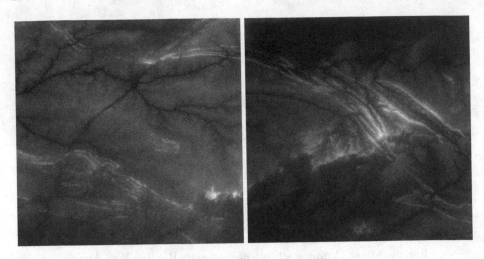

Fig. 4. SRTM30m file examples

required (see Eq. 1). The resulting slope can be either positive (ascending) or negative (descending) and is measured in percentage (%).

$$slope = \frac{destination\_altitude - source\_altitude}{distance} * 100 \qquad (1)$$

Regarding road topology, different metrics were considered such as road speed limit, number of lanes or road types (e.g., highways, streets, secondary roads), among others. This information was retrieved from the Overpass API provided by OpenStreetMap, using the Overpass Query Language (Overpass QL).

Figure 5 shows an example in which different routes between a source and a destination have been calculated. All routes are represented in the Topology Graph Database (TGD) as a directed graph. Each colored bubble represents an OSM node and each link between two nodes stores the properties of the road connecting them. In this example four routes were obtained. The shortest one is displayed in yellow, the fastest in blue and the eco-route in green. The fourth one, displayed in black, is a valid but not optimal route according to the selected

Table 1. Calculated routes. Path and related metrics: Distance (D), Estimated Travel Time (ETT), Estimated Fuel Consumption (EFC).

Route Id.	Path	D (meters)	ETT (minutes)	EFC (liters)
1	A, B, F, H	**10525** (*shortest*)	21,05	0,75
2	A, C, D, G, H	11212	26,91	**0.58** (*eco-route*)
3	A, B, E, H	10825	**18.56** (*fastest*)	0.69
4	A, B, E, F, H	10913	21.83	0.71

criteria, i.e., shortest distance, lower travel time and lower fuel consumption.
Table 1 displays these routes along with their paths and estimated metrics.

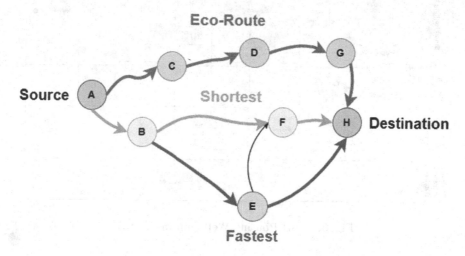

Fig. 5. Graph generated for the four routes retrieved by the SRS.

5 Workflow

The workflow of the proposed framework is illustrated in Fig. 6 and involves
all its components. The process begins when the user selects the source and
the destination of the trip using the WBM. Then, the SRS parses this input
and sends the corresponding requests to the routing services supported by the
RS component. Once they return the calculated routes, they are individually
processed according to the following steps:

1. All the OSM nodes of each route are retrieved.
2. The road segments connecting these nodes are obtained.
3. The geospatial information for each node is retrieved using the TES.
4. For each road segment, its length, speed limit, number of lanes and restrictions
   are obtained.
5. The slope of each road segment is calculated using its length and the elevation
   of the two nodes it connects.
6. All the route information is stored in the TGD.

Once all the routes have been successfully processed and stored in the
database, three different queries allow calculating which one is shorter (minimum total distance), faster (minimum total travel time considering each segment
length and speed limit), and more eco-friendly (less fuel consumption considering
each segment length, speed limit and slope). Finally, the result of these queries
is graphically displayed on the web-based map, allowing users to select the route
that better fits their preferences or needs. Additionally, directions are provided
for the selected route.

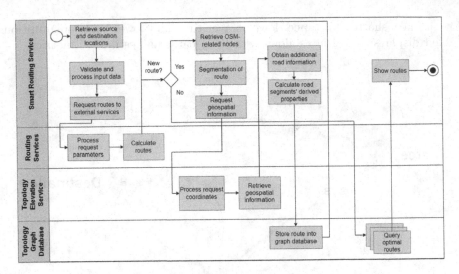

Fig. 6. Smart Routing Web App workflow.

6   Conclusions and Future Works

The work presented in this paper introduces a Smart-Routing Web App aimed at helping users plan their road trips considering not only the fastest or the shortest routes (already provided by most navigation apps), but also the most eco-friendly one, i.e., the less fuel consuming (and thus, less contaminating) route. Although some of the existing route planning apps already provide users with eco-routes, their estimations about fuel consumption/savings do not account for important aspects such as the road slope. In order to cope with this limitation, the proposed framework builds on different route planning and topological data services to obtain more precise metrics on the different routes available for a given trip, namely: estimated distance, travel time and fuel consumption. In the paper, both the structure (loosely-coupled component-based architecture) and the behavior (workflow) of the developed framework have been presented, along with an illustrating example.

Building on this preliminary work we plan some future extensions, including: (1) increasing the precision of the travel time and the fuel consumption estimations by considering both the traffic conditions (e.g., using the information provided by the MapBox API [29]) and the specific features of the vehicle used for the trip (e.g., using FASTSim: the Future Automotive Systems Technology Simulator [30]). Traffic conditions may significantly affect the speed profile in some segments and, as a consequence the travel time and the fuel consumption, e.g., under congestion. Similarly, the specific features of the vehicle (weight, idle consumption, etc.) have a significant impact on fuel consumption and cannot be neglected; (2) considering city-specific limitations such as zero-emission zones; (3) replacing the graph database instance by an in-memory graph projection to enable route caching and shorten query execution times; and (4) integrating the proposed tool into an API for easy remote access.

Acknowledgements. This work was supported by Project TED2021-132696B-I00, funded by MCIN/AEI/10.13039/501100011033/ and by ERDF A way to build Europe. José R. Lozano-Pinilla thanks the Junta de Extremadura for its Recovery, Transformation and Resilience Plan (funded by Next Generation EU), currently supporting him with an INVESTIGO contract.

References

1. Google Maps, Google. https://www.google.es/maps/. Accessed 14 July 2023
2. Ericsson, E., Larsson, H., Brundell-Freij, K.: Optimizing route choice for lowest fuel consumption - potential effects of a new driver support tool. Transp. Res. Part C: Emerg. Technol. **14**, 369–383 (2006). https://doi.org/10.1016/j.trc.2006.10.001
3. Kono, T., Fushiki, T., Asada, K., Nakano, K.: Fuel consumption analysis and prediction model for "Eco" route search. In: 15th World Congress on Intelligent Transport Systems and ITS America's 2008 Annual Meeting (2008). https://trid.trb.org/view/902235
4. Zeng, W., Miwa, T., Morikawa, T.: Prediction of vehicle CO2 emission and its application to eco-routing navigation. Transp. Res. Part C: Emerg. Technol. **68**, 194–214 (2016). https://doi.org/10.1016/j.trc.2016.04.007
5. Zeng, W., Miwa, T., Morikawa, T.: Application of the support vector machine and heuristic k-shortest path algorithm to determine the most eco-friendly path with a travel time constraint. Transp. Res. Part D: Transp. Environ. **57**, 458–473 (2017). https://doi.org/10.1016/j.trd.2017.10.001
6. Zeng, W., Miwa, T., Morikawa, T.: Eco-routing problem considering fuel consumption and probabilistic travel time budget. Transp. Res. Part D: Transp. Environ. **78**, 102219 (2020). https://doi.org/10.1016/j.trd.2019.102219
7. Aguiar, A., et al.: MobiWise: eco-routing decision support leveraging the Internet of Things. Sustain. Cities Soc. **87**, 104180 (2022). https://doi.org/10.1016/j.scs.2022.104180
8. Vamshi, B., Prasad, R. V.: Dynamic route planning framework for minimal air pollution exposure in urban road transportation systems. In: 2018 IEEE 4th World Forum on Internet of Things (WF-IoT), Singapore, pp. 540–545 (2018). https://doi.org/10.1109/WF-IoT.2018.8355209
9. Ghaffari, E., Rahmani, A.M., Saberikamarposhti, M., Sahafi, A.: An optimal path-finding algorithm in smart cities by considering traffic congestion and air pollution. IEEE Access **10**, 55126–55135 (2022). https://doi.org/10.1109/ACCESS.2022.3174598
10. Xiaofeng, S.: Improved Energy-efficient Routing Architecture for Traffic Management System Using a Hybrid Meta-heuristic Algorithm in Internet of Vehicles. (2022). https://doi.org/10.3233/JHS-222003
11. Alfaseeh, L., Djavadian, S., Tu, R., Farooq, B., Hatzopoulou, M.: Multi-objective eco-routing in a distributed routing framework. In: 2019 IEEE International Smart Cities Conference (ISC2), Morocco, pp. 747–752 (2019). https://doi.org/10.1109/ISC246665.2019.9071744
12. Rydzewski, A., Czarnul, P.: Recent advances in traffic optimisation: systematic literature review of modern models, methods and algorithms. IET Intel. Transport Syst. **14**, 1740–1758 (2020). https://doi.org/10.1049/iet-its.2020.0328

13. Winkle, T.: "Safety Benefits of Automated Vehicles: Extended Findings from Accident Research for Development, Validation and Testing", Autonomous Driving, Berlin (2016). https://doi.org/10.1007/978-3-662-48847-8_17
14. Use eco-friendly routing on your Google Maps app, Google. https://support.google.com/maps/answer/11470237?hl=en. Accessed 1 Apr 2023
15. Heckmann, R., Gaspers, L., Schönberger, J.: Development of an eco-routing app to support sustainable mobility behaviour. Innov. Metropolit. Areas (2022). https://doi.org/10.1007/978-3-662-60806-7_20
16. Google Maps is expanding its eco-friendly navigation feature to Europe, TechCrunch. https://techcrunch.com/2022/09/06/google-maps-is-expanding-its-eco-friendly-navigation-feature-to-40-more-countries/. Accessed 1 July 2023
17. OpenRouteService. https://openrouteservice.org/. Accessed 10 July 2023
18. Open Source Routing Machine, OSRM Project. https://project-osrm.org/. Accessed 20 July 2023
19. Open Source Routing Machine, GitHub. https://github.com/Project-OSRM/osrm-backend. Accessed 14 July 2023
20. GraphHopper, GraphHopper. https://www.graphhopper.com/. Accessed 23 July 2023
21. GraphHopper, GitHub. https://github.com/graphhopper/graphhopper. Accessed 26 July 2023
22. Open-Elevation API. https://open-elevation.com/. Accessed 10 July 2023
23. Elevation API Google. https://developers.google.com/maps/documentation/elevation/overview. Accessed 13 July 2023
24. Open Topo Data. https://www.opentopodata.org/. Accessed 30 June 2023
25. Overpass API User's Manual. https://dev.overpass-api.de/overpass-doc/en/. Accessed 20 June 2023
26. Containers Modeling Language (CML), GitHub. https://github.com/elpiter15/CML. Accessed 4 July 2023
27. Shuttle Radar Topography Mission, NASA. https://www2.jpl.nasa.gov/srtm/. Accessed 10 July 2023
28. 30-Meter SRTM Tile Downloader. https://dwtkns.com/srtm30m/. Accessed 4 June 2023
29. Mapbox API. https://docs.mapbox.com/api/overview/. Accessed 20 July 2023
30. FASTSim: Future Automotive Systems Technology Simulator, National Renewable Energy Laboratory (NREL). https://www.nrel.gov/transportation/fastsim.html. Accessed 20 July 2023

Author Index

© ICST Institute for Computer Sciences, Social Informatics and Telecommunications Engineering 2024
Published by Springer Nature Switzerland AG 2024. All Rights Reserved
A. L. Martins et al. (Eds.): INTSYS 2023, LNICST 540, p. 259, 2024.
https://doi.org/10.1007/978-3-031-49379-9

Printed in the United States
by Baker & Taylor Publisher Services